Modern Movements Among Moslems

Modern Movements Among Moslems

by

SAMUEL GRAHAM WILSON, D.D.

GYAN

Published by

Gyan Publishing House
5, Ansari Road
Daryaganj, New Delhi-110002
Phone: 011-47034999, 9811692060
E-mail: books@gyanbooks.com

Distribution Network
gyanbooks.com
India, USA, Canada, UK, Australia, France

ISBN : 978-81-212-6024-4 (PB)
First Published, 1916

2nd Impression 2021

Printed at: Gyan Press, Delhi.

Modern Movements Among Moslems
Author: Samuel Graham Wilson

By

Samuel G. Wilson, D.D.

Bahaism and its Claims. A Study of the Religion Promulgated by Baha Ullah and Abdul Baha.

12mo, cloth . . . . net $1.50

"Dr. Wilson lets the light in on its doctrines and rites, its pantheism, its polygamy, its political opportunism, its boast of love contrasted with its abusive language and its vindictiveness, its assassinations, and its quarrels and schisms."
—*Presbyterian Banner.*

Modern Movements Among Moslems. 12mo, cloth . . . . net $1.50

An important and exhaustive study of the many modern movements (quite unknown to earlier Mohammedanism) which mark the progress and propaganda of the Islam of to-day. Dr. Wilson writes out of a wide experience, and with first-hand knowledge.

Persian Life and Customs. With Incidents of Residence and Travel in the Land of the Lion and the Sun. Popular Edition. Illustrated. 8vo, cloth . . . . net $1.25

"This is not merely a book of travel, but of long observation in Persia. The author has studied with much care the condition of Persia and its future possibilities."—*The N. Y. Tribune.*

"A comprehensive, up-to-date account of a once famous land."—*The Living Church.*

Modern Movements Among Moslems

By

SAMUEL GRAHAM WILSON, D.D.

Thirty-two Years Resident in Persia

Author of "Persian Life and Customs," "Bahaism and Its Claims," etc.

NEW YORK CHICAGO TORONTO

Fleming H. Revell Company

LONDON AND EDINBURGH

PREFACE

THE Western world is showing increasing interest in Moslems. The great movement which has developed so marvellously in Eastern Asia affects Moslem peoples as well. Recent political upheavals in the Near East resulted in the proclamation of Constitutional governments in Turkey and Persia. In one year three autocratic Moslem rulers were dethroned. A spirit of Nationalism is growing. Events have followed in quick succession, leading up to the participation of Turkey in the World War. Her call has gone forth to all Islamic peoples to engage in a Holy War of deliverance. The Ottoman Empire occupies a unique position in the great contest of arms.

Study of Islam as a religion has made great progress in recent times; critical examination of its history and traditions by eminent scholars has thrown much new light upon it. Its present remarkable advance in Africa and Indonesia and the entrance into it of modernist influences from Western civilization have engaged the attention of all students of religion. The awakening of the Christian Church to its duty to evangelize the Moslems and its undertaking work to this end is enlisting another large element to consider Islam. So it has come about that the statesman, the historian, the sociologist, the theologian, the missionary give thought to the affairs of the Islamic world as never before. Contemporary literature indicates the spread of this interest, especially new periodicals in different European languages which are devoted exclusively to Islam. Even fiction is seeking its themes and plots among the followers of Mohammed.

Residence in the Near East, for a generation, in personal contact and converse with Moslems, with opportunities of travel among them in Persia, Russia, Turkey, Syria, and Egypt, and study and observation of contemporary events, supplementing knowledge of the history and doctrines of Islam, have given Moslem peoples a large place in my vision and thought. For this reason, when I was elected to deliver the course of lectures on the L. H. Severance Foundation before the Western Theological Seminary of the Presbyterian Church, at Pittsburg, Pennsylvania, I chose a subject connected with Islam. These lectures on "Modern Movements Among Moslems," in a much enlarged form, constitute the present volume. Study about the Moslem world has a fascination for me, and I trust this review of present-day events and movements in the life, thought, religion, society, and politics of Mohammedan lands may arrest attention and inspire efforts for the welfare of these millions of our fellow-men.

S. G. W.

CONTENTS

I

INNOVATIONS IN ISLAM

THE modern age is one of movement and change. The Moslem world is swept by currents of thought and life. The action and reaction of influences local and worldwide are affecting Islam. The Faith, to the Moslem, has intimate relation to all affairs, whether political, social, or religious. I wish to review Modern Movements among Moslems, whether these have been set in motion within Islam or from without, whether they have resulted in its deterioration or reform, in its decline or progress.

As a preliminary question, it is well to inquire how far it is possible to influence Islam by new forces, external and internal, and to what extent this has occurred. Is Islam changeable or not? Do Moslems vary their belief and worship? Has the mode of interpreting and executing their Law remained stationary? True conceptions of the past and the present will show what it is reasonable to expect in the future.

It is a common conception that Islam is fixed and stationary. It is said to be its boast that "it is always the same,—inflexible, neither requiring adaptation nor capable of it." Concerning this, Principal Fairbairn says: "It is the most inflexible of all positive religions. A religion, to be permanent, must be progressive,—

capable of formal without essential change. But a system in which the form is as divine as the spirit, the institution as the truth, is a system which can allow no change, no progress. Islam is an elastic spirit placed in an iron framework. The progressive is sacrificed to the stationary" (*Contemporary Review,* Vol. XL, p. 806). In accordance with this opinion are the words of Sir William Muir ("Caliphate," p. 594): "Swathed in the bands of the Koran, the Moslem faith, unlike the Christian, is powerless to adapt itself to varying time and place, keep pace with the march of humanity, direct and purify the social life, and elevate mankind." And with the philosopher and the historian agrees the statesman. Lord Cromer writes ("Modern Egypt," Vol. II, p. 202): "The Moslem stands in everything on the ancient ways, because he is a Moslem, because the customs which are interwoven with his religion forbid him to change." Lastly I quote the opinion of the great traveller in Arabia, Palgrave ("Arabia," Vol. I, p. 372): "Islamism is in itself stationary, and was framed thus to remain. It justly repudiates all change, all development. To borrow the forcible words of Lord Houghton: 'The written book is there, the dead man's hand, stiff and motionless; whatever savours of vitality is by that alone convicted of heresy and defection.'"

Undoubtedly these views state correctly the genius of Mohammedanism. Such has been the orthodox position. It asserts that "no advance, no change has been admitted into orthodox Islam during the past thousand years" (Stanley Lane-Poole). Islam, as settled from the traditions by the great Imams, Abu

Hanifa, Shafi, Ibn Malik, and Ibn Hanbal, must remain fixed.

But this is only one side of the shield. Historically and actually these dicta of our great writers are but partially true. Let it not be considered strange that I should take as a subject, " Movements Among Moslems." For remarkable modifications have taken place in Islam in the past, and conspicuous changes are occurring and are being attempted at the present time. It is all the more interesting to consider these movements because of the idea that is in many minds that Islam is immovable.

In his own day the Prophet exercised his authority to make modifications, such as changing the Kibla from Jerusalem to Mecca and introducing the semi-idolatrous and superstitious rites of the pilgrimage around the Kaaba. After his death many things were added on the authority of traditions,—reputed sayings of the Prophet, created to suit circumstances. The details of the system had not been fixed, and disputes over doctrines, forms, and polities culminated in fierce and bloody struggles. Persecution fixed the religion and made disputes dangerous. The spirit arose which is shown in the story told of Omar, that he appointed a commission of six to settle certain points and decreed that the minority, if any, should be decapitated. Under such persuasion to agreement, unanimity would doubtless prevail. But notwithstanding the often arbitrary rule of the Caliphs, Islam has been influenced and modified. Some changes have been wrought from within; more have come through the influence of converted races; not a few from the creeds and philosophies of rival and alien peoples. Most modifications have been received unconsciously by accommodations and adaptations. Doctrines and rites have been assimilated which seem even contrary to the spirit and to the letter of the Faith. The conceptions of Mohammedans have varied and do vary. So much is this the case that "The Report on the Special Preparation for Missionaries to Moslems in the Near East" says: "One cannot obtain a complete knowledge of Mohammedanism from books, especially those that deal with its early history and the claims and contents of its Faith. The modern missionary meets and deals with a *modified Mohammedanism,* and it is this he should know and understand."

Only from a knowledge of what changes Islam has undergone in the past, can it be rightly estimated what may be the effects of the present-day movements. And only from the knowledge of the latter and the conditions that prevail can the agents of the Christian propaganda rightly direct their efforts and exert their influence.

SUFIISM MODIFIES ISLAM

One element which has permeated and modified Islam is Sufiism. This is universally recognized. Sufiism is a pantheistic mysticism. It is a philosophy, almost a religion, which has been added to and mixed with the religion of the Prophet and wrought a strange transformation. Its first great development was in Persia. Persian thought and literature are imbued and permeated with it. And the influence of Persia on Mohammedan thought has been without measure.

The Arab historian Ibn Chaldoun says: "The majority of those who taught and preserved the sacred traditions were Persians, and the same is true of our systematic theologians and commentators on the Koran." Many of these were pantheists in philosophy, and they sought to find a basis for it in the new religion by explaining texts of the Koran in accordance with it. By Sufiism the rigid monotheism of Islam has received a pantheistic mode among millions of its votaries. The simple creed, "There is no God but God" has come to mean to them, God is the only being,—the universe is but a mode of God's existence. As the poet Jami says (Browne, in "Religious Systems of the World," p. 327),

> "Thou art absolute being, all else is but phantasm,
> For in thy universe all things are one."

The absolute supreme Being, perfect Goodness, perfect Beauty, manifested the world that he might be known and loved, according to the saying of the Koran, "I desired to be known, therefore I created the world." The first creation was the Primal Intelligence or Will, and from it and through it came into being all spirits, intelligences, and the elements. Man's soul is from God and "verily unto Him do we return." Belief in the *tohid,* or unity of God, means to hold to, and to desire to attain to, union with Him as the aim of all things. Man is God. Mullah Jalal-ud-Din exclaims to his spiritual Guide, "Oh, my Master, you have completed my doctrine by teaching me that you are God and that all things are God." The waves when they settle down become the sea, so men are the waves of God and after death return to His bosom. Hence the injunction, "Adore God in His creatures" (J. P. Brown: "The Dervishes," p. 333). Since all is God, there is no idolatry, for all worship is rendered to the One, though maybe with imperfections.

Sufiism gives allegorical and mystical interpretation to the doctrines and rites of Islam. It delights to picture the relation of the soul to God as that of Lover and Beloved, the enraptured, entranced one contemplating the Supreme Beauty. All the imagery of love and the thrill of amorous passion set forth spiritual communion. The delights of the senses, the intoxication of wine and hasheesh, are symbols of divine things. The great Persian poets, Fardusi, Saadi, Hafiz, and Nizami, abound in praises of wine and love. One party considered them unorthodox. Fardusi was on account of this accusation refused his reward for his poem and burial in the public cemetery. A Shiah Mujtahid destroyed the first monument erected over Saadi's grave at Shiraz. Hafiz, now regarded as a saint and his tomb as a shrine, was at first refused burial by Mohammedan rites. Finally they drew lots to settle it. A child opened at random upon the following verse of Hafiz:

> "Withhold not thy foot from Hafiz;
> For though he be drowned in sin,
> He fareth to heaven."

He was considered a libertine, fond of wine, women, and music. Sufis pretend that his amorous and bacchanalian poetry is allegorical. He has the fortune to be "adored by both saints and sinners." It requires much credulity to believe that their antinomian verses relate to spiritual desires. Even this summer, a Moslem writer (*Islamic Review,* July, 1915) interprets the secularism and pessimism of Omar-i-Khayyam as spiritual and orthodox. In truth, Sufis are free from the Law, and not only from its rites but from its restrictions on conduct. Shams-i-Din says (quoted in Canon Sell's "Sufiism," p. 64):

> "The man of God is beyond infidelity and religion,
> To the man of God infidelity and religion are alike."

The "Masnavi" of Jalal-ud-Din says: "When one is out of the Kaaba, he looks towards it, but for him who is in the Kaaba, it imports not what direction he turns." One in God's love need not fulfil the Law.

Sufiism involves a different conception of salvation from Islam. Salvation, according to it, is to be freed from self, to be in union with God, by means of increase in the knowledge and love of Him. Man the seeker after the Truth is a traveller on life's journey. The goal is God. The Way has various stages or degrees. Beginning with the Law, obedience to the Shariat, the traveller passes to the Path of Mystic Rites, bringing purity, then to Knowledge, immediate communion with God, and further on to the stage when he is in Truth itself, united to God. The last stage is called *fana,* which is usually translated "annihilation." The word is interpreted by Al Sarraj, a philosophic mystic (R. A. Nicholson, Roy. Geog. Soc., 1913, p. 61), to mean a "passing away," in opposition to the word *baga,* "continuance," a passing away of conscious thought of self, a passing away from passions and desires and even perceptions and the concentration of all entirely on God. Others regard it as such an entire absorption of self in God that the individual can say, "I am God."

The means of progress in the Way are contemplation, meditation, adoration, remembrance of God, induced and aided by rites peculiar to Sufiism. After the first stages, ordinary forms of prayer and worship and reading of the Koran are neglected, and emphasis is placed on the inner light, "the eye of the heart," as the instrument of direct communication with God. The ritual used to incite this condition is called the Zikr. This includes various recitations, repetitions, and physical and mental gymnastics, by which the mind is fixed on God and the emotions and nerves excited. The formula for repetition is varied, but the most common words are the name Allah, repeated 1,001 times, or the ninety-nine names of God, or the first clause of the Creed, the kalima, "La illa ill Allah." These words are repeated until an ecstatic or hypnotic stage is reached. This zikr is pronounced by no less an authority than Professor Margoliouth to be a compound of "various hysterical and hypnotizing processes." The zikrs are of two kinds, silent and vocal. They are sometimes accompanied by a variety of motions, as swaying, whirling, dancing, or by ejaculations, singing, or howling like a dog. Musical instruments are used either for the soothing effect or to give vivacious movement. The order of the Maulavis have a band of six or more instruments. This is a striking innovation, for tradition says that Mohammed stopped his ears when he heard the music of a pipe. Some orders prepare for the zikr[1] by long periods of solitude, fasting, and vigils. The disciples, who are called darvishes or fakirs, when in this state of trance see visions, experience ecstasies, are excited to frenzy, or fall into unconsciousness. In this state some of them perform wonderful feats, such as eating, without pain, red-hot coals, handling and placing in their mouths red-hot irons, eating live snakes and scorpions, pounding their bodies with rocks, or lying prostrate to be trodden upon by the Sheikh's horse.

ORDERS OF DARVISHES

The one who has passed through the stages and attained oneness becomes a Sheikh or Murshid, to guide others to attain. The disciple must submit his will to the Sheikh's will, vow to obey him and forsake self, surrender all control of his thought and personality to the Sheikh. Certain classes of darvishes take vows of poverty and beg from door to door. From this the name is derived, *dar* meaning door in Persian. There are many Orders. A very few of them have the vow of celibacy as the Baktashi had at first. But this is contrary to the genius of Islam. Tradition reports that Mohammed said: "When the servant of God

[1] Some students of Islam attach considerable value to its mysticism and to more spiritual forms of the zikr as a means of soul-uplift. Among these are Prof. D. B. Macdonald and Rev. G. Swan of Egypt. The latter (*Moslem World*, 1912, p. 380) expresses the conviction that the study of the aims and effects of the zikr might aid the evangelistic missionary, and that Christians, by imitating it or by finding a substitute for it, might disclose a source of satisfaction to the heart. He puts the query whether it is not in it that the secret power of Islam lies. Most observers despise the zikr as a religious rite of little value.

marries, he perfects half his religion," and "One prayer of a married man is worth seventy of a bachelor." Sheikh Abdul Kadir, the founder of the Kadiris, had four wives, some concubines, and forty-five children. A Nakshbandi Sheikh told Dr. Hughes that he had wished to remain celibate, but his disciples insisted that he should perfect his religion by taking a wife. Asceticism is practised by neglect of the body and indifference to worldly comforts. A Persian darvish, half naked, covered with rags and vermin, suffering from hunger and exposure, said to me: "Will not this subjection of my body purify my soul?" It is common for darvishes to live in *takias* or lodges, sometimes in the crowded city, sometimes in solitary spots.

The traditions attributing the founding of orders of darvishes to Abubekr or Ali are no doubt apocryphal. But Sufiism certainly manifested itself early in the history of Islam. By the second century this innovation began to creep in. Perhaps the first order was that founded by Sheikh Alwan, a Sufi celebrated for his knowledge and worth (A.H. 149, A.D. 766). The movement met with great opposition as contrary to the orthodoxy of Islam. Some Sufis were punished as heretics. In A.D. 923 Al Hallaj, a disciple of Al Junaid and of Imam Reza, uttered the celebrated words, "I am the Truth, I am God," and was put to death for blasphemy. But Al Junaid claimed that they were not breaking with Islam, and said: "Our system of doctrines is firmly bound up with the dogmas of the faith, the Koran, and the Traditions." Imam Al Gazzali, called the Plato of Moslems, secured recognition in Islam for Sufi mysticism as a system in opposition to scholasticism. Ibn Tufail accomplished the same in the West, i.e., Spain and North Africa. Palgrave says ("Essays on Eastern Questions," p. 52): "The Darvishes, secretly subverting the very foundations of Islam, have nevertheless, thanks to legists like Abu Hanifa, doctors like Ahmad al Ghazali, and Sultans like Bayazid II, succeeded in vindicating to themselves a sufficient though not an unquestioned reputation for Orthodoxy. Different orders were organized from time to time and spread throughout Islam. Each founder gave a distinct practice and rules to his order. The coming to the throne of Persia of a Sufi dynasty, in 1501, was the signal for an effort to suppress the darvish orders in the Ottoman empire, as the enemies of Sunniism. In 1656 the suppression of the orders was again attempted, by the government combined with the Ulema, and aided by the popular passion of the orthodox Sunnis. Again on the destruction of the Janisaries, 1826, the darvishes of Constantinople were exiled and some of the Sheikhs of the Bektashi executed. But all these attempts came to naught.

Of late years the growth of the darvish orders in number and influence has been striking. Dozy says: "The influence which Sufiism has exercised over the Moslem world, and which in our day is rather increasing, has been extremely great." Since his time there has been a greater increase. Now Von Kremer says: "Sufiism is the preponderating element in Moslem civilization." The system is spreading in Turkey and Syria. Abdul Hamid is said to be a member of the Rufai, or Howling darvishes, as well as of the Sanusiyah, and to have often attended the zikrs (Ramsay: "Impressions of Turkey," p. 150). The present Sultan, Mohammed V, is of the Maulavi order. There are two hundred lodges in Constantinople. Professor Macdonald says, in "Aspects of Islam": "To the bulk of the population of Egypt, their real religion is Sufiism as represented in the zikr." Simon says: "Nearly every devout Mohammedan in the Dutch East Indies is a member of such an order" ("Progress, etc.," p. 145). In North Africa public sentiment strongly insists on every person being a member of some order, and pressure is used to accomplish this end. In some provinces every one is an initiate. The majority of the people of the Sudan belong to a darvish order. The opposition of the mullahs has been silenced and conquered, for as Dr. Hughes says ("Dictionary of Islam," p. 116): "There is scarcely a maulavi or learned man in Islam who is not a member of some religious order." The separate orders number well-nigh a hundred.

If Sufiism was a natural expression of religious conception among the Aryans and owes its origin to Hindu, Greek, and Persian philosophy, its propagation in Islam is a striking instance of Persian conquest over the religion of its conquerors. The Semitic races, as well as the Turanian, African, and Malay, have adopted Sufiism. Even if it did not spread from Persia as a reaction against Islam, but took its inception subsequently and independently in Islam, it is anyhow a foreign element and one that has influenced the whole fabric of the religion, its doctrines, its worship, its life. It shows how foreign elements have been and can be introduced into the system of Mohammed. It shows that the need was felt of something more than Islam provided; that Islam had not that which would satisfy the religious instincts of the heart, that man desires to draw near to God and to find a Path, a Way of Approach, and that he knows that the performance of rites and the merit of his own works do not secure him this access. It shows that the Moslem heart yearns for that which the Christian finds in his union with Christ and communion with the Holy Spirit and in his worship of the Father in spirit and in truth, not in a formal prayer-ritual.

SAINT-WORSHIP

Another modification and corruption of Islam is seen in the prevalence of saint-worship. Veneration of the Imams, regarding them as manifestations of God, and rendering them honours as semi-divine, has prevailed among Shiahs and their sects; the development of creature worship among the Sunnis is connected with the spread of the darvish orders. Many Sheikhs or Pirs are regarded as Valis, blessed spirits, possessing superhuman powers, capable of working miracles of healing by the touch, the breath, or the saliva. Votive offerings are brought to them to procure their intercession for blessings. Kissing their hands, with the expression "I repent on your hands," is common, with accompanying trust in their mediation. It is believed that pardon is secured through them for the living suppliant and for the dead.

Ill-gotten gains receive purification through their pronouncement, a percentage being retained. These Sheikhs are friends of God; they see visions and dream dreams for the guidance of the people. Sheikh-al-Akbar Ibn Arabi claimed that his book was revealed to him in a dream by the Prophet Mohammed. They are credited with interpreting dreams, exorcising evil spirits, empowering charms and talismans against witchcraft, sickness, theft, snake-bite, and all calamities. Some are supposed to have spiritual power over souls as kings have over temporalities. God makes known to them His will with regard to the actions of men and all the purposes of men come under their cognizance previous to their being carried out in deeds (Brown's "Dervishes," pp. 80-81).

The takia of the order, the cave or hut of the darvish, or especially the tomb of the venerated Sheikh, becomes a shrine. For example, Bagdad is called the City of Saints. In that seat of the Abbasides are many sacred tombs, including that of Sheikh Abdul Kadir Jilani. Professor Siraj-ud-Din refers ("Vital Forces," p. 168) to the "divine honours paid to this great Pir," and adds, "There is nothing more soul-stirring in Mohammedan worship than to hear these prayers and hymns chanted in the service of the Pir Sahib,—continued until early morning." These dead Sheikhs are invoked everywhere; vows are made to them; healing is expected from them. Especially the pilgrim expects the blessing. He salutes the grave, prostrates himself, kisses it, holds sacrificial feasts at it, endows the shrine, carries earth away from the grave to rub on the sick or a pressed cake of it to place under his forehead, when he prostrates himself in prayer. These shrine tombs are very common. For example, near my home, at Tabriz, on a ridge of the mountain, there is one called Ainal-Zainal, the reputed grave of two descendants of Ali. To visit this on seven successive Fridays is said to be equal to a pilgrimage to Mecca. So in the surrounding villages, at Sofian, Sardarud, Ilkachi, on the Ujan, on Mt. Sahend there are others. So everywhere in travelling one sees Imamzadahs and zayaretgahs. So not only in Persia, but all over the Islamic world, these centres of superstition and creature-worship are scattered. Though unauthorized by the Koran or Shariat, this innovation has spread far and wide in Islam. The transformation wrought in the religion by this doctrine of human mediation and intercession is striking. On the part of the Shiahs it is very deep-rooted. Imam Husain is deemed a real atoning mediator who by his death at Kerbala has merited the position of availing intercessor. (See writer's article, "The Atoning Saviour of the Shiahs," *Presbyterian and Reformed Review,* V. 1891.) This is constantly kept in mind by the Muharram month of mourning, the Passion Play, and the Readers of Lamentations. The saint-worship has spread everywhere among the Sunnis in Turkey and Arabia. In Afghanistan "adoration of the Pirs is universal and constitutes the religion of the masses." In Beluchistan Pir worship at pre-Islamic shrines is widespread. In truth, shrines of pagan saints are usually turned into Moslem ones. In Algeria and Maghrib and among the Berbers

Maraboutism is a special characteristic of Islam. Revered marabouts swarm everywhere and the tendency to deify men and worship saints has eclipsed the primitive faith (" Encyclopedia of Islam "; Arts.: Afghanistan, Algeria, Beluchistan). In other parts of Africa the same is true. There, as well as in Malaysia, these Sheikhs and the maalims or teachers have a powerful influence. They are representatives of God and inherit the reverence given to the heathen sorcerers. In Java the drosky driver, even with a European passenger, dismounts when he meets one of them. Says Mr. Simon: "They are worshipped as demi-gods. Many people look upon them as their god. For they are Allah's friend and work miracles before one's very eyes; their curse brings misery; their blessing happiness. They know the hearts of all men." Their supposed influence as intercessors is very real. As Professor Macdonald says, " In the lives of the saints we find them exercising again and again flat pressure upon Allah " (" Vital Forces," p. 234). To many a Moslem the Vali has become more real than the Prophet; the Sheikh more powerful than the mullah; the zikr more efficacious than the namaz (prayer-rite); the Path more holy than the Law; the brotherhood of the Order more intimate than the fellowship of the Faith.

THE GLORIFICATION OF MOHAMMED

Another modification of Islam is seen in the glorification of Mohammed. Wahabis, stating the primitive doctrine of Islam, deny Mohammed's pre-existence, his power of present intercession, and the lawfulness of the reverence given to his person and his tomb. The majority of Moslems, disregarding the accusation of sacrilege, are increasing in this tendency. The traditions which have grown up may be seen in the "Life of Mohammed," the *Hiyat-ul-Qulub,* translated by my predecessor in Tabriz, the Rev. J. L. Merrick. The traditions referring to the creation and the pre-existence of Mohammed are received by Sunnis as well as by Shiahs. According to these the first creation was the Light of Mohammed—the Nur-i-Mohammed. Before all else it was created from the Light of God. This Light of Mohammed existed alone through several periods of seventy thousand years and its dwelling-places and experiences are described with the details of a Milton. When God decided to make the worlds, He divided the Light of Mohammed into four portions and from these created the Word, the Tablet, the Throne, and from the fourth portion the angels, the heavens and the earth, and all intelligences. So Mohammed was before all things and from him were all things made. It is the Sufi doctrine of the Primal Will, the Arian doctrine of Christ, of which it is an evident imitation. In Shiah Islam, Ali and the other Imams are exalted almost to the rank of divinity, but orthodox Islam has not been content without the apotheosis of Mohammed. Not only is there ascribed to him an unparalleled glory in the pre-existent state, but there is an idealization of his earthly life. His sinlessness is taught, contrary to the plain statements of the Koran itself and of the Traditions, which, in the deathbed scene, among his last words report prayers for pardon. That which would be sin in other men is made to be only a sign of divine favour to him, who was granted every privilege, even though contrary to the Law. He is regarded as the mediator not only at the Day of Judgment but now and under all conditions,—the intercessor, supreme and all-efficient and availing for his sinful followers. One cry for pity in the name of Mohammed blots out the sins of two hundred years. "Ya Mohammed," says Dr. Zwemer, "is the open sesame to every door of difficulty—temporal or spiritual. Sailors sing it while hoisting their sails; hammals groan it to raise a burden; the beggars howl it, to obtain alms; it is the Beduin's cry in attacking a caravan; it hushes babes to sleep, as a cradle song; it is the pillow of the sick and the last word of the dying; it is written on the doorposts and in their hearts as well as since eternity on the throne of God; it is to the devout Moslem the name above every name ("Islam: A Challenge," p. 47). Professor Siraj-ud-Din, a convert from Islam, now professor in Forman Christian College, Lahore, says: "No Mohammedans, except perhaps the Wahabis, are truly unitarian; all others have been led to deify Mohammed more or less. . . . Hymns to the Prophet are sung most enthusiastically and devotionally. Their whole nature is stirred up and their whole heart goes out in worship and adoration when these hymns are sung. The entire popular religion as well as literature is filled with the deification and glorification of Mohammed. One popular hymn runs thus:

"'In every flower and in every plant,
The Light of Mohammed is reflected.'"

("Vital Forces," pp. 167-68; comp. pp. 228-30). Professor Simon testifies that a similar exaltation of the personality of Mohammed has occurred in Malaysia. The same is seen also in the manner of celebrating the birthday of Mohammed (molud) with increasing enthusiasm and devotion. Prof. Stewart Crawford declares that in Syria (*International Missionary Review*, 1912, p. 608) it amounts to "a practical deification of the Prophet." The worshipper, "with all the florid rhetoric of Oriental imagery," in direct address salutes Mohammed "with enthusiastic expressions of loyalty and devotion, and associates himself with the heavenly beings in adoration for his person." Thus that which we see in Persia occurring with reference to Ali is occurring all over the Moslem world in reference to Mohammed.

Besides all this, which seems so like an imitation of Christianity, there is that other importation into Islam, in an earlier age, of the doctrine of the uncreated Koran, on the Eternal Tablets—an eternal Word which was made a book and stayed among us,—a doctrine which caused such fierce and bloody contests and which finally became a criterion of orthodoxy. It is an innovation in Islam as strange as it is embarrassing to the unitarian Moslem who would find fault with the Logos doctrine of John's Gospel.

MOHAMMEDAN CLERGY

Another modification of Islam in the course of its history is the development of a clergy—of various ranks and classes. It is the claim that there are no priests in Islam. This was true, as it was true also of primitive Christianity.[1]

Islam was modelled on the synagogue as was the Church. Islam has developed a clergy, with gradations and ranks. These vary in different countries. In Persia there are first the *talabas,* theological students; then the mullahs, who, if assigned to be leaders of prayers, are called *peesh-namaz,* or, if preachers, *vaiz.* Many mullahs are connected with the local mosque in the village or the ward of the city, and act like pastors in performing marriages, funeral services, as well as tending to matters of divorce and inheritance. One lucrative portion of their work is the writing of deeds and contracts. They also solve questions of conscience for the people. Of higher degree is the Kazi, who is a judge in matters coming under the Canon Law. Still higher in rank is the Mujtahid, who preaches in his special mosque, is professor for the talabas, decides questions of the Canon Law, and judges in civil and criminal suits which pertain to it. Over the Mujtahids of each city and province are the Chief Mujtahids who reside at Kerbala and Najef, the centres of the Shiahs, direct the religious affairs of the sect, issue binding fatvas or decrees, and train the mullahs in higher studies. The Persian Mujtahid has more independent influence and

[1] The word *hieros* is not once used of ministers of the Church in the New Testament. The Christian presbyter is only a "priest" in the way that the latter word is a contraction of the former. The word used by Mohammed in Surah V, 85, for the Christian clergy is *kassisin,* the equivalent of presbyter, elder, Syriac Kashish-a,kasha, Persian Kashish. The word *kohen,* priest, was used by the Arabs as the equivalent of sorcerer.

power than the Ulema of Turkey. The Shah has no religious authority over him, and he is not dependent on the state for authorization. He has more control over property right, endowments, and tithes, and is less accountable for religious funds than in Turkey. In Turkey the grades of the Mohammedan clergy are even more numerous. (See H. Dwight's "Constantinople," pp. 213-14.) The *softas,* or students, are trained in theology and Canon Law in many schools, the chief of which are at Damascus, Aleppo, Brusa, and Adrianople. Over all these are one at Constantinople and the Al Azhar at Cairo. In Constantinople the mosque schools have from ten thousand to twenty thousand students, half of whom are studying Sacred Law. Grades whose duties are almost wholly religious are the Imam, the leader of prayers, and the Khatib or mudarris, the mosque preacher. Four degrees higher than the Khatib is the Mufti, who resembles the lawyer among the Jews in New Testament times. From this grade are appointed the Kadis; seven ranks higher is the Grand Mufti, Chief Judge according to Canon Law; and five grades higher yet is the Sheikh-ul-Islam, the head of the religious clergy and of the religio-civil judges. The Sheikh-ul-Islam is ex-officio Minister of Public Worship and does not change with the other ministers of the Sultan. He is also official Interpreter of the Shariat. His decision for the time is effective, even if it be a fatva deposing a Sultan. But decisions by him have not binding force on others of the Ulema. He continues to wear a long white robe and a yellow turban with a grey *aba*, cloak, though the viziers have changed to European dress. All these higher grades are called Ulema, Doctors, the *alim* or learned. There is in Turkey no ordination. The diploma is the authorization and prepares one for appointment, but in Central Asia the binding of the turban on the head is a sign of authorization. In Turkey the duties of many of the Ulema are both religious and civil, but in Persia as well as in countries like Russia, where their civil duties are more restricted, it is more easily realized that their prime function is religious. In the thought of the people they are the clergy. Dr. Dwight facetiously refers to them as "the Ulema who deny that they are priests, yet act like them." Palgrave, after stoutly maintaining the non-priestly character of the Mohammedan mullahs, says: "Still social fact recognizes what dogmatic theory denies. Gradations and classifications exist and the functions are intimately connected with and even essential to the religion." And as regards India he regretfully admits ("Essays, etc.," p. 138) that "Sacerdotal superstition, so proper to the Hindu, has re-arisen and afflicted Islam with its taint, so that we see the Indo-Mohammedan investing the Kazi with a semi-priestly character and function." Mr. S. Khuda Bakhsh of India says (quoted by Dr. Zwemer in *Missionary Review*): "In its decadence Islam is priest-begotten and priest-ridden." Mr. Simon says: "The Moslem has been delivered over bound hand and foot to his priesthood in matters that concern his welfare equally in this world and in the next" ("Vital Forces," p. 87). "They have an unholy power over the masses of the people. A quiet nod from these masters of Islam is quite sufficient for an outbreak of fanaticism in the name of God" ("Progress of Islam, etc.," p. 164). Justice Amir Ali continually refers to the mullahs as clergy. He specially refers to those of the Shiahs as the "Expounders of the Law who have assumed the authority and position of the clergy in Christendom." Professor Becker of the Hamburg Colonial Institute ("Christianity and Islam," pp. 50-51) says: "The force of Christian influence produced a priestly class in Islam. . . . This influence could not create an organized clergy, but it produced a clerical class to guard religious thought and to supervise thought of every kind." In Malaysia and Africa, and among the ignorant in many Moslem lands, the custom is prevalent for the mullah or mualim to write charms, talismans, and amulets, use incantations, divination, astrology, and magical arts, thus degenerating into the status of the *kohen* or soothsayer of Mohammed's times. Besides all this the mullahs have in some countries added the last resort of priestcraft, selling indulgences for cash. The mualim of the East Indies (Simon, p. 82) has a list of fees for the ransom of the souls of the dead. For a fee of thirty dollars he will testify on the Day of Judgment that the dead man has been to Mecca; for another fee certify that he was a blameless Moslem; for ten dollars all his sins will be blotted out; for the "instruction fee" a certificate is given that the man knew the entire Koran, though the fact be otherwise; another fee will insure the dead man an animal to ride on in the Day of Judgment; for five dollars redemption-money a son who died a heathen can be received into Islam and paradise after his death. For all these fees, amounting to about seventy-five dollars, salvation is assured to the departed and protection to the survivors from being tormented by his ghost. So far has Islam changed in Indonesia. That the rewards of priesthood are enjoyed by some of them is seen in the High Sherif of Mecca. It is said that this functionary has a paltry income of $400,000 a year with an added *mudakhil* or graft of $1,200,000, and that his Vali has $800,000. Every guide must pay them a fee of $250 a year. The drawers of the water from Zem-Zem; the doorkeepers of the Kaaba, the cameleers who transport the pilgrims,—each pays his fee. Though most of this money must be passed up to the coterie at Constantinople to secure the tenure of their positions, yet when the Vali was arrested by the Young Turks in October, 1908, and taken to Constantinople, he had amassed a million in money and an untold treasure in jewels (Simon, p. 121).

Besides the regular mullahs, Islam has a kind of priest in the Sheikhs of the darvish orders, whom I have described above. Palgrave confirms what I have already said, that they "not infrequently arrogate to themselves supernatural and mystical powers." They act as mediators of God's blessings. They introduce the *murid* or neophyte to communion with God, taking, as it were, for a time the position of God to him. The Shiahs have, in addition to these, a clerical class called Marseyakhans, who are influential and numerous. Their business is to tell stories of the martyred Imams during Muharram, Ramazan, and at funerals. Tears that are shed at the recital of these lamentations are very meritorious, bringing forgiveness. These tears are sometimes caught in bottles.

In all these we see large additions to original Mohammedanism. They show how it has been greatly modified. Bosworth Smith says ("Mohammed and Mohammedanism," p. 211): "As instituted by Mohammed it had no priest and no sacrifice. In orthodox Islam there is no priestly caste, and therefore no fictions of apostolic succession, inherent sanctity, indissoluble vows, or powers of absolution." How changed it is! We now have an apostolic succession in the line of Imams, inherent sanctity in the Sayids, or Sherifs, vows and absolutions connected with the Pirs, offerings at the tombs to secure the mediation of the living or of the dead saints, and even the sale of indulgences in Islam. Kuenen says (quoted in *Missionary Review,* 1889, p. 302): "The Moslem seeks what his faith withholds from him, and seeks it when the authority which he himself recognizes forbids him to look for it."

THE CANON LAW, OR SHARIAT

The Sacred Law was for a thousand years the religious, civil, and criminal code of Islam. It purports to be founded on the Koran and the Traditions, which are reports of the life, conduct, and words of Mohammed,—what he said, what he did, and what he allowed to be done without rebuke. Traditions are regarded as authoritative by all sects of Islam, Sunnis, Shiahs, and Wahabis, but they receive different collections of traditions as valid. Out of 500,000 traditions from 4,000 to 6,000 are selected as true, and about the authenticity of these, even Doctors of the same sect differ. A third foundation of Law is the *ijma,* the agreement or unanimous consent of the Mujtahids in a decision or interpretation of what is Law. A fourth foundation is *kiyas* or inference, reasoning from analogy from what is in the accepted law.

A small portion of the Law is found in the Koran itself. Only two hundred verses out of six thousand are about legal matters. It has no elaborate system. Stanley Lane-Poole says ("Studies in a Mosque," pp. 152-58): "Mohammed never attempted to arrange a code of laws. His scattered decisions are few and often vague. It is surprising how little definite legislation there is in the Koran. Mohammed had no desire to make a new code. He seldom appears to have volunteered a legal decision, except when a distinct abuse had to be removed; and the legal verses of the Koran are evidently answers to questions put to him."

It has been commonly supposed that the traditions upon which the Mujtahids founded their codes were at least of Arabic origin, however much or little may have been founded on Mohammed's instruction. But as the result of scientific research and modern study of the origin of Mohammedan Law, it is coming to be clearly recognized that Roman Law lies at the basis of and is the source of the Shariat. The learned Dr. I. Goldziher, professor in Vienna University, whom I had the privilege of hearing discuss Islam at the Congress of Arts and Sciences at the St. Louis Exposition, has made a study and exposition of this subject. The laws in the Koran and Arabia were utterly insufficient for the new Arab theocratic empire. In taking charge of the conquered provinces, the Arabs adopted from and incorporated with their ordinances the system in vogue among the people over whom they were ruling. The substance of the Law was from "alien sources—from contact with foreign elements" ("The Historians' History of the World," Vol. VIII, p. 296). "The first impulse to the creation of a Mohammedan system of law was given by contact with the great spheres of civilization—the Roman and the Persian. The influence of Roman Law on the sources of a legal system in Islam is witnessed by the very name given to jurisprudence in Islam in the beginning (*fikh* equals *prudentia; fakih* equals *prudens,* lawyer). The influence extended both to the principle of legal deduction and to particular legal provisions. In regard to property the new government had to take over many ordinances of Roman Law, not only particular laws but principles of law." Among such principles, he instances that of legal deduction from analogies, *kiyas,* the opinion of the jurists or *rai*, which is a literal translation of *opinio,* and regard for public utility and interests or *istalah,* the equivalent of *utilitas publica.* "The influence exercised by Roman legal method in the system of legal deduction in Islam is more important than the direct adoption of particular points of law" (Goldziher, quoted in Khuda Bakhsh: "Essays Indian and Islamic," p. 393). Professor Macdonald, another investigator in this department, agrees with these opinions. He says that the Moslems "learned willingly of the people among whom they had come. Roman Law made itself felt. It was the practical school of the court that they attended. These courts were permitted to continue in existence till Islam had learned from them all that was needed. We can still recognize certain principles which were so carried over. That the duty of proof lies upon the plaintiff and the right of defending himself with an oath upon the defendant; the doctrine of invariable custom and that of the different kinds of legal presumption. These as expressed in Arabic are almost verbal renderings of the frequent utterances of Latin Law" ("Development of Muslim Theology, etc.," p. 84). An eminent jurist writes in the *Moslem World* (1912, p. 354): "The Law of Justinian lies at the base of the Moslem shariat." The latter "resembles in a most striking manner the common principles and even the specific rules of Roman Law." Some of the words are almost translations of it. The methods of judicial procedure were adopted from it. "The more developed rules of intestate succession resemble it; the inheritance is divided legally into parts similar to the Roman;—in the developed law of contract we find echoes of the Roman Law; even *vakf*, endowment, contains much that resembles it." It is even shown that the foundations of the Shariat to which we referred, namely the Ijma or Consensus of the Mujtahids and *Kiyas*, or Deduction by Analogy, had their counterpart in Roman Law.

Thus, says Professor Becker, of the Hamburg Colonial Institute ("Christianity and Islam," p. 34), "In a few centuries Islam became a complex religious structure, accurately regulating every department of human life from the deepest problems of morality to the daily use of the toothpick and the fashions of dress and hair. It had high faculties of self-accommodation to environment, was able to enter upon the heritage of the mixed Greco-Oriental civilization in the East" (*Ibid.*, p. 98). Professor Becker discovers also a large influence of Christian doctrine and ritual. He says (p. 73): "The state, society, the individual, economics and morality, were thus collectively under Christian influence during the early period of Mohammedanism. Christian ideas came into circulation among Mohammedans . . . as utterances given by Mohammed himself." "The development of ritual was derived from pre-existent practices which were for the most part Christian" (p. 83): such are the ceremonies of marriage, funerals, preaching, and the niche in the mosque wall. We have been long accustomed to recognize that Islam received its philosophy and science, medicine and art from the Greeks, Syrians, and Persians, and was greatly influenced by Neo-Platonism and by the dialectics of Aristotle, in its theology. To these we must add this conviction also, that its Canon Law, the Shariat, so holy and sanctified in their eyes, is largely the result of borrowing from the Romans and Persians.[1] Laws and usages adopted from them were made to appear a part of original Islam. And traditions were invented to suit the circum-

[1] Goldziher says further that "contact with the people and religion of Persia had an influence which was very important in the development of its legal system. It is hardly possible to overestimate the importance of the part played in the development of Islam by Persia." Von Kremer mentions Rabbinical Literature as an influence on Islam, besides the Roman-Byzantine Law and daily intercourse with the subject nations.

stances and words put into the mouth of Mohammed or an incident narrated as occurring in his life to give the sanction of authority to them. After several centuries this Shariat became crystallized and stereotyped and came to be regarded by the Ulema and by the whole Islamic world as the unalterable divine law.

The nineteenth century witnessed remarkable action regarding the Shariat. Several Moslem states broke away from its observance, and introduced modern civil and criminal codes. In Persia the common law, called the *urfi,* has been determined by the Shah, his ministers and custom, and administered by Hoikims, the judge-governors of the provinces and the districts. These have regard to the provisions of the Shari but do not follow it. Indeed a condition of friction and opposition has existed between the governors and the Ulema, the Shah's government trying more and more to restrict the operation of the Shariat.

In Turkey the reforming Sultans, as they are called, Sultan Mahmud and Sultan Abdul Mejid, largely set aside the Shariat. Under the influence of European civilization and chiefly through the "Great Ilchi," the British ambassador, Lord Strafford de Redcliffe, the Hatti Sharif of Gulkhana was promulgated in 1839 and the Hatti Humayun in 1856. These decrees were designed to turn the face of Turkey toward progress and granted a large measure of civil and religious liberty. These were followed by the promulgation of codes, modelled on the Code Napoléon, and by the establishment of civil courts. This inaugurated a system foreign to Islam, and brought the administration of law largely under direct control of the state. It limited the courts of the Ulema, the Mahkama, to such special subjects as are treated in the Koran, as marriage, divorce, and inheritance. The Ulema were greatly dissatisfied. But even when Sultan Abdul Hamid, in his strong reaction, abolished the Constitution of 1876, he confirmed the secular Courts and Codes. "The greater part of the new law," says Jurist, "is not in accordance with the Shari." In regard to penalties, the change is strikingly evident. The old penalties are simply disregarded. Modern ideas are conformed to. Instances of conflict between the Kazis and the judges are not uncommon. For example, a Moslem was found guilty of eating food during the fast of Ramazan. The Kazi condemned him to have melted hot lead poured down his throat. The governor declined to inflict the penalty, and referred the case to Constantinople, where it was pigeonholed and forgotten. In another case the penalty decreed was that the man's tongue should be pulled out. Compliance was refused by the Executive. The only resource of the Kazi was to say, "My duty is to decide according to the law, yours is to execute. My responsibility ends." An example in the change of law is seen in commercial transactions. The Shari forbids not only usury, but all interest, profit on loans and deposits, insurance, annuities, conditional contracts, dealing in futures and even a bona-fide sale of crops before the harvest time or advanced payment on the same. Even certain exchanges of one commodity for another are illegal. In accordance with this I have known Moslems to deposit money solely for safety and refuse to take any interest on it. In Egypt in 1901 the postal deposit law was put into operation by Great Britain. Of the depositors 3,195 refused to take interest. Following this the Grand Mufti issued a decree that it was permissible. The next year 30,000 Moslems, including 94 mullahs and Sheikhs, took advantage of the privilege (Gairdner's "Reproach of Islam," p. 200). Though this antiquated law does not fit into modern commercial life, yet the banking business flourishes. The law is the cause of all kinds of disguises and subterfuges and of fictitious transactions having the appearance of the real. Even a usurious rate of twenty-four or thirty-six per cent is collected. Some person desired to sell a future crop of wheat; a cat was brought in, around the neck of which a stalk of wheat was tied. A bill of sale of the cat was written out in due form and phrase, it being understood that in the transfer of the cat, the crop was made over to the purchaser. Not only in Persia and Turkey but practically everywhere the Shari is being set aside. Even in Afghanistan the process has begun. A decree of Amir Habibullah has been issued abolishing the punishment of cutting off the hand. The reason assigned for this change was that he had been in danger of the loss of his hand from blood poison and it had been saved to him by an English surgeon. In Egypt, between 1876 and 1883, the French Codes and Courts were established. Throughout the whole of North Africa the Shari is superseded. In India it is only applied in a certain defined sphere. Such is the case in other countries under European jurisdiction.

Aside from the action of governments there is a tendency among the Ulema to accommodate the Shari to existing conditions. By strict construction every non-Moslem land or land under non-Moslem rule is a Dar-ul-Harb, a land of war, and it is the duty of Moslems to attack and fight against it. But in India the Ulema have decreed that a country in which some of the peculiar customs of Islam prevail can be considered a Dar-ul-Islam, and the Muftis of Mecca have confirmed the principle. Regarding the jihad they have decided that it is not to be entered upon "unless it is likely to be successful." When there is no probability of victory, proclamation of a jihad is unlawful. Strictly the law forbids Moslems to have Christian troops as their allies, but not only now but at other times Moslems have fought "Holy Wars" against Christians with the help of Christians. Even in Byzantine times this was so, and Egyptian Moslems helped the Crusaders in their invasion of Palestine (Margoliouth's "Mohammedanism," p. 86). Strictly the proclamation of the jihad was the prerogative of the one caliph, but it has become a power attached to each independent Moslem ruler in conjunction with his Sheikh or Mujtahid. The law of the succession to the caliphate is in abeyance. It was restricted to the Arab tribe of the Koreish. But victory of the Osmanli Sultanate has given to a Turk the name, prerogative, and prestige of the caliphate—by the power of the sword—as one of the spoils of war. So it has continued four hundred years, abrogating the Law and Traditions in so fundamental a matter.

MODIFICATIONS IN RELIGIOUS CUSTOMS

There are a large number of modifications in Islam which affect its religious customs among millions of its adherents. These also show that Islam is not the fixed, uniform, and inflexible thing it has been deemed. I shall briefly indicate some of them. It was the law of Islam that idolaters should be exterminated, while peoples of a Book, as Jews, Christians, and possibly Zoroastrians, might be tolerated as zimmis or rayats, subjects. According to this law idolatry was exterminated from Arabia. But in India, Moslem rulers finally tolerated idolatry in their subjects, though after persecutions. Moslems also marry Hindu women who have not accepted Islam. Moslem Emperors married Hindu, Rajput, ladies. The Sunnis of the Turkish Empire regard the people of the Book as pure and will buy bread and meat from them, but the Sunnis of India, following the Shiahs, regard Christians as unclean ceremonially and contact with them and eating their food as an abomination. The Law is changed according to environment. In China Moslem women do not wear the veil and do bind the feet; men wear the queue. They include the old Chinese feasts in their calendar.

In India Islam has taken up many elements of Hinduism. Not only is this seen in the sects like the Sufis, who mingle the fire-worship of the Persians and the Pantheism of the Hindus with some tenets of Islam, look upon Ali and Mohammed as incarnations of the Supreme Spirit, and acknowledge the Koran only in a spiritualized sense (C. R. Haines: "Islam as a Missionary Religion," p. 93), but among the more orthodox Moslems. Even the caste system has affected them. Tribes of Hindus and other races have accepted Islam, but retained their caste, with their customs, and do not intermarry with Moslems of other castes. Moslems of a certain caste will draw water from a well with Hindus of the same caste, but not permit Moslems of a lower caste to use the well (Dr. Wherry: "Christianity and Islam, etc.," pp. 108-09). There are Mohammedan castes which refuse to eat beef, stick to certain trades, wear Hindu dress, rarely go to the mosque, but take part in Hindu festivals and openly worship idols and many gods. The Mohammedan Rajput Hindus preserve unaltered the social customs of the clan (T. W. Arnold: "International Congress of History and Religion," Vol. I, p. 314). The sayids of India are as strict to maintain the purity of their blood as the Brahmans and exclude intermarriage with other Moslems. In the Punjab, the Shariat regarding marriage is a dead letter. There is no dowry and no inheritance for daughters. One-sixth of the Moslem widows remain widows through the influence of Brahmanism (Arnold: *Ibid.*, p. 314). Moslem villagers may be seen utilizing the Hindu astrologer and even praying to the idol god to give his wife a son. Not only the accustomed saint-worship but demonology and witchcraft have corrupted the original faith (*Imperial Gazetteer of India*, p. 435). The sect of Pachpiriyas is a fusion of Islam and animism, worshipping five local saints or gods. The Egyptian fellahs celebrate the cult of Bubastis as if honouring a Moslem saint. In Algeria the Mohammedan law has failed to replace the old tribal customs. Superstition, magic, and relics of paganism hold sway. Circassians, too, retain much of the old heathen religion and worship gods many ("Encyclopedia of Islam," p. 835). In the East Indies, Islam has mixed with animism to such an extent as to be thoroughly corrupt and is called Javanism. Magic has become as a divine institution. Spiritualism has been adopted and ancestor worship and angels and prophets have been substituted for their ancestors. The worship of spirits is not abolished. The Shariat has become mixed up with animism. Mr. Simon says: "The old and new jurisprudence have been amalgamated. Malay common law was given elbow-room, with unscrupulous adaptation" (pp. 200 and 66). In some respects, as in regard to slavery and the treatment of women, Malay custom has improved Islam. The mode of receiving new converts has been modified. As the heathen tribes often have circumcision, it has no further significance. The *kalima* is not even committed to memory, though but a sentence in length. The convert is asked, "Do you wish to become a Moslem?" On his answering "Yes," a lemon is squeezed over his head as a rite of purification (Simon, p. 110). Regarding Islam in Annam, M. Doutte says (Margoliouth: "Mohammedanism," p. 40): "In our colonial empire we have a good example of Islam entirely changed and brought back to quite primitive belief, among the Chams."

ISLAM DOES UNDERGO MODIFICATIONS

It is evident, therefore, that Islam has in the course of its history undergone many modifications. These changes have been of varying degrees of importance, from simple accommodations to the customs and ways of peoples to such beliefs and practices as compromise the monotheism of the Faith. Of some things we have been able to see the origin and the process by which they obtained admission. Of others this is not possible, only it is evident that they were not in primitive Islam. Islam has shown power of adaptation. And in order to get a true conception of it as a religion this needs to be emphasized. This fact has been obscured, though students of Islam have not overlooked it. T. W. Arnold calls attention ("The Preaching of Islam," p. 371) to "the power of the religion to adapt itself to the peculiar characteristics and the stages of development of the people whose allegiance it seeks to win"; and Oscar Mann ("Great Religions," p. 58) speaks of it as showing a marvellous adaptability in shaping its religious ordinances to old customs. Stanley Lane-Poole ("Studies in a Mosque," p. 169) makes the emphatic statement that "the faith of Islam has passed through more phases and experienced greater revolutions than perhaps any other of the religions of the world." Professor Goldziher ("Historians' History," p. 298) says on this theme: "The first step which Islam took on its victorious career taught it to accommodate itself to an alien spirit and to mould its intellectual heritage by influences which seem absolutely heterogeneous to a superficial observer. It was a borrower. That it makes inflexible protest against the influence of foreign elements is an illusion." Bosworth Smith ("Mohammed and Mohammedanism," p. 255) says: "It may be safely said that there is nothing more extraordinary in the whole history of Islam than the way in which the theory of . . . the stereotyped and unalterable nature of its precepts, have by ingenuity, by legal fictions, by the Sunna, and by *responsa prudentum,* been accommodated to the changing circumstances and the various degrees of civilization. . . . It is quite possible that where so much has been done already, more may be done in the future and means be found of reconciling the laws . . . with the requirements of modern society."

THE PROCESS OF CHANGE

What are we to expect will be the process of change in Islam? One possible method that lies open is by Ijma, the consensus of opinion of the Ulema. The Shiahs follow the interpretations of their Mujtahid, and there is no legal reason why this method cannot be utilized among Sunnis, for tradition affirms that Ijma cannot err. This is a legitimate way of escape from the bonds of tradition and the Shariat. Professor Macdonald, while believing that this may be the solution, suggests that a more probable alternative is for Moslems to take refuge more fully in the mystical way and follow Islam as an abstraction but Sufiism as the reality to live by ("Aspects of Islam," p. 112). Some have suggested that Islam may undergo change by revelations through Pirs,

Sheikhs, and Valis, since they profess to have this power, and belief in them is increasing. Professor Margoliouth finds a loophole for progress in the Moslem simply allowing to pass into desuetude any undesirable rites or injunctions; for to formally deny or reject a law is regarded as infidelity, but simple disobedience or neglect is pardonable ("Mohammedanism," p. 129). Judging by past history, the causes of change will be varied. Some changes, as the assumption of the caliphate by the Turks and the modification of the doctrine of the jihad in India, have been the result of conquest. At other times they have come through compromise with the conquered. Most modifications, whether due to Greek philosophy, Roman Law, Persian Sufiism, to Christianity or to the Aliites, whether from internal or external influences, have been received without formal action or decision. It is possible that Islam may be changed by definite revolts and reforms, which shall cause schisms from the orthodox Sunnis. There are some indications of this.

In the present age Islam is undergoing further changes. There is movement. There is a condition of unrest and dissatisfaction, of misgivings, fear, and anxiety. New thoughts, ideals, and aspirations are clashing with old tenets, prejudices, and superstitions. It is a period of controversy. Doctrines and policies are in debate. Many are moving from the old moorings. Contentment with their condition, civilization, and environment have passed away. Old-time arrogance and pride are gone. Self-assurance is weakened. Many lament the conditions of the Moslem world as one of decadence and of material, social, and intellectual inferiority. They feel that Islam and Moslem peoples are both at a low ebb. Different parties assign diverse reasons for these conditions and propose different remedies according to their various attitudes toward the modern age.

Some cry out: Hold to the Old Faith! Observe the Law and the Traditions and Almighty God will bless our people and give our armies victory as of old. Our weakness comes from ignoring the Shariat.

Others cry out: Back to Mohammed! Back to the Koran! The Traditions have led us astray.

Others, with a free use of criticism and of rationalism, would interpret in accordance with the spirit of Islam and reconstruct it in conformity with modern ideas and twentieth-century conditions and culture.

Others again, counting themselves superior to creed and law, and setting them aside by allegorical interpretations, would have all to walk in the divine Path by means of mystical communions and hypnotic exercises.

Others, feeling that only a new divine Guide and a new revelation can solve the perplexities and right the wrongs of the age, have fixed their faith and hope on Mahdis, Imams, and so-called Lights.

Others would adopt Western political institutions and learning as the framework for a reformed Moslem state, subordinating affairs of Islam to national progress and civilization. With a secularistic spirit, they would side-track religion, unless perchance it be to use it for nationalistic purposes.

None of these parties are animated by a spirit of

friendliness to Christianity, though all of them are willing to take advantage of Western military and industrial science and some of them of all the Christian world can furnish, except the Gospel.

Lastly there are some, all too few, in the Moslem world who are earnest inquirers and who are learning to look to the Lord Jesus Christ as the panacea for their ills. This day of unrest in Islam is a special opportunity for Christian missions. It is a fit time to bring the impress of the Gospel, the impact of Christian truth to bear on Islam. We cannot rely on our civilization to Christianize it. Islam, be assured, will find a way to adopt our civilization and remain Islam. Special and mighty and immediate efforts are necessary if we wish to draw them Christward. This day of Movement is a crisis in their spiritual history.

I wish to present to your consideration Modern Movements among Moslems. I will consider:

First, those movements which spring from and are inspired by doctrines or aspirations within Islam itself, as Wahabism, Pan-Islamism, and Moslem Missions, especially as carried on from Mecca and by the Darvish Orders.

Secondly, those connected with eschatalogical hopes, as the Return of the Imam, or Mahdiism.

Thirdly, those movements inspired by or due to the impact of Christian civilization, as Neo-Islam.

Fourthly, Political Movements in Moslem Lands.

II

THE REVIVAL IN ISLAM

I HAVE referred to the fact that Islam is being moved by opposing currents of thought. Zealous leaders have come forth, antagonistic to each other, yet all professing the purpose to assist the Faith and the Faithful. I will first of all describe a vast conservative movement.

A remarkable phenomenon of the last century was a revival in Islam. As a religion, Islam, at the end of the eighteenth century, was like a palsied, decrepit old man. It showed signs of disintegration and decay. No less an authority than Palgrave ("Essays on the Eastern Question," pp. 114, 115), describing its condition, writes: "Where the Caliph and the Koran retained their apparent, they had lost their real supremacy. Throughout the Turkish Empire, the most distinctive precepts of the Book were publicly set at naught, nowhere more than in Constantinople itself. Nor were the sacred cities themselves, Mecca and Medina, much better. The wine taverns of the janisaries, the raki shops of the citizens, the prostitutes of the Hejaz, the Bi-lillahs of Bagdad and Cairo had become recognized institutions; opium-eating, too, was next to universal; the mosque stood unfrequented and ruinous, while the public schools and Colleges of Mohammedan Law had fallen into dreary decay. An eclipse, total it seemed, had spread over the crescent, foreboding disaster and extinction."

But this expectation was not fulfilled. On the contrary, there came about a renewal of religious loyalty and zeal, manifested in a closer adherence to the Shariat, the Sacred Law, a more strenuous maintenance of its creed and observance of its rites, an aggressive propaganda and a determined effort to renew and strengthen the power of Islam, both religious and political. The reasons for this awakening were partly religious, arising from regret for the low condition of the Faith; and partly political, from chagrin on account of the weakness and inferiority of Mohammedan peoples and determination to yield no further to the influence or the pressure of Christian governments. The result was, writes Palgrave (*Ibid.*, p. 123), "that Mohammedan fervour has been thoroughly rekindled within the limits which its half-extinguished ashes covered and the increased heat has by natural law extended over whatever lies nearest but beyond the former circumference." Claude Field, the author of "Mystics and Saints in Islam," describes the movement as the "almost miraculous renaissance in Islam which is now proceeding in Turkey and other Mohammedan lands."

WAHABISM

The impetus to this awakening came from Wahabism. The influence of this puritanic reformation has been deep and widespread. It deserves study. It is the judgment of Oscar Mann ("Great Religions of the World," p. 58) that "almost the whole of the modern progressive movement of Mohammedans may be traced directly or indirectly to it."

Wahabism took its name from its founder, Mohammed Ibn Abdul Wahab. He was the son of a village Sheikh in Central Arabia and was thoroughly educated in Islamic theology at Basra and Medina. The divergence of Moslems from the primitive standards of rigid monotheism and simplicity of life had deeply affected him. He started his career by a protest against the cult of Sad, at Inayah, where saint-worship prevailed. His cry was back to the Koran and the primitive Law of the Sunna. He even rejected the interpretations of the orthodox schools of the Sunnis. He stood for a literal interpretation of the Koran and affirmed the right of interpreting it, even contrary to the Imams. He abhorred Sufiism. He demanded the strict observance of the prayer-rite, fast, and tithes-giving. He denounced the reverence paid to the saints, the Sheikhs, and even to Mohammed, and all invoking of their mediation as well as making pilgrimage or offerings to their shrines or perambulating their tombs and all the superstitions connected with them, and the use of the rosary. He limited the festivals and forbade the celebration of Mohammed's birthday. He denounced luxury in dress and habits and the use of silk, jewels, gold and silver ornaments, and strictly prohibited wine, tobacco, gambling, and Oriental vice. In a word, he aimed to reform doctrines, purify worship, and purge out innovations and corruptions. He protested against the liberty granted to the infidels, that is, the Christians, whom he pronounced unclean abominations. The ordinary Moslems were no better, being *musrik,* polytheists, even as the Christians. He thoroughly approved of and made use of the primitive Islamic method of promoting reform, namely, by the power of the sword. All unbelievers, even Moslems, who did not reform were to be killed. The jihad was indeed holy and the warrior, dying fighting for the faith, passed into Paradise; and to make firm the soldier's assurance a written order on the gate-keeper of the heavenly mansions was put into his hand, with the injunction, "Kill and strangle all infidels who give companions to God."

The message of the reformer was at first rejected. He was driven from place to place. But finally Ibn Saud, the ruler of Daraiyah, believed. Ibn Abdul Wahab gave promise to Ibn Saud that if he would draw the sword in the cause of pure Islam, he would make him sole ruler in Najd and the first potentate in Arabia. Sheikh Saud accepted the terms, married the reformer's daughter, and became the commander of the new jihad and the founder of a conquering dynasty. He and his successors, from 1760 onward, brought into subjection the neighbouring tribes, offering conversion or extermination. Kerbala, the shrine of the Shiahs, was despoiled of its treasures and destroyed, with its relics and the golden dome over the tomb of the Imam Husain. Mecca and Medina, the sacred cities, were subdued, 1803-04, and compelled to reform, the dome of Mohammed's grave and all the objects of veneration were destroyed, and ceremonies which were innovations on primitive Islam were prohibited.

The desecration of the holy cities and the inhibition

of pilgrimage to all who were not of his sect, aroused the Sunni Caliph or Sultan. At his command, Mehemet Ali, the Khedive of Egypt, and Ibrahim Pasha subjugated the Wahabis, and their Sheikh, Abdullah II, was sent to Constantinople and beheaded in front of St. Sophia (1819). Two small Wahabi states survived, one with a capital at Riyad, another at Haiel in Najd, with a population of 1,500,000.

The influence of the Wahabi movement extended beyond Arabia and was greater in its religious than in its political aspect. It was introduced into India by Sayid Ahmad of Oudh, who claimed to be the Mahdi. His propaganda to purge out Hindu superstitions from Islam excited fierce fanaticism. He raised a jihad against the Sikhs, captured Peshavur in 1830, and maintained an insurrection for four years. He declared that India was a Dar-il-Harb, a land of warfare, and that jihad against the British government was obligatory. The influence of Wahabis is still felt in India and the sect continues near the northwest frontier. Another sect, called the Faraisis, arose in India, animated with the same spirit.

In Sumatra a like movement was started about 1837 by a pilgrim returned from Mecca. He began the correction of the errors and abuses of Moslems, especially striving to abolish the use of opium, tobacco, and betel nut. From this propaganda grew up the Padri sect. They proclaimed the jihad against the heathen Bataks, destroyed their villages, outraged their women, sold their children into slavery, and killed every male who would not accept Islam.

Wahabism bore fruit in Africa. Osman Danfodio,

chief of the Fulahs, learned the doctrine at Mecca, and on his return preached it. He succeeded in arousing the people, founded Sokoto and the Fulah kingdom, subdued several heathen states and forced them to embrace Islam. Wahabism was also the inspiration of the Sanusi, of whom I shall speak later (Arnold: "Preaching of Islam," pp. 230, 265, 299).

Wahabism greatly influenced the whole Islamic body. Just as the Protestant Reformation was followed by a counter-reformation in Roman Catholicism, so Wahabism was the instrument for arousing the Sunni Moslems. Its influence, true to its own spirit, has been thoroughly reactionary. That return to primitive Islam is the hope of the world's regeneration has been the inspiration of modern conservative movements. Of it T. W. Arnold (*Ibid.*, pp. 345-46) says: "It has given birth to numerous movements which take rank among the most powerful influences in the Islamic world. It is closely connected with many of the modern Moslem missions; the fervid zeal it has stirred up, the new life it has infused into existing religious institutions, the impetus it has given to theological study and to the organization of devotional exercises, have all served to awaken and keep alive the innate proselyting spirit of Islam." Similarly Canon Sell says (*Missionary Review*, October, 1902, p. 732): "Its religious teaching, and still more its narrow fanatical spirit, have spread into many lands and influenced many peoples." Palgrave, who lived and travelled in Turkey and Arabia in close contact with Moslems, writes: "The whole school of Islamic teaching has been modified by it; not only the common people but also many of the highest and best educated classes, even the Sultan (Abdul Aziz) himself, are distinctly inclined to the stricter school, and so are most of the principal Ulema." He finds in it a principal cause of the "Mohammedan revival—a worldwide movement, an epochal phenomenon, before which the lesser laws of race and locality are swept away or absorbed in unity, which we can no more check nor retard than we can hinder the tide from swelling" ("Essays," p. 140). He declares that in the middle of the last century "the energy and breadth of the revival embraced every class from the Sultan Abdul Aziz down to the poorest hammal or porter on the wharves and every Mohammedan race in the Ottoman empire" (*Ibid.*, p. 123), "with the public adhesion of all and the sincere adhesion of the masses." This was evidenced by a repair of the mosques and *madressahs*, schools, a stricter observance of the fasts and prayers, a thronging of the shrines, and increase of pilgrimage to Mecca. There was also a reform of the habits of drunkenness among the soldiers.

This spirit was also a reaction against the introduction of European laws and customs by the reforming Sultans, Mahmud II and Abdul Aziz in his first years. A strong feeling of opposition to these measures existed not only among the Ulema on account of the Western code, but also among the beys and proprietors, because they had been deprived of their lands and feudal privileges by the new regulations. So political conservatism and zeal for Islam went hand in hand. Dissatisfaction with the new codes led to a partial return to the jurisdiction of the Mahkamah or Courts of the Sacred Law. Opposition to the patronage given to the infidels led to the casting out from employ of many Europeans who about 1850 had overrun the Turkish service, and the employment in their places of Moslem doctors, civil engineers, and administrators. Rushdi schools which had been started for the whole population, including Christians, were transformed into strictly Mohammedan schools, with teaching of Islam and Islamic languages. The Sultan Abdul Aziz became sympathetic with the reactionaries. The Grand Vizier, Ali Pasha, said to a British official: "What we want is an increase of fanaticism rather than a diminution of it." Notwithstanding these symptoms, the political reformers retained superior influence in the government till the promulgation of the Constitution of 1876. After its abrogation by Sultan Abdul Hamid, he openly became the chief of the reactionaries, and made it his whole aim to strengthen the Moslem element of his empire. This aim soon assumed a wider scope and developed into a movement to which is given the name Pan-Islamism.

PAN-ISLAMISM

Pan-Islamism is a movement with the purpose and endeavour to unite for defensive and aggressive action. It aims to combine by the ties of the religion Moslems of every race and country, in the work of conserving and propagating the faith and of freeing it by means of political and military force from alien rule and thus making it again a triumphant world power. It has a religious side and a political side. On the religious side it is conservative and would strenuously maintain Islam. Yet it would have a platform broad enough to include all sects and parties. On the political side it would weld into an alliance all Moslem peoples and governments.

This scheme is in accordance with the nature of Islam. Mohammed apparently designed that all believers should constitute one nation, not intending that racial or national aspirations should assert themselves. Great effort even was made to spread the Arabic and make it a universal language. Islam has much to draw it together in unity:—a simple creed formula—La illah ill' Allah, Mohammed rasul Allah—No God save God; Mohammed is the Apostle of God—A common Koran, Kibla and Kaaba; a Capital, Mecca, the centre of Pilgrimage, with its unifying influence; a common language of worship, a common prayer ritual, a common calendar—a sense of brotherhood which excludes distinctions of race and colour.

By including military action in its programme, Islam was acting entirely according to its nature. The Crusades were contrary to the Gospel of Christ, but an organized movement for warfare is harmonious with the genius and history of Islam. Such a movement is facilitated in this age by the very civilization introduced by the infidels, for ease of communication and transit bring the widely separated sections of Islam into closer contact, and even the peace maintained by Christian governments in Asia and Africa gives opportunity for the spread of ideas and plans. Uniting Islam in a great final struggle is in accordance with its alleged prophecies, and the ever-present hope of its complete triumph. A Holy War is expected to precede the judgment and by means of it all authority is to pass into the hands of Moslems. The year A.H. 1300 (1882) was regarded from these prophecies as a crisis destined to bring greater weakness or renewed strength.

DIVISIONS OF ISLAM

One difficulty to be overcome was the condition of division into sects and nationalities. Islam has not been a unit since the twelfth year after the Prophet's death, nor since the second century of the Hegira has it maintained outward unity. It has abounded in opposing sects whose hostility ofttimes unsheathed the sword. There is an erroneous impression abroad about the unity of Islam. Few people recognize the multiplicity of sects there are in it. Mohammed is reported by tradition to have said that the Jews have 71 sects, the Christians 72, and the Moslems would have 73. It would excel even in the number of sects, and in truth more than twice the above number have been listed. The Mohammedans are no solid mass of severe monotheists. Besides the sects of Aliites or Shiahs, such as Ismieliyahs, Borahs, Zaidis, Fatimites, Sufis, Usulis, Akhbaris, Sheikhis, Nusairis, Kuzil Bashis, etc.; Sunnis include Kurds who do not keep the law; Arab tribes who worship jinns; Indians who worship idols; Africans and Malays who are still fetish-worshippers; Rationalists and free-thinkers; Dunma Jews and Stavoirite Christians. Islam is a heterogeneous mass whose divisions hold to their differences as tenaciously as do any sects in Christendom. New movements have led to new schisms. The Wahabis, the Babis, the Sudan Mahdiists each in its turn created antagonisms. The enthusiasm, courage, and fanaticism of their followers, which urged them on to war and conquest, were expended largely in hostility to the governments of Islam, for each of them regarded the authority of its leader as supreme and called upon Sultan and Shah to submit to them.

Overcoming racial jealousies and hatred was also a problem. These exist among Islamic peoples just as between Christians. By race Moslems have been divided into 80,000,000 Caucasians, 70,000,000 Mongol-Turks, 44,000,000 Malay-Dravidians, and 36,000,000 Negros or Negroids. Arabs, Turks, and Kurds have their racial and political antagonisms. Iran and Turan did not forsake their age-long warfare by accepting Mohammed. The national ambitions of the Albanians and Egyptians are in opposition to those of the Ottomans. Berbers and Arabs fought through centuries and the Berbers twelve times threw off the yoke of Islam. Even in Central Africa Islam has not had influence enough to overcome the national peculiarities of the races who have adopted it. Professor Westermann declares (*International Review of Missions,* October, 1912, p. 648) that "the national consciousness of the Sudanese is stronger than their religious attachment. The Hausa and Fulah have lived together for centuries side by side, but their relations continue to be entirely strained, while the Tuareg are equally unfriendly to them both."

Pan-Islamism aimed by a spirit of accommodation to smooth over differences. It was not reformatory, it did not emphasize doctrinal unity, but rather confederation for action—a union for the defence, propagation, and glory of the Faith.

These difficulties did not seem insuperable and the task was entered upon with strong determination. The leader of this movement was Abdul Hamid, Sultan and Caliph. It is said that during the first years of his reign he hesitated as to whether he should support the liberal or the reactionary side. But soon it became evident that he had determined to make his government a Moslem administration, to magnify Islam and repress Christians. The rebellion of Arabi Pasha in Egypt and the claims of the Mahdi in the Sudan had a tendency to accentuate Moslem desire for supremacy and to lead them to deplore Christian prestige. Abul-Huda, the chief of the Rafai darvishes—the Sultan's astrologer,—gave advice to revive and strengthen the influence of the caliphate. So around it the propaganda was made to revolve so as to throw the shield of religion over the political aims.

THE CALIPHATE

The office of Caliph, or supreme Head of the Moslems, has pertained to the Osmanli Sultans for four centuries. In 1517 Salim I conquered the Mamelukes of Egypt. Living in subordination to the latter, treated as underlings and at times almost as prisoners, and used to further their political ends, were the successors of the Abbaside Caliphs of Bagdad, who were permitted religious authority only. The last of these

Mutavvakul ceded to Sultan Salim his rights and titles as Caliph of the Prophet of God, Commander of the Faithful, Imam of Moslems, Refuge of the world, and Shadow of God, which the Sultan now bears in addition to King of kings, Arbiter of the world's destinies, Lord of the Two Continents and Two Seas, and Sovereign of the East and West. The insignia of the office, the possession of which has high significance, were transferred to him, namely, the standard or cloak of the Prophet, some hair of his beard, and the sword of the Caliph Omar. At the same time the Sherif of Mecca tendered his allegiance and brought to Salim the keys of Mecca and Medina and transferred to him the guardianship of the Sacred Cities.

Thus, by the power of the sword, the Osmanli Sultans became caliphs, ignoring however two essential requisites according to accepted Sunni tradition, namely, that the Caliph should be of the Arab tribe of Koreish, and, secondly, that he should be elected to the office. The latter is fulfilled nominally at the accession of each Sultan, when the form of an election is observed by the Ulema of Constantinople and the Sultan is invested with the Caliphate. The other condition is ignored, though a list, which named descent from the Koreish as among the qualifications, remained posted in all the great mosques, even of Constantinople, until ordered removed by Abdul Hamid. The Khavarij held that it was not necessary that the caliph should be of the Koreish ("Spirit of Islam," Amir Ali, p. 525). By legists and scholars generally the Sultans are regarded as usurpers, yet they are acknowledged practically because they are the most powerful defenders of the faith. Still considerable bodies of Moslems have never acknowledged them, as the Shiahs, and the subjects of the Sultans of Morocco, Zanzibar, and Oman, and of the Wahabi Sheikhs of Arabia. Before the time of Abdul Hamid, Chinese Moslems cared nothing for the Turkish caliphate nor did they recognize the Sherif of Mecca. Yet such distant rulers as the Amirs of Bokhara and Khotan, the Sultans of Atchin and Panthay have sent envoys during the last century. European governments with Moslem subjects have acknowledged him as supreme, and the United States has seen fit to send an envoy to consult about the Sulus of the Philippines.

The greatest strength of the caliphate is with the ignorant populace. Some of them regard him as the emperor of all Europe, holding in subjection to himself all Christian states, who acknowledge his sovereignty by sending him tribute and keeping delegates at his Court. The kings of Europe cannot be crowned without first obtaining his permission and sometimes have to come in person to obtain it; not even the emperors of Russia and Great Britain are exempt from this necessity. The Emperor of Germany came to do obeisance to the Sultan and brought presents of horses in token of his subjection. The Sultan will one of these days overthrow these Christian governments (Simon: "Progress of Islam, etc.," p. 28; "Turkey and Its People," by Pears, pp. 75, 86; "Turkey and the Armenian Atrocities," E. M. Bliss, p. 75). A Moslem, and he not a fellah but a mullah in St. Sophia, told Sir Edwin Pears that Queen Victoria was a faithful servant of their Padishah, but it was not plain why he allowed the governor of England to be a woman.[1]

Among the qualifications for the caliphate, character scarcely finds a place. He is to be a " just person " and supposedly God-guided. Yet Abdul Hamid had the astrologer Abul Huda as his constant adviser. This astute magician is said to have worked in collusion with Izzat Pasha, who showed him telegrams from various quarters before the Sultan had seen them. He thus many times astonished his Padishah. Morality has not been required nor expected as a qualification of the caliph. Of course, without question, he has legally the privilege of having three or four hundred concubines in his haram, and can even count the massacring of tens of thousands of Christian subjects as a holy work. But even Moslem law cannot justify the horrible practice which many Sultans successively followed of celebrating the binding on of the sword of Osman by putting to death all the royal brothers. Mahmud II ordered his seventeen brothers to be bowstrung. They were interred in St. Sophia around the newly made grave of their father. This practice was general (Pears: *Ibid.*, pp. 8-10) and was continued without concealment until the middle of the nineteenth century. How Moslems can look upon such a line of assassins as their religious chiefs can only be accounted for by their habit of divorcing religion from morality. Justice Amir Ali says

[1] This ignorance is equalled by that in Persia which attributes to the Shah's visit to Queen Victoria a matrimonial purpose, as their traditions do to the coming of the Queen of Sheba to Solomon.

(" Spirit of Islam," p. 470) that the Sunnis do not demand that the caliph be just, virtuous, or irreproachable; that neither vices nor tyranny justify his deposition. But some of them, as the Omayyad Walid and the Abbaside Mutavakul, have been deposed by popular revolt against their iniquities. It had happened among the Osmanlis several times before Abdul Hamid.

Sunnis claim that there can only be one caliph at a time, regarding as unlawful the existence of contemporary caliphs as the Omayyads at Granada, the Abbasides at Bagdad, and the Fatimites at Cairo.

The claim of the Sultan, weak legally and historically, was rendered more insecure and ineffective at the beginning of his reign, by the fact that the Sherif of Mecca and the Arabs were inclined to repudiate him. After the Russo-Turkish war some of the Arabs declared that the Sultan had forfeited his claim through his defeats and that the caliphate should return to the Koreish tribe (H. H. Jessup: " The Mohammedan Missionary Problem," p. 21). The Sherif Sheikh Husni, an Anglophile, was ready to make good his claim, and it was supposed that he was encouraged to do so by the British. The Sherif was disposed of in true Oriental style by means of an assassin, and a supporter of the Sultan was put in his place. Henceforth the religious side of Pan-Islamism was promoted from Mecca as a second centre (" Fall of Abdul Hamid," F. McCallagh, p. 23).

Abdul Hamid carried on his propaganda in no half-hearted way. He put his untiring energy into it both in his own dominions and in the whole Islamic world.

He called together in secret session many Sheikhs and planned schemes. His agents were sent everywhere on secret missions. They were liberally supplied with funds. Generous presents were sent with them to the heads of various sects, orders, shrines, and holy places; pensions were given to mullahs, sayids, and influential darvishes. It is asserted by Salib el Khalidi that the Sultan spent half his revenues for Pan-Islamism. Influencing and intriguing with the subjects of other governments was no small part of the effort, which included not only the preaching of union but the encouraging of fanaticism and rebellion. Hurgronje says ("The Holy War, etc.," p. 29): "It secretly worked as a disturbing element; it often would oppose the normal development of a mutually desirable relation between the governing and the governed." The agents used were at one time the able diplomat, at another the learned mullah, or again the darvish mendicant or the Khoja, dressed as a darvish. Turkish consuls were established at many points, whose manner of life, however, somewhat interfered with the scheme, for it was often an offence against Moslem morals. In Turkey the Ulema were urged to engage yet more zealously in strengthening the faith of the people, proclaiming the waxing of the Crescent and the increasing glory of the caliphate. Above all they were urged to be diligent in convincing the faithful concerning the merit to be acquired before heaven by robbing and killing the Christians. The *dallals* or guides to the pilgrimage were made efficient agents. Formerly they had been ignorant and untrained men who came from Mecca, collected the dues for the

Kaaba, guided the pilgrim caravan to Mecca, and acted as guides while there. At this time a different type of men, ably trained propagandists, were assigned to this service and went everywhere preaching.

The press was enlisted in the cause. Not a few journals were its advocates. These papers and books fostered disloyalty to other governments, proclaiming the triumph of the Crescent. Abdul Hamid even went so far as to have denunciations of Great Britain printed in his palace and distributed in Afghanistan and Arabia. A part of the propaganda consisted in taking children of prominent families from India, Java, and Sumatra to Constantinople to be trained in loyalty to the Ottoman caliphate. This was forbidden by the colonial governments. The result of "this skilfully planned agitation, carefully engineered from the Palace (Sir William Ramsay: "Impressions of Turkey," pp. 136-39) was all through Turkey a further increase of Moslem power and fanaticism." As Palgrave had noticed it in the previous reign, so Sir William Ramsay speaks of it under Abdul Hamid. Sir Charles Elliot also says: "In this decade, 1880-90, a tendency prevailed to accentuate the Sultan's position as caliph—to make it a vital reality. There was kept before the minds of the Moslems the idea that the Sultan was the head of all Islam on the one side as opposed to all Christians on the other" (Sir Charles Elliot: "Turkey in Europe"). Abdul Hamid made his Moslem subjects believe that their misfortunes were due to the interference of Europeans. Hurgronje testifies to the spread of this propaganda, saying: "There is *certainly a very pronounced Pan-*

Islamic tendency in all classes of Mohammedan society."

COMBINATION OF SUNNIS AND SHIAHS

An important factor of the scheme was the bringing of the Shiahs of Persia into co-operation. This was the more important owing to the geographical position of Persia, lying between the Moslems of India and Afghanistan and those of the Turkish Empire. For both political and military reasons Persia's co-operation was most desirable. The agents of Pan-Islamism showed marked activity, and their presence was continually reported in the bazaar rumours. Their chief was a remarkable man named Sheikh Jamal-ud-Din, whose life-story is a marvellous exhibition of a powerful personality—a man who left his mark on the political and religious life and history of Afghanistan, India, Egypt, Turkey, and Persia. He was a sayid born at Asadabad, near Hamadan. At the age of ten he began his wanderings, studied in various cities, and became erudite in almost the whole range of Moslem learning. As a youth he passed some time in Afghanistan and a year or two in India, where he acquired some knowledge of English and Western science. After making the pilgrimage to Mecca, he returned to Afghanistan and, rising to the surface in one of the civil wars, became Prime Minister during the brief reign of Amir Mohammed 'Azam. Fleeing thence, he led a life of varied experiences, influential in many places among the literary and official classes. Expelled from India as a precaution against his political intrigues, and from Constantinople through the jealousy of the Sheikh-ul-Islam, he settled in Egypt and gave lectures on Mohammedan theology, philosophy, law, and science, having great influence and fame. He was driven thence by the Khedive at the instigation of the orthodox mullahs and of the British Consul, in 1879, who objected to his activities in connection with the Egyptian Nationalists. After the defeat of Arabi Pasha, he was expelled from India, and came to America to obtain naturalization, but did not remain to carry out this plan. Next he became an editor in Paris, and carried on controversy with Renan and also with the British Government. After residing as a diplomat-at-large at Petrograd, he accepted in 1886 the invitation of Nasr-ud-Din Shah, came to Persia, and was made Minister of War. Later he organized a reform movement and preached much about it at the mosque of Shah Abdul Azim. In this he offended the Shah, so he took refuge at the sanctuary of this mosque. Dragged from there by order of the Shah, he was expelled to Turkey. After a visit to London and various negotiations with its cabinet, he finally took up his residence in Constantinople, where he was a guest and favourite of Abdul Hamid and the active Apostle of Pan-Islamism. In this, he did much, says Professor Browne ("Persian Revolution," p. 30), "to awaken the independent Moslem States to the imminent peril and the urgent need of combination to withstand the aggressions of the great European Powers," and "to create a sense of brotherhood and community of interest among them." His Arabic biographer says of him: "The goal towards which all his actions were directed and the pivot on which all his hopes turned, was the unanimity of Islam and the bringing together of all Moslems in all parts of the world into one Islamic empire under the protection of one supreme Khalifa. He raised up a living spirit in the hearts of his friends and disciples." He founded at Mecca a Pan-Islamic Society, called Umm ul Kura. It printed and circulated its rules and constitution, but was suppressed by Abdul Hamid, because it suggested Kufa as an alternative seat of the caliph (Browne: *Ibid.*, pp., 2-14). The plan was laid to bring the Shiahs into harmony with the Sunni Caliph. This was a bold and difficult scheme. The age-long alienation and bitter enmity, the bloody wars between the adherents of the Imam Ali and those of the four "rightly directly caliphs" made reconciliation seem impossible. Yet the lessening of Shiah hatred in latter years gave hope, and it was by smoothing over of differences rather than by a change of convictions that they expected to bring about concord. There was an example before them; for a union of Sunnis and Shiahs had been accomplished in the Muridism of Mullah Mohammed and Sheikh Schamyl of Daghestan. Both Persia and Turkey felt the necessity of doing something in the face of the aggressive Christian Powers who were pressing in on both sections of Islam. Sheikh Jamal-ud-Din corresponded with the Shiah Mujtahids of Kerbela and Persia. He also sent envoys to work secretly among the Persians, especially among the officials of liberal tendency, upon whom distinctive Shiahism sat lightly. His plea was stated in these words: "If all the Mohammedan nations would only unite, all the nations on earth could not prevail against them." One of these envoys was Mirza Hasan Khan, with whom I had conversation in Tabriz at the house of Yusuf Khan, Mustashar-i-Doulah. Another promoter of Pan-Islamism was Prince Haji Sheikh-ur-Rais, the author of "Ittahad-ul-Islam" ("Union of Islam").

The effects of these negotiations were evident. Some of the influential Shiah Mujtahids of Kerbala and Najef, as well as officials like Amin-i-Doulah and Mustashar-i-Doulah, the Foreign Agent at Tabriz, became advocates of the scheme, and of an arrangement whereby the Persians should recognize the caliphate of the Sultan and the Turks recognize the Shah as head of all the Shiahs, and that both should work in harmony. An account of these negotiations is given in a poem by Mirza Aga Khan. Of the answer of the Mujtahids, he writes (Browne: *Ibid.,* p. 412):

"From Persia and Irak they wrote: 'We have washed from our hearts the dust of dissension;
We will all sacrifice our lives for the Holy Law, we will all swear allegiance to the King of Islam.'"

To allay antagonism and promote unity of feeling, all customs which tended to perpetuate enmity should be discontinued. In accordance with this, Shiahs were to be no longer molested in their pilgrimages. They in observing the mourning of Muharram and the Passion Play, though they might curse Yezid, would not transfer the rancour to the modern Turks. They would drop the festival of Omar and no longer dress up an effigy to represent that caliph and heap indignities upon it. They would no longer make any one to represent this enemy of Ali and treat him with contumely and maledictions, as *Omara laanat olsun* ("Cursed be Omar"). The effect of these efforts at reconciliation were plainly observable in Persia in better relations between Sunnis and Shiahs and were felt in Russia and India as well. But the Shah of Persia did not take kindly to the scheme. It was doubtless evident to him that the prominent negotiators were Old Babis and that they and Jamal-ud-Din did not wish him good. In passing it may be remarked that the Sultans of Morocco and Zanzibar, too, refused to listen to the envoys of Pan-Islamism.

HAJIS AS PROPAGANDISTS

Besides all this, the propaganda was carried on from Mecca by the Sherif and the Ulema. Abdul Hamid cultivated the friendship of the Arabs. As an aid in binding them and the holy cities to the Osmanli caliphate the Hajaz railway was planned and completed to Medina. It was made by the labour of 7,000 soldiers. The Khedive of Egypt and the Shah of Persia joined in the enterprise. A Prince of India spent $200,000 on the Medina Station. Popular interest was aroused and personal subscriptions solicited. Large contributions were received from India, Java, and the whole Moslem world. Lucknow sent $140,000 and Rangoon and Madras $300,000. Peculations from the fund were put at $3,000,000. Yet in spite of this and the Beduin robbers, it was carried to completion. One specialty of its trains is the prayer-car for the pilgrims. The idea of Pan-Islamism is one congenial to the Arabs, for Mecca is a hotbed of Islamic fanaticism and its atmosphere is surcharged with hatred of Christianity and with assurance of the final triumph of Islam over the Christians, even though it is the present kismat that the infidels oppress the faithful. The new High Sherif was in communion of purpose and idea with the Sultan. The power which lay in the schools of Mecca and of the mullahs who went forth from them was more actively exerted to revive Islam. Increasing effort was made to incite the Hajis. These pilgrims come from all parts of the Mohammedan world to be present at the annual feast of sacrifice, and to perform the rites around the Kaaba and other sacred places. Each race and language has its special groupings and mosques, and are brought under instruction with an aim to indoctrinate, inspire, and excite them to stronger faith and fanaticism. Every year one hundred thousand of these devoted pilgrims kiss the black stone and, notwithstanding the fact that they are fleeced unmercifully, swindled and deceived at every turn, notwithstanding the fact that exposure to the broiling sun, cholera, plague, and the treachery of the Beduins prevent thirty-eight per cent from returning to their homes (see Keane's "Six Months in Mecca"), yet the Haji is more than all others a fanatic. Even among the Persians, though they have suffered specially as Shiah heretics, the most fanatical class of the population are the Hajis. They are most ready to treat with scorn and contumely the Armenians or Nestorians, to revile them as infidels, and to gather their honourable robes about them lest they be defiled by their touch. The Hajis return to their Sunni communities, bound as never before to Mecca, with a deep idea of the unity of Islam and a determination to promote it and to defeat and destroy the Christians. This is strikingly true of the Malays, of whom Simon and Hurgronje testify, saying that "every Haji is an agent of Moslem propaganda; they return home inspired with the idea of living and dying for the realization of that unity." They are permeated with the thought of the greatness of Islam, of their position and blessedness in being members of it. They are firm in their belief in its power and its unparalleled influence in the world. They have caused Pan-Islamic principles to penetrate the Moslem millions of Java and Sumatra and even the most remote mountain villages. They are assured that the Supreme Caliph, the Rajah of Stamboul, will one day deliver them. Christians are helped by the devil, their science is of the devil, their machine-guns are called the devil's guns, and they will go to the devil. Their destruction is at hand by the power of the Prophet, for they are inferior in power as well as cursed in their faith, being like unclean beasts. In some such words is described to us (Rev. G. Simon in "Islam and Missions," p. 87) the attitude of East-Indian Moslems. No wonder that its outcome is disloyalty and insurrection.

In Russia Pan-Islamic influence is widespread. A journal advocating it is published in Petrograd, called "The World of Islam," and another is issued by the Academy of Kazan. Agents have travelled far and wide among the Tartars along the Volga. Others have gone through the Crimea, Caucasus, the Kirghiz Steppes, and Turkestan, and inflamed the bigotry of the Moslems, inculcating hatred of Christians and collecting funds for the Sultan. In Bokhara the propaganda is reported to have been very successful and the Amir to have become a leader in the movement. The twenty millions of Moslems in Russia are united and desirous of attaining to the religious and political ideals of Pan-Islamism. In India the propaganda has been active. Abdul Hamid sent his emissaries. A paper was printed in his palace, called Peik-Islam, for circulation in India. The Sultan's name was introduced into the Khutbas, or prayer service, in some provinces.

In Africa, the propaganda had wide ramifications. Lord Cromer saw its activities and describes it in his reports and in his "Modern Egypt." The great darvish orders to which I shall again refer, are active advocates of its main principles, and have won the people to adhesion to them. One of Sultan Abdul Hamid's special agents was Sheikh Jaffar, chief of the Madaniyah darvishes in Tripoli and Algeria. He was a strong supporter of Pan-Islamism and had his headquarters at Stamboul, whence he sent out his messengers ("Islam and Missions," p. 66). The Sanusi Sheikh at first denounced the Osmanli Sultans for their friendliness to and imitation of Christians, but later was reconciled and strove for the same programme. Regarding North Africa, Canon Sell affirms (*Missionary Review*, 1912, p. 739) that "the Pan-Islamic movement is having a power such as has not been seen since the early days of the Arab conquest." Dr. Washburn wrote in 1909: "There seems to be a general movement in North Africa and all over Asia, even in China, the full significance of which we cannot understand. But one thing is clear . . . a determination to maintain their faith on the part of Moslems."

PAN-ISLAMISM AN ANTI-CHRISTIAN MOVEMENT

The Pan-Islamic movement aimed to oppose and conquer Christianity. It strove not only to promote things Moslem but abolish and destroy things Christian. Its policy of repression was evident in the Sultan's dominions. The condition there was well described as "an increasing stringency directed against Christian education, and increasing hostility to the use of books by the Christians" in order to "cripple their intellectual powers, . . . an increasing vigilance to prevent Christians from exercising their religion . . . and to restrain Christianity." (Quoted in E. M. Bliss: "Turkey and the Armenian Atrocities," p. 367.) The censorship of Christian books was made very strict, not only on certain kinds of books but even on words and ideas. The censor prohibited the use of the word *rasul,* apostle, for Christ's disciples, claiming that the title should be used exclusively for Mohammed; that the phrase "guidance of God" should not be used in reference to Christians, for they had not that blessing. Even books coming *in transitu* to Persia were seized. Some volumes of the "Life of Henry Martyn" in English were burnt at Trebizond by the Turkish officials, who thus showed an oversight of the interests of their Islamic neighbour. Books such as Shakespeare, "Universal History," and encyclopedias were taken from our cases. But while zeal for the law led to their confiscation, the higher law of self-interest often led to their being sold in the bazaars of Trebizond. In search for these unclean books, it chanced that once a ham was discovered. What should be done with this abomination? While officials were deliberating on this, the question was settled by a dog snatching it and running away with it. Once an agricultural machine was landed at a certain port. Accompanying it was a description of it which fell into the hands of a Turk who could read English. He was struck with horror and rushed off to report to the police that the machine was a terrible one guaranteed to make "eighty revolutions a minute." A panic followed. Guards were posted and a telegram for instructions sent to Constantinople. The machine was ordered out of the country instanter.

Interference with and repression of Christian work in Turkey was reflected in Persia. Not seldom some action of the Shah's officials could be traced to a report received of some anti-Christian action of the Osmanli government.

Repression of the worship and education of Christians was not enough; Christian officials were dismissed by the Sultan. It is definitely stated that they were offered continuance in their civil and diplomatic posts on condition of accepting Islam; that those in arrears of taxes were tendered remission on the same condition. All this was a part of Abdul Hamid's programme to convert the Christian rayats.

Massacres of the Christians had a religious end. They were inspired by religious fanaticism, as well as designed to repress political and revolutionary activity. The latter were not sufficient cause for general massacre. Indeed the forcible conversion to Islam of seventy or more villages of Yezidees or devil worshippers of Kurdistan was carried out, though there could not be any political danger from them. Sir William Ramsay declares his belief that the Armenian massacres were part of the plan of Pan-Islamism—a deliberate plan to crush Christianity. In any case they were promoted and carried out as an anti-Christian campaign. Not only in Turkey but elsewhere the whole spirit of the movement was against the religion as well as against the governments of the Christians. It may readily be admitted that there is much in the political dealings of Christian Powers, their aggressions and selfish diplomacy, to excite hatred, but there is very little in their conduct towards Islam as a religion to call for reprisal. They have treated it impartially and justly, sometimes favoured it. Nevertheless the Pan-Islamic propaganda increased the hatred for Christians as well as the desire to overthrow Christian domination everywhere. Sheikh Abdul Hak of Bagdad but voices the feeling of the multitude when he fulminates a defiance, saying: "Christian peoples! The hatred of Islam is irreconcilable! We abhor you more than we did in the early period of history. Our most ardent desire is that the day may soon dawn when we shall wipe out the last traces of your supremacy." The *Ijtihad*, a Moslem journal, says (Dr. Howard Bliss in *International Review of Missions*, 1913, p. 647) the Christian is "the curse of the world. To reason with him, to lead him back to salvation, and when that is impossible, *to remove his existence*, is the most sacred duty and the holiest piety of the faithful. Oh, Christian nations!

We are now hating you. We want you to understand that we hate the civilization and the extraordinary development which has made you so wealthy and so powerful." [1]

TURKISH MASSACRES OF CHRISTIANS

The idea is said to prevail in England that "the Turk always showed a contemptuous toleration for his Christian subjects." Of the contempt there can be no doubt. Sir William Ramsay says ("Impressions, etc.," p. 206): "Armenians and Greeks were regarded as dogs and pigs; their nature was to be Christians, to be spat upon if their shadow darkened a Turk, to be outraged, to be mats on which he wiped the mud from his feet. The Turk then did not mind what religion these dogs belonged to and he was as far as possible from the wish to make them Mohammedans." But with this contempt was also persecution. Sir Edwin Pears says ("Turkey and Its People," p. 350): "Until the nineteenth century the policy was one of constant worry with occasional Bartholomew massacres" (*Ibid.*, p. 42): "I doubt whether at any time since Mohammed conquered Constantinople a quarter of a century has passed without a big massacre." In another place this close student of Turkish history writes (*The Nineteenth Century*, 1913, p. 278): "I assert that ever since the Turk entered Eu-

[1] This abhorrence is revealed in the incident that Sheikh Othman of Batavia was severely criticised for praying for the Queen of Holland at the time of her coronation. Another celebrated sayid, Salim ibn Ahmad of Arabia, defended him with the remark that it was merely an external performance to conciliate the infidels, but God knew what was in his heart.

rope, say five hundred years ago, the whole course of Turkish history . . . was a period of Mohammedan fanaticism, during which tens of thousands of Christians died for their faith. The persecutions under which the Christians suffered after the capture of Constantinople, in 1453, were so continuous and striking as to terrorize the sufferers. They were far greater in each century before 1800 than during the last century. Their history under Turkish rule was a long and terrible persecution for their faith. On three occasions every Christian in Constantinople was threatened with death. In 1512 Salim I proposed to kill them all unless they would accept the Mohammedan faith. The Grand Vizier averted it. One-half of the churches of Constantinople were left to the Christians at the conquest, but before a century all but one were taken from them." Some were bought back with money. Or if instead of the ones of which they were dispossessed, they were permitted to build, they must be of wood that they might quickly decay or be burnt down.

A mere recapitulation of the massacres in the nineteenth century fills one with horror; such infernal brutality and devilish lust, rapine, murder, and barbarity surpass description. In 1822 the Greeks of Chios were almost exterminated. The Turkish rabble hurried to the scene and enjoyed the slaughter as a picnic. Thirty-two thousand boys and girls were sold into slavery, 30,000 of the people were killed, and 30,000 fled into other lands; but 15,000 remained in this most prosperous island. In 1844 10,000 Nestorians were massacred by the Kurds; in 1860

30,000 Christians of the Lebanon were slaughtered by the Druses; in 1876 the massacre of 40,000 Bulgarians aroused the indignation of Europe and brought about the Russo-Turkish war; in 1894-96 200,000 Armenians perished either by slaughter or consequent deprivations. In 1909, under the Constitution, occurred the massacre of Armenians at Adana. "Every man that could be found was shot, hacked to pieces, or thrown into the flames of the burning houses and shops. No Christian woman's honour was spared." Churches were destroyed. In city and villages all were hunted down. Twenty-eight thousand were slain. Twenty-one out of twenty-five trained Protestant pastors were massacred. It was more fiendish than the preceding massacre.

MASSACRES CAUSED BY RELIGIOUS FANATICISM

Moslem fanaticism was the fundamental cause of these massacres. They were ordered by the Sultan, the Caliph of Islam, instigated by harangues of the mullahs declaring the merit of killing and outraging Christians. They were enjoined by proclamations in the mosques. The Moslems robbed, desecrated, and burnt the churches as well. When they made a holocaust of the Urfa Cathedral, within which were eight thousand innocent victims, many of them women and children, the Moslems "mockingly called on Christ to prove himself a greater prophet than Mohammed." In the time of trial, tens of thousands were compelled to choose between death and Islam. Tens of thousands chose death. Thousands, alas, denied the faith especially to save their wives and daughters from the vile hands of the wretches who maltreated them in a horrible manner or carried them off to their harams or sold them as slaves and even compelled them to become promiscuous concubines. In the midst of all the slaughter and rapine, all that was required of a man was to raise one finger as a sign of acceptance of the Moslem creed and he was safe. At least forty thousand under compulsion became Moslems in 1894-95.[1]

Such is a brief summary of Turkish atrocities against the Christians; a record which well qualifies him to be called the unspeakable Turk. Yet we are assured, by one who knows, that the Turk shows improvement. Sir Edwin Pears, for forty years the sterling representative of Great Britain in Constantinople, after condemning the Sultan and these massacres in burning words, assures us that there has been a decrease in the fanaticism of the Turks. The brutality, bloodthirsty savagery, monstrous cruelty, bestial

[1] E. M. Bliss: "Turkey and the Armenian Atrocities," chap. xxvi. Dr. Bliss gives details. At Chunkush, in the province of Diarbekr, there were 6,000 Christians; 880 were butchered, the rest were compelled to become Moslems. At Senerek nearly all the grown men, 750, were killed, and all the women and children were distributed to the Moslem harams. At Urfa most of the Christian men were compelled to become Moslems and to put up a white flag as a sign of it. After a month, some houses were found without the white flags and 1,500 were killed as apostates. At Albislaw nearly all accepted Islam; at Adianam out of 800 all were slain but 20 who denied the faith. At Arabkir, of 18,000 Christians, all were plundered and burned out of house, 4,000 were killed, the rest accepted Islam. At Tadem, of 1,800, 250 were killed, the rest became Moslems. In all, 100,000 to 200,000 perished; 40,000 accepted Islam.

sensuality from which Christians suffered in our day were exceeded in the atrocities of the sixteenth, seventeenth, and eighteenth centuries. Even the massacres of the Greeks in the beginning of the nineteenth century surpassed in inhumanity and horror the indescribable massacres of the Armenians. This being so, we might hope, at such a rate of progress, that after several millenniums the lives of Christians, were any left, would be safe under the Turks. Victor Hugo has an expressive line which runs

> "The Turks have passed here: All is ruin and mourning."

These unpunished massacres of Armenian Christians were exulted over as a victory for Islam. Even in far-off Mandaling, the Moslems announced that they would treat the Batak Christians in exactly the same way (Simon, p. 39).

THE HOLY WAR

An instrument was ready at hand for Pan-Islamism. This was the Jihad, or Holy War. Abdul Hamid counted on making effective use of it. The Law of Mohammed, both in the Koran and the Traditions, commands fighting for the Faith. War is a religious duty. Their prophet enjoins: "Kill those that join other Gods with God wherever ye shall find them: but if they shall convert, then let them go their way" (Surah IX, 5). Some would interpret this to mean only the heathen of Arabia, but this is untenable, for verse 29 says: "Make war upon such of those to whom the Scriptures have been given, i.e. Jews and Christians . . . who profess not the profession of the truth until they pay tribute out of hand and be humbled." Surah VIII, 40, commands: "Fight against them until religion be all of it God's." Mohammed declared: "Fighting in the way of God is a divine duty. When your Imam orders you to go forth to fight, then obey him." By command of Mohammed, says Bosworth Smith ("Mohammed and Mohammedanism," p. 177), "religion became warlike and war became religious, with the whole world for a battlefield." Islam conquered and spread by the sword. All Moslem historians affirm it. The Persians call themselves "guluj mussalmani" ("Mussulmans by the sword"). It remained for European apologists, like T. W. Arnold, to attempt, however unsuccessfully, to show the contrary. In the jihad the Moslem warrior gave the option of (1) Islam, (2) Subjection, (3) Death. Under the second condition Christians must live in abject submission, under the lordship of the Moslem, inferior in legal status, paying a special tax, regarded as *zimmis* or *rayats* (cattle). If they assert themselves, seem desirous of freedom, or are supposed to be planning release or to be sympathizing with the enemy, they come under the ban of the jihad and they and their families can be killed and maltreated without mercy. Dr. G. Herrick, a lover of the Turks as a race, condemns their jihad in these words ("Christian and Mohammedan," p. 119): "These orgies of carnage and arson, attended by treachery and falsehood, by infernal cruelty and beastly lust, are the natural fruit of Mohammed's ethical teachings and example at Medina."

The Holy War is in force "till the resurrection," and only expediency limits it while non-Moslem governments exist in the world. It is a permanent statute of Islam for aggression and propagation as well as defence. According to the Shari, it should always exist against non-Moslem countries "until they submit," and until every Dar-ul-Harb is converted into a Dar-ul-Islam, an abode of Islam. Submission to European rule is abnormal, unlawful, only a temporary trial. The "Moslem Dictionary," published in India (quoted by Dr. Zwemer, *Missionary Review,* 1913, p. 102), says: "This is an abode of Islam, although it belongs to the accursed ones and authority belongs externally to these Satans." Only expediency holds them in check. For a new interpretation has been given to the law by the Ulema of North India, that the jihad is lawful only when there is "a probability of victory to the armies of Islam." This accords with the saying of the Koran: "Ye are in no wise bound to rush upon your destruction." Fear and not loyalty prevents the jihad, for, as Professor Petrie says of Egypt ("Ten Years in Egypt," p. 180), "the fellah looks upon the unbeliever as a miserable minority; and it is the unpleasant fact that they cannot be crushed at present which prevents his crushing them and asserting the supremacy of Islam."

The jihad is invoked not only against non-Moslems but also against heretics, as the Shiahs and the Wahabis. The Shiahs claim that there can only be a true jihad when the Imam appears to issue the call: Sunnis ascribe the authority to the caliph. In practice, the Shiah Mujtahids proclaim it and even mullahs in Africa and Indonesia declare local jihads. It has been invoked in the Atchin and other insurrections and in frequent fanatical uprisings; in the rebellions in China; in the Wahabi campaigns in India; by Sheikh Abdul Kadir and Schamyl in their stubborn defences in Algeria and the Caucasus; by the Sudan Mahdi; in every important war of Turkey, except possibly the Balkan War. The Sheikh Sanusi issued a call to the jihad against Italy in Tripoli, 1912. In it salvation and blessing are promised to all "who extend the dominion of the Faith with the sword's sharpness, as the Koran has commanded, 'Battle with unbelievers.' For Paradise lies under the shadow of swords; the martyr feels death only as the light pressure of the finger when he is filled with the hot desire for it. By God's grace, it is the last step to the presence of God. The breath of Paradise fans him and the houris seek to draw his gaze on themselves when he lies wound-covered. Up then, worshipper of God! pour wealth and blood into the fight! God has commanded the jihad! Endurance! Endurance! God is near to help" (*Missionary Review,* 1912, p. 790).[1]

The effect of such proclamations is to excite religious fanaticism in a superlative degree, filling the soldier with fiery zeal to slay as God's service, for has not the Prophet said "the fire of hell shall not touch the legs of him who shall be covered with the dust of battle in the way of God"? Indifference to death and dauntless courage are engendered. The

[1] Mr. Simon (p. 141) tells of a Javanese, bent on suicide, who rushed in and wounded several Dutch soldiers and shot the sentry. Suicide would have been accounted a great sin for him, but killing Christians was a merit, deserving a heavenly reward, so he committed this act of holy warfare to enter Paradise.

jihad is a tremendously effective weapon, as in days of old.

With such a propaganda, such principles, such a following, and such a weapon, Pan-Islamism loomed large. The ideal of the Caliph Abdul Hamid seemed to have borne fruitage. The successful campaign against Greece in 1897 sent a thrill of joy through the vast body of Moslems to the farthest extremity. Every mosque was illuminated throughout India, even to the smallest village in the Deccan (Aga Khan: *Edinburgh Review,* 1914, p. 3). It was one cause of the Tirah rising. The Greeks were conquered; the Armenians decimated; the Arabs brought into order and conciliated; the Sanusiyahs working in harmony; the Shiahs friendly; the Moslem leagues fanatically active; the Christian Powers flouted; the Colossus of the North humbled by Japan; the Sultan's prestige among Moslems was at its zenith. Pan-Islamic ideals seemed to them about to be realized. Even European writers did not regard their military aspirations as impossible. Edward Dicey viewed as reasonable ("The Egypt of the Future," quoted in C. R. Watson's "In the Valley of the Nile," p. 218) the "widespread Moslem belief that the time is at hand when Islam might resume her career of conquest and might fulfil her mission of exterminating all unbelievers, no matter what creed they may profess." Oscar Mann wrote ("Great Religions of the World," p. 58): "We see a fermentation going on in Islam from one end to the other. What is not possible if some gifted man succeeds in inspiring these tremendous masses!" Some, on the other hand, called it a "rope of sand" (Dr.

G. Herrick), a "chimera" (Dr. W. S. Nelson), an "impossibility" (Prof. E. G. Browne), "with no prospects of realization" (J. Simon). These estimates seem undoubtedly true from a military point of view. But its possibilities could not be accurately determined and Christian Powers cautiously watched developments.

Events which followed revealed its failure as a political power but its reality as a religious conviction, and intensifies its anti-Christian bitterness. The apparent purpose of Russia and Great Britain to divide Persia, the annexation by Austria of Bosnia and Herzegovina, the declaration of independence by Bulgaria, the Italian war and the loss of Tripoli, the Balkan War and its direful consequences, the seizure of Morocco,—all together impressed Moslems with the thought that Christian governments had formed a plot to destroy all Moslem governments. In consequence Turk and Arab emissaries were sent through India and Russia. Intense feeling was created. Sympathy with Turkey was profound, for, as the London *Times* said (April 19, 1913), "the Moslem looks upon Turkey as the embodiment of the temporal power of Islam and does not desire to see Islam reduced to the position of Israel, a religion without temporal status." A Mohammedan graduate of an English University was so affected by the news of the battle of Lulu Burgas that he felt like committing suicide. In India inflammatory speeches were made, bombs were purchased, *fatvas* for boycott were issued, large sums were subscribed to help Turkey. Popular meetings passed indignant resolutions. Protests and petitions were sent from the London Colony and from the Transvaal Moslems. The Indian Moslem press denounced the conspiracy to overthrow Islam, the British policy in Persia, the aggressions of Russia, Italy, and France. Egypt seemed a hotbed of sedition. Moslem Leagues were multiplied. A thrill of sympathy and excitement went even to the remotest corner of Zanzibar ("Vital Forces," p. 197). Agitation and discontent were manifested everywhere. Pan-Islamic feeling was tense and aggressive. Remembering the Crusades, who can tell but some spark might set on fire the Islamic world? We soberly and rightly calculate that the devotees of Islam cannot prevail in warfare against the armouries of Europe. Without our science, Islam is hopelessly outclassed as a fighting power. But Islam might find her opportunity in a divided Christendom. Even some great Dreibund might equip and finance Pan-Islam. Besides this, the point is not as to where the final victory would be. It is rather as to the purpose and possible attempt of the Moslem world. They await the time to strike. God is great! Victory is His! "A consciousness of victory," says Mr. Simon (p. 223), "pervades the whole Mohammedan world. Islam's unfavourable position politically has not affected it, because the feeling has its origin in the religious conceptions of Islam, more especially in the doctrine of the holy wars which are to usher in the Last Day. It has a feeling of invincibility." Notwithstanding its collapse, at present, it is Julius Richter's judgment that "the deep and strong conviction that has grown up into the very fabric of Mohammedanism, through thirteen centuries of victory and success, of a call to world-wide dominion, cannot be uprooted by the reverses" it has met. *The Comrade,* the Moslem journal of Calcutta, voices their sense of unity and strength when it says (quoted by Dr. Zwemer, *Missionary Review,* 1914, p. 176): "Mussulmans have just begun to perceive that Islam is a living source of spiritual and social cohesion, binding all Moslems in an indissoluble unity of hope, purpose, duty, and endeavour. Moslems have never felt its vital strength as keenly as they feel it to-day. The sufferings of the parts have revived in the whole its sense of organic unity." Palgrave ("Essays," p. 125) writes: "So strong indeed is the bond of union that in the presence of the infidel the deep clefts which divide Sunni and Shiah are for a time and purpose obliterated," and it is "roughly welded into one formidable weapon of attack on the common foe, the uncircumcised foe, governed and governing." Aga Khan, who is loyal to Great Britain, writes (*Edinburgh Review,* 1914, p. 4): "All sections of the Moslem world are moved. There is between them and their fellow-believers in other lands an essential unity which breaks through differences of sect and country." The *Tanin* of Constantinople, even after the failure of the call to the jihad, expresses its belief in the reality of Pan-Islamism as follows:

"The wish to abolish existing misunderstandings between the various Mohammedan elements and to establish as between them a defensive force that will permit them to give reciprocal protection to each other, is not anywise the result of vast and chimerical schemes, but rather the outcome of most natural necessity and most convincing logic. The movement among the Moslems toward union and solidarity, which had as its object the respect of the political and national rights of others, the respecting of the national frontiers, and a united effort against common enemies, has taken during these late years as a result of events a form so serious as to make it most illogical for certain indifferent individuals to shrug their shoulders over it. The spread of ideas of this sort among elements that have for centuries looked askance at each other, has proved that a new and very powerful movement is manifesting itself in Islam.

"Thus it happens that Turkey, who in the campaign of 1877-78 was compelled to guard her Persian frontier, on this occasion beheld the whole of Persia, as soon as the jihad was proclaimed, rise to her feet with her Ulemas, khans, and tribes. The Moslems have for a long time been awake, but the movement will have to be progressive, for the time necessary for them to prepare to move in common at a given moment, has not yet passed by. Everybody in the Moslem world has been awaiting a time that should strengthen this current and hasten its development. This chance, which we were hoping for in heaven, we have at last found on this earth."

III

ISLAMIC MISSIONS

ANOTHER aspect of the Islamic revival is a renewal of zeal in propagating the Faith. Islam has always been a missionary religion, and it retains this characteristic in a marked degree and both by the sword and by the word it continues to increase its numbers. True its opportunity to use force has largely passed from its hand. The restraint of Christian governments prevents it. But numerous examples have occurred in modern times. Some thousands of Greeks in Chios and of Armenians in Turkey were made Moslems under threat of death. The Kaffirs were forced into Islam by the Afghans. The jihad against the Battaks in 1821-28 became "a bloody and savage war of conquest" in which they tried to impose their faith on the heathen (Arnold, *Ibid.*, p. 300). But in Achin and Sumatra some regions were kept for centuries from becoming Moslems that they might continue to be legitimate fields for slave trade, for it was considered that they had a God-given right to make plundering raids on the defenceless heathen and sell them into slavery (Simon, p. 206). Osman Danfodio, to whom I have already referred, led his army (1830-40) against the heathen Hausas, the tribes around Sokoto, Yoruba, and Senegambia, compelling them all to embrace Islam. He carried the faith to the Gulf of Guinea and to the West as far as the Atlantic. Four powerful Mohammedan kingdoms of the present day owe their religion to his sword (Arnold, pp. 265-67). The Tijaniyah Darvishes, a militant order founded by Sidi Ahmad of Tijani, Algeria, have forced Islam by the sword upon tribes from Nigeria to the Gold Coast. A number of pagan states were converted by their jihads. The Tijaniyah appear now to be reconciled with France. The Sheikh receives a salary and wears the badge of the Legion of Honour. The Sheikh of the Tabbiyah order, the Sherif of Wassan, is the son of an Englishwoman and was educated in a French school. Yet Professor Westermann declares that " Even now among the ruling races of the Sudan, the Holy War—that is, force—is regarded as the natural and normal means of conversion and as more effective than preaching (*International Review of Missions,* 1912, p. 285). Mungo Park narrates (Arnold, p. 285) that the following message was sent by the Moslem king of Futa Toro to his pagan neighbour: " With this knife Abd-ul-Kadir will condescend to shave the head of Damel, if Damel will embrace the Mohammedan faith; and with this other knife Abdul Kadir will cut the throat of Damel, if Damel refuses to embrace it." A young Arab said to Captain Burton at Abeokuta: " Give guns and powder to us, and we will soon Islamize those dogs." The Mohammedan ruler in Bambara sent out teachers with an armed force to convert the heathen to Islam and, in case they did not receive it, to lay waste their villages. On receiving it, a fifth of the spoils was to be paid to the ruler.

But now, for the most part, Moslem propaganda is carried on by persuasion. The two movements mentioned, Wahabism and Pan-Islamism, have stirred up a fervent missionary spirit, the former by renewing primitive faith; the latter by strengthening the solidarity of believers, giving them a sense of their unity and so inspiring them with boldness in witnessing for their religion. The geographical situation now favours the spread of Islam more than Christianity. The latter has converted all the races in contact with it in Europe and in contact with its colonies in America and Australia. Now separating us from the African pagans and the heathen nations of Asia stretches the great mass of Mohammedanism. Only in South Africa does Christianity have the advantage of close contact. The advantage of peaceful penetration and gradual assimilation through proximity lies with Islam. Influence across the seas is not so intimate and effective.

The most striking and, from a Christian point of view, critical progress of Islam has been made in Africa. I have described the warlike advance. Much also has been accomplished in a peaceable way. Moslem traders and shepherds are in the habit of settling down in new locations, marrying among the people, and gradually acquiring an influence among the negroes. Their somewhat higher culture and the social standing and dignity which come from the possession of property, create admiration. Marabouts or teachers go about, write charms, use magic, work faith cures, and adapt themselves to the superstitions and habits of the tribe. They ingratiate themselves with the chief, acquire a standing with him, marry his daughter; or, if not, on the contrary, if he is obdurate, they instigate rebellion against him and supplant him. Merchant and marabout alike enter into relationship with the different families by marriage and soon a community is established. If there is a European sovereignty, they sympathize with the black man against this new oppressor and tax-collector, counting themselves fellow-sufferers, and the negro, soon forgetful of the rapacity and cruelty of the slave-traders, feels grateful. Above all, the Arab or North African adopts the newly converted negro into the brotherhood of Islam, in which there is no colour line.

Then, too, the Christian missionary, if there is one, is of the same race and religion as the foreign subjugator. If the Moslem were the ruler, he would take advantage of it to further his religion, but the European administration is neutral in principle, and so upright at times that he leans backwards. Or perchance he thinks Islam a better faith for the black man or is simply careless and indifferent. He is surrounded by Moslem secretaries, clerks, interpreters, and agents. They have some education and more clothing than other natives. Through them all government business is transacted. The subaltern army officers are Moslems, and new recruits are circumcised to make them acceptable to the older ones. If a school is established, it teaches Arabic and the books of Islam. So in court, in camp, in school, the heathen sees the Moslem preferred and the Christian ignored. He finds it to his advantage to become a Moslem. Besides all this the Moslem appears to a better advantage under Christian rule than usually, for he is restrained from showing his bad qualities, such as oppression, violence, slave-trading. To some provinces the Christian missionary is prohibited entrance, but the Moslem goes everywhere and has the roads and safety of Christian administration to assist him. In the Sudan for many years missionaries were prohibited, but Gordon College at Khartum, the memorial of that Christian saint, is a Moslem institution, in which Islam is taught by Sheikhs from Al Azhar. The Koran is a text-book, and Friday, not Sunday, the school holiday. Professor Westermann says: "The College exerts a powerful influence in favour of Islam."

The strongest influence in Africa for Moslem propaganda is wielded by the orders of darvishes. I have already told of their origin. As an offshoot of Persian Sufiism, they should be latitudinarian and friendly to Christians. So were the Kadiriyah, and they continue somewhat so in Africa. The Bektashi of Turkey are Alivis, and were very tolerant, teaching that "the paths leading to God are as numerous as the breaths of His creatures." Sir Edwin Pears tells of one of their Sheikhs who said he regarded the Christians as brothers, and removed his turban and showed the sign of a cross embroidered upon it. Yet even Bektashi joined in massacring the Armenians. Another darvish Sheikh was a member of a Masonic lodge in Constantinople. Yet the new orders of darvishes are actively hostile to everything Christian and European. Some of them are fighting orders, as the Tijaniah and the Mahdiists of the Sudan; some hold to non-intercourse and opposition to foreign influences. Among these are the Sanusiyah, who adhere to puritanic practices like the Wahabis. Of them Canon Sell says: "The object of the founder was to erect an impassable barrier to the progress of Western civilization and to the influence of Christian Powers in Moslem lands" (*Church Missionary Intelligencer*, January, 1899). They are ardent adherents of Pan-Islamic principles and are notable as the most zealous and powerful propagators of Islam, by peaceable means, that the world has ever seen. The future of their large and influential organization may yet show more wonderful development.

The founder of the order of Sanusiyah was Sidi Mohammed Ibn Ali as Sanusi, an Arab of Morocco. He studied theology at Fez and other madressas. He was initiated into many orders,—"finally acquiring the degree of Master Sufi and passing through the ordeal of fire" (Achmad Abdullah, a Sanusiyah, *Forum*, 1914, p. 679). He lectured at various places in North Africa and latterly at Cairo. Here his teachings offended the Ulema by their mystical and puritanical tendencies. He was anathematized and narrowly escaped death by poison. Proceeding to Mecca, he received instructions from the Mufti and had as his Murshid or Guide the Grand Sheikh of the Kadiriyah, Al Fussi. On the latter's death, Sanusi was disappointed in not succeeding to the headship, so he founded a school and order of his own and taught in Mecca till 1843. Forced to leave there by theological disputes, he returned to Africa and propagated the order called after him Sanusiyah.

Sheikh Sanusi strove for a return to primitive Islam. Following Ibn Abdul Wahab, his great aim was to purify and revive Islam and correct abuses. He denounced prayers to the Valis or saints, pilgrimages to their shrines and undue honour to Mohammed. He rejected the use of tobacco, coffee, and music, rich clothing and ornaments, but his conscience found no offence in tea and perfumes. Yet he held on to Sufiism and to worship by means of the zikr. His formula for producing the hypnotic trance is by the repetition first of "Allah" 100 times; secondly, the kalima or creed, with additions, 300 times; and thirdly, the prayer, "O God! Bless our Lord Mohammed, his family and friends," 1,000 times. Their oath is "By the Truth Sidi-es Sanusi." The book of the Sheikh is described as a frenzied writing, recounting the stages of ecstasy which lead to oneness with God. "In the first stage the adept will see 7,000,000 green stars of surpassing loveliness; in each succeeding stage there will be different-coloured stars, until in the bliss of oblivion he beholds constellations of a glory beyond words" (Salib ul Khalili, in *Spectator*). The Sanusiyah are classed by Goldziher as a fifth school, distinct from the four orthodox schools of the Sunnis.

The centre of the order was established at Jagbub, where the Sheikh procured large estates and had as many as 2,000 slaves to work them. There also was at one time a college, with 750 students preparing for religious work, under Sheikh Mohammed ash Sherif. Settlements or colonies of the darvishes were made in many places in those semi-civilized Moslem countries, the lands were cultivated, and schools for boys and even girls established. The chief of each *zawiya,* or lodge, became governor of the district round about, combining temporal and spiritual authority, receiving tribute and offerings to such an extent that large funds were accumulated. The order has increased greatly. Zawiyas exist in all countries from Morocco to Egypt, in the Sudan, around Lake Chad, and, it is said, even in Turkey, Arabia, and Malaysia. The entrance of Sultan Ali of Wadai and Sultan Sayid Baldas of Krej into the order has added to its influence. The populace about the zawiyas is initiated as adherents, so that six million are estimated to be affiliated. To call these zawiyas monasteries gives a wrong impression, for though they may practise austerities, yet celibacy is not commanded. They are bound by a secret oath and have passwords and signs.

Mohammed-as-Sanusi first married a woman named Manna, whom he received as a present at Mesaad and soon afterwards divorced. Another wife was Fatima. Their son was called Mahdi, and he had this sign at least that he was the son of Mohammed and Fatima, as tradition says the Mahdi should be. He was also credited with the physical marks which were requisite. He refused to accept appointment from the Sudanese Mahdi as one of his Khalifas. He died without fulfilling a mission, but rumour says that he is in concealment and will appear to fulfil his work as Mahdi. Another son was a diplomat, but a debauchee. After the death of the founder in 1859, the seat of the order was moved farther into the interior, to Gouro or Borku, beyond Wadai. The present Sheikh is reported to have made arrangement with the Italian Government, whereby he will have autonomy within his sphere, paying tribute to Italy, and having the title and emoluments of Governor-General and at the same time be the Sultan's religious representative.

The influence of the Sanusiyah has been very great in strengthening the faith and arousing the zeal of the Moslems of North Africa, awakening within them a spirit of intense loyalty and devotion. All through that vast region many Moslems were ignorant of their religion, steeped in superstition, and addicted to practices contrary to Islam. Many had retained their heathen practices and beliefs mixed with Mohammedan rites and conceptions. These they have instructed and confirmed and developed into strong Moslems. Among these were many tribes or parts of tribes that had remained heathen. Sanusiyah preachers and schools have converted them. In some instances they have bought slaves, educated and Islamized them and sent them back to their own tribes. At a single time they purchased from the Moslem slave-dealers two thousand persons. Thus their influence as a proselyting agency has been very effective through a wide stretch of territory. The results of their labours and of the Kadiriyah order and similar peaceful orders, as well as the militant ones, coupled with the influence of traders, teachers, and soldiers, penetrating from the North, from Egypt, from the Arabian seacoast and Zanzibar, and even in Cape Colony itself, have been to give Islam such victories in Africa—such progress in numbers and in power as to startle the Christian Church. The campaign has been aggressive, rapid, successful. Thousands of square miles, numerous and powerful tribes as well as millions of the weak and unorganized masses, have been brought under the banner of Mohammed. Vast regions which for centuries lay beyond Arab influence have lately been brought under it, and this has come about owing to the peace and security which European domination is maintaining. This Mohammedan awakening and advance in Africa has created a veritable crisis which calls loudly to the Christian world to be up and doing. For though Islam in Africa is an inferior and degraded system, adapting itself to the passions and superstitions of the heathen, yet it fills them with zeal, bigotry, and pride and makes the task of the Christian Church in accomplishing their evangelization a herculean one. Hear what Achmad Abdullah writes (*Sunset Magazine,* 1915, p. 99): "Nowadays when Christian missionaries discover a new and very pagan tribe in Central Africa, and return after a year or two with money collected at home to distribute the blessings of Christianity and a sample line of cheap gin, they discover that the Moslem has been there ahead of them and the pagans greet them with the resounding shout of La illa ill' Allah."

Another principle taught by Sheikh Sanusi was intense hostility to everything foreign to Islam. He inveighed against the innovations brought in from Christian civilization. He forbade all intercourse with Christians and Jews. Because Sultan Abdul Aziz was friendly to Christians and was adopting Western ways he rejected his caliphate and denounced him and the Turks as bad Moslems. He is said to have affirmed that he would crush out the Christians and Turks in one common destruction (Pears: "Turkey, etc.," p. 300). But when Abdul Hamid took up a fanatical policy, the Sanusiyahs united with him in the Pan-Islamic propaganda. In 1886 the Sultan was received into the order and in 1898 was acknowledged as caliph by the Sheikh, who sent his official representative to Constantinople (A. R. Colquhoun: *North American Review,* 1906, p. 910).

The Sanusiyahs do not make converts by the sword, but they undoubtedly have as one of their objects to use the sword, if opportunity offers, to deliver Mohammedan lands from the infidels. The Sheikh is ready for the jihad when victory seems assured. He is striving to unite Africa against the white man's supremacy. His zawiyas are storehouses of ammunition. Supplies of rifles and some cannon have been received from some unknown European sources. He has large funds, the offerings of his followers, which are used for the purchase of arms. The Sanusiyahs are encouraged to enlist in colonial regiments and secure European drill. Much intrigue is carried on among Mohammedan regiments of European Powers in Algeria, Egypt, Tripoli, and the Sudan, to make them disloyal. Youths are sent to Europe for education in military art. Reports even say that there are manufactories of arms in the oases in charge of graduates of European technical schools. The Sheikh has a devoted intelligence department in his strolling fakirs. (Compare "The Moslem Menace," *Nineteenth Century,* September, 1907, by Capt. H. A.

Wilson of the British army.) The centre of African Pan-Islamism, Wadai, was taken by the French in 1910 and can no longer be used as a base for preparation against European rule. They may not listen to the call to the jihad by the caliph in Constantinople, but they will listen when the call goes forth from their own Mahdi. M. Hanataux, former French Minister of the Interior (Zwemer's "Islam, etc.," p. 170), says: "The religious orders of Islam are yet keeping their powder dry for the day of the great slaughter and the great victory." Achmad Abdullah (*Sunset Magazine,* 1915, p. 99) says on this point; "Another invisible force at work is the incredible number of Mohammedan lodges with which Asia, North and Central Africa are honeycombed. Call them darvishes, call them Sanusiyah or gentle dreaming Sufis, they all work towards the same object. Some of them experiment in practical magic, some of them are mystics, some of them are literati, poets, grammarians; some of them are beginning to make powder, bullets, and guns."

The Mohammedan awakening is showing itself in the propagation of the Faith in other countries. In Russia the mullahs are carrying on a widespread and continuous itinerary, confirming those who need it and drawing in new converts, to whom pecuniary assistance is given ungrudgingly. Not only heathen Votiaks, Voguls, and Tsheremis on the west of the Ural Mountains are being converted, but even some Christians. At Atomva ninety-one families of the Orthodox have embraced Islam and fifty thousand who had joined the Russian Church have returned to

Islam since the proclamation of religious liberty. New mosques and schools are being built ("Islam and Missions," p. 257). A great mosque has been erected at Petrograd, the Moslem press is active, Moslems sit as members of the Duma; new rights and privileges are being petitioned for and received.

In China, agents from the West have been visiting all the Moslem communities, preaching in the mosques and trying to revive Islamic faith and enthusiasm. There has been much stir. Training schools for propagandists have been organized, and the one at Peking has as its head a graduate of Al Azhar. An impetus has been given to the study of Arabic. The relationship with Western Asia is drawing closer. A Turkish missionary has gone to China to reside and preach Islam, but the effort to establish Turkish consulates failed. Yet success is not altogether unalloyed. Several mullahs some years ago returned from Mecca and began a revival. But the movement was opposed. The mullahs organized a New Sect. Strife and bitterness arose. The conservatives made complaint against the New Sect and the Viceroy put them under the ban. When China was at war with Japan, 1896, the Old Moslems took advantage of the confusion to proclaim a Holy War against the Chinese. Then the New Sect took their revenge and were instrumental in bringing about the execution of thousands of the others. Yet the slaughter was small compared with that meted out to the Moslem rebels in 1862-74. Despite these rebellions, the usual attitude of the Moslem Chinese is to practise conformity, and to worship in the Confucian temples and to take part in the service to the idols. Now under the Republican government they have cut off their queues (H. H. Ridley: *Moslem World,* 1913, pp. 386-90; *Missionary Review,* 1912, p. 722 ff.).

In India a striking fact is the awakening of the Moslem community to its own backward condition. They are showing a feverish desire to make up for their past neglect of privileges of modern civilization, and to regain a status superior to the Hindus. They are gaining in numbers much faster than any religion except the Christians, partly because they are more prolific than the Hindus, and also by the remarriage of their widows. They are gaining converts from the Hindus, to win whom they are showing much zeal. However, many of the conversions of Hindus to Islam are what are named by Mr. Takle ("Islam and Missions," p. 213) "love episodes—either elopements of Hindu girls or the taking of Hindu widows into Moslem harams." Moslems are also beginning to work among the low-caste people, not without success. This is not the work of individuals only, but societies or *anjumans* have been formed who work through paid agents. The Moslem League promotes religious and political interests alike, supporting schools and preachers, and publishing literature. They have specially requested collectors to inform them of any Moslem orphans, that they may not allow them to fall into other hands. In Lahore a Society for the Assistance of Islam was formed in 1885. It maintains schools, orphanages, and the Islamic College, repairs mosques, strengthens the wavering, strives to win back converts to other faiths, and interferes in every possible way with the work of missions. It is also directed against Hinduism, which in the form of the Arya Samaj has been receiving some converts from Islam. This society, as well as those at Lucknow, 1894, at Cawnpore, and at other points, is making special efforts to educate the mullahs and to prepare them for the controversy and to propagate the Faith. The apologetic of Islam,[1] including the history of Christianity, are added to the curriculum, with English and the sciences. At Lahore there is also the Mohammedan Book and Tract Depot to distribute publications in defence of the Faith and the Koran in cheap popular editions. English books in favour of Islam or which lend themselves to Moslem propaganda, as Carlyle's "Hero as Prophet," are published and sold. Magazines are issued by different societies. Some journals have made a business of publishing all the evil reports about Christians which are to be culled from the press (Farquhar's "Modern Religious Movements in India," pp. 347-52). In a word, the Moslems in India are alert for defence and aggression. They are active in the use of modern methods for the propagation of their religion.

In Malaysia, the conversion of the heathen to Islam goes forward continuously. It has been marvellously successful in point of numbers, though lacking in transforming or elevating influence. The modern roads open up the way. Darvishes and traders penetrate on them to the heathen interior heretofore un-

[1] In a new program of study for softas in Stamboul the "Szhar-ul-Hak," a criticism of the Bible and apologetic for Islam, is included.

approachable. One method of the Moslem is to adopt an overbearing and lordly air, despising and scorning the heathen, so the latter becomes a Moslem to rise to the level of him, considering it a favour to be received. The heathen also sees that Islam is the one thing with which the Dutch Government does not interfere. He interprets this fact to mean that the Christian is afraid of Islam. The Moslem assures him that this is true and that the Sultan is greater than six kings. The converted pagan is full of pride, fanaticism, and craftiness. However, the Dutch missions have given Islam a check and converted thirty thousand Mohammedans. Islam has, I believe, never converted any considerable body of Christians except those who were subject to its government. But curiously enough, at the present time, such conversions are occurring to a limited extent. I refer not to the Wofing, England, movement, which is almost negligible. But in Abyssinia some Christian tribes have partly gone over to Islam and are in danger of being won over entirely. In South Africa, too, Malay and Indian Moslems through marriages with white women by the Moslem rite, which in law is regarded as concubinage, and through the adoption by them of Christian children and orphans, are making a noticeable increase to the Moslem community. These half-breed children are all raised as Moslems. Again East-Indian coolies who have come to British Guiana and Jamaica have become a danger to the Christian and heathen coolies in these places and attentive efforts are necessary to prevent Islam from propagating itself in the New World. Already these immigrant Moslems number 158,000. Most of them are in Brazil. They have seven Arabic newspapers.

Another sign of the times is the organization among Moslems of foreign missionary societies. In Egypt the "Society for Invitation and Instruction" has opened schools for the training of missionaries to go to heathen and Christian lands to invite to Islam. A similar attempt in Constantinople, called "The Society for Knowledge and Instruction," failed because the founder wished the language of the school to be Arabic, but the government decided it should be Turkish. Islamic congresses to consider the advancement of Islam have been held in Mecca, Egypt, Russia, and India. The Mecca congress was wise enough to consider the ailments of the religion. Fifty-seven reasons are said to have been mentioned for its decay, with the object of finding remedies for them. That in Cairo, 1907, was called by Dr. Gasprinski to "promote the moral, social, and spiritual regeneration of Islam" by a non-political, non-military movement. In India, with delegates from Turkey and Egypt present, 1910, the congress approved of missions in China and Japan. Missionaries were located in these lands. A deputation was sent to Japan headed by a professor of Lahore Government College. The first Japanese converts were Baron Hiki, his wife and daughter, who took the names Ali and Fatima. A Japanese officer, Jama-Oka, has been converted through his admiration of the warlike spirit of Mohammed. He made the pilgrimage to Mecca and a prolonged stay in Constantinople (*Missionary Review,* October, 1910, p. 722). Another convert started a monthly journal,

'Al Islam. Professor Barakat Ullah started the *Islamic Fraternity,* published by Chinese Moslem students in Tokyo. Both were soon discontinued (*Moslem World,* 1914, p. 312). The press in all Moslem countries has a wide and strong influence. A number of weekly journals have been started for the propaganda; two important ones are in Constantinople. "The Spirit of Islam," by Sayid Amir Ali, is being translated into Japanese. The latest sceptical and liberal literature is being distributed to show that Christianity is undermined. The Taarifi Moslemin has sent a delegation around the world to report on what will further the interests of Islam. It has a world-wide vision as never before.

What a powerful aggressive opponent Islam is! It is the greatest anti-Christian force in the world today. It is vigorous, active, determined. It is making progress, winning victories, planning other victories. No easy work lies before the Church if it would stem the tide of Mohammedanism and convert these masses to Christ. Christians should appreciate the greatness of the task. It is indeed a challenge to faith and only a faith which overcomes will undertake it. Such a faith will not falter.

The aggressiveness of Islam and its increase are calls to us to immediate and all-embracing efforts. A revived Islam, newly incited by the spirit of Mohammed, must be met by a revived Church inspired by the Spirit of Christ. Who can doubt the issue!

IV

MAHDIIST MOVEMENTS

THE coming of the Mahdi is a living hope in Islam. Mohammed foretold the advent of one who would "fill the earth with equity and justice, even as it has been filled with tyranny and oppression." This Mahdi, "a guided or directed one," and therefore able to be the Guide of men, "will reign over the earth seven years" ("Dictionary of Islam"). All Moslems await his coming. The Sunnis hold that he has never yet appeared. But Shiahs believe that he has appeared once and his return is imminent. All believe that Jesus will accompany him. The Tradition runs that Mohammed said: "The Mahdi will descend from me . . . a man of my tribe and of my name." The followers of Imam Ali, the fourth caliph, believe that he was by right the first caliph and that the office was hereditary in his line. His descendants in succession were recognized as Imams or caliphs by the Shiahs until the twelfth, but some recognized these only until the seventh, Jaffar-i-Sadik, and followed his son Ismiel, hence were called Ismieliyah. The Ismieliyahs expected the return of Ismiel as the Imam Mahdi and the Fatimides of Egypt regarded Obeidullah as that return. The former, who now prevail in Persia, are called the Sect of the Twelve. Under the oppressive caliphs of Bagdad the doctrine of the Mahdi developed among the Aliites. The first one who was acclaimed Mahdi was Mohammed, son of Ali by the Hanifite wife, and his Khalifa was Mukhtar. His followers, accounting that he had not died but simply disappeared, remained at Radwa near Medina, and awaited his return until their death. Husain, the grandson of Zaid, raised a standard as Mahdi, but the caliph had him hanged on a gibbet. The Abbasides came into power as caliphs with the aid of Ali Muslim and the Aliites, who believed they were aiding the Mahdi. Caliph Mansur named his son Mahdi either to engage the loyalty of the Mahdiists, or possibly to deride their claims. Each of the twelve Imams was hailed with expectation by his secret followers, till poison carried them off one by one. The last one, Mohammed Abul Kasim (A.H. 329, A.D. 940), at Suraman Ra near Kufa disappeared into a grotto, departing to a land called Jubulsa or Jabulka. Expecting his immediate return, his faithful followers day by day went forth from their villages, armed and on horseback, to meet him. At midday prayer one hundred horsemen led forth a horse saddled and bridled to the shrine at Hillah, with trumpets and drums sounding. At the door they cried out: "In the name of God, come forth, O Lord of the Age!" Till the time of evening prayers they voiced their appeal,—but returned disappointed (Darmesteter: "The Mahdi," p. 42).

So have they waited. The Sarbedarian kings of Khorasan in the fourteenth century, the Safavian

Shahs at Ispahan, the Kajars at Teheran, have kept two horses in the royal stables, splendidly caparisoned and in readiness for the appearing of the Mahdi and his lieutenant Jesus the son of Mary, who is to destroy Dajjal the Anti-Christ. The new Constitution of Persia was established to last only till the appearing of the Imam Mahdi. At the mention of his name the pious Shiah adds a prayer: "May God hasten his glad advent." The dynamic of these movements is hope,—hope that springs eternal in the human breast,—a hope of amelioration, of material good, bound to a coming deliverer.

Through the Moslem centuries, this hope has caused the appearance of many claimants, followed by numerous wars, the downfall and rising of kingdoms, and the establishment of various sects. Conceived in the religious enthusiasm or maybe the ambition of the leader, born of the traditional expectation, nurtured in the discontent and unhappiness of the people, developing soon into a military struggle, characterized by fierce fanatical warfare, they have ended either in subjugation through fiery persecution or in a triumph, bringing political supremacy to the Mahdi or his successor, who continued the same old tyrannical oppression with no social amelioration. The Ismieliyahs, the Karmatians, the Druses, the Assassins, and the Nusairiyahs reaped their crop of fanaticism from the soil of Mahdiism. The dynasties of the Fatimides and of the Almohayes were founded by Mahdis. After a claimant by lack of success had proved himself an impostor the hope revived again in a succeeding generation; though some, as the followers of Sayid Mohammed of Jeypore ("Dictionary of Islam," Art.: "Ghair-i-Mahdi"), may declare that the Imam Mahdi has come and gone in the person of their leader and no other is to be expected.

Our own age has seen Mahdis not a few. Such a one was Sayid Ahmad of Punjab, who fought against the Sikhs in 1826. Another was Sayid Mohammed Husain of Persia, who appeared among the Ali Allahis. I had an appointment to receive him as a visitor. My tea-urn was boiling and I awaited him four hours before sundown. It reached the third hour and passed on towards sundown. Still no heavenly visitant deigned to take off his sandals in my hallway. On the morrow I was informed that the Governor-General had the intention to seize this divinity and he had escaped. His followers fought against the Shah's forces in Mezanderan, believing themselves invulnerable till cold lead convinced them. Another such divine leader was Sheikh Kadir Agha of Maragha. A Mahdi lately rose in Somaliland; the Sheikh of the Sanusiyahs was regarded as another. Mahdis or their forerunners are constantly rising in Malaysia, making attempts against Christian rule. In 1882 the people of Borneo expected the Imam and cut in pieces all the Christians and heathen. Schamyl of Daghestan had much the same character. In Syria, living in restraint at Acca, is Sheikh Ali Nur-i-Din, called Insan-i-Kamil ("the perfect man"), who is regarded as a manifestation of Mohammed and his essence as divine. Intoxicated by Sufiism, he led his followers into Pan-Theism, saying: "There is nothing but God." He claimed to possess all the divine attributes and was honoured as a Vali by Moslems (*Missionary Review of the World,* 1914, p. 200). These and other attempts to move the Islamic world by the fulfilment of its hopes need not detain us, for they failed to have a conspicuous and lasting influence. Leaders of rebellions are fond of taking this title and giving a religious aspect to their political schemes. But several of these movements have been remarkable in themselves and have made or are making a place in the religious and political life of Islam.

THE BABI MOVEMENT

The first of these is the Babi movement. The Sheikhis (of whom I shall speak, p. 155) had aroused keen expectation of the manifestation of Imam Mahdi. Haji Sayid Kazim of Resht, successor of Sheikh Ahmad Ahsai, is said to have discoursed much of the promised appearing, the signs which would precede it, and his characteristics. Announcing the "True One," he said: "I see him as the rising sun" ("Trav. Narrative," p. 239; "New History," pp. 31-32, 341). Shortly afterwards Mirza Ali Mohammed announced himself as the Expected One. Born at Shiraz, the son of a cloth-seller, he served his apprenticeship in a shop at Bushire. After receiving an ordinary primary training, he afterwards attended the lectures of Haji Kazim at Najef and Kerbala. He did not acquire the correct use of the Arabic. He was of dreamy and devout disposition. His first book, the "Ziyaret-Nama" ("Pilgrim-Guide"), shows no consciousness of a mission, but deep veneration for the Imams and longing for the Return (Professor Browne, in *Journal of Royal Asiatic Society,* 1899, p. 901). From such longings and contemplations developed the idea that he had communion and communication with the Imam. In the "Best of Stories," a homily on the Surah-i-Yusuf, he definitely announces himself, at the age of twenty-four, as the Bab, the Door of communication. This was in 1844, A.H. 1260, about one thousand years from the disappearance of the Imam. Though he did not then break with Islam nor declare the Koran abrogated, he affirmed that God would accept no one except he came to the Bab by the Bab; and he called himself "This well-favoured Arabian youth in whose grasp God has placed the kingdoms of heaven and earth" (*Ibid.*, p. 907).

In announcing himself as the Bab, Ali Mohammed was using a term familiar to Shiahs. It had been applied to several representatives of the absent Imam, after his occultation or disappearance. Abu Jafar Mohammed, who had assumed the title Bab, was put to death in the reign of Caliph Razi. In the numerous trinities of the Nusairiyah, the third person is called the Bab; as Maana, meaning; Ism, name; Bab, door. One of the trinities is Ali, Mohammed, and Salman Farsee ("Asian Mystery," pp. 57, 111, 131). It was a term applied to Ali, also, in the Traditions as in the one cited by the Bab himself at his examination subsequently at Tabriz. He was asked, "What is the meaning of the name Bab?" He answered, "The same as in the holy tradition, (in which Mohammed said) 'I am the city of knowledge and Ali is the gate thereof.'" From this name the followers were called

Babi. The first disciples, full of zeal and devotion, spread the message of the advent far and wide through Persia. Their assurance of faith and enthusiasm kindled responsive fire in many hearts. Soon the Bab made more exalted claim for himself and at the shrine of Mecca announced himself as the Mahdi or Kaim, the long-absent Imam, and finally as the Nukta, the Point of Divinity, in some sense a Manifestation of God. The number of his disciples grew apace. Some were dreamers, mystics, religious enthusiasts who had lived in expectation of the Advent; others were the discontented in whose hearts the oppressions and injustices of the rulers and the clergy had caused a longing for that reign of righteousness in which iniquities would be righted. These were reinforced by those who hoped in some change to serve their own interests. (See Mirza Kazim in *Journal of Asia*, 1866.) By the time the Bab had returned from Mecca to Bushire the news had been carried to the bounds of Persia. In Shiraz even the call to prayer, *azan*, had been made in the Bab's name. The government was alarmed. The Bab's apostles, sent from Bushire, August, 1845, were forbidden to preach. The tendons of their feet were cut. The Bab was brought to Shiraz in chains. Thence he escaped to Ispahan, where the Governor, Minuchihr Khan, believed on him and befriended him. The Shah's Government was supremely interested in these developments. If the claim of the Bab were admitted, the Shah had nothing to do but to lead forth the waiting steed from the royal stables, mount Ali Mohammed on it, resign his throne to the Imam, and enlist under his banner. Instead of this the Shah and his government determined to treat him as a self-deceived and dangerous enthusiast. He was conveyed under guard to the extreme northwest of Persia and confined in the fortress of Maku and afterwards at Chirik in Salmas, 1847-50, but during the greater part of the time permitted to write his books of Revelation, called the "Bayan," and to correspond with his followers. (See writer's article, "The Bayan of the Bab," *Princeton Theological Review,* 1915, pp. 633-55.)

The death of Mohammed Shah was a signal for revolts and disturbances in many parts of Persia, on the part of claimants for the throne and dissatisfied noblemen. In this confusion the Babis, incited by persecutions and anxious to take immediate advantage of disturbed conditions to bring about the triumph of their cause, collected in armed bands. Collisions soon occurred with the Persian authorities, which developed into insurrections at Sheikh Tabarsi in Mezanderan, at Zenjan, and at Niriz in Fars. The Babis fought with fierce courage, undaunted by the overwhelming odds and superior arms of the troops who attacked them. They threw up fortifications and, aided by their women, endured sieges for some months. Savage brutalities were enacted by both parties, the cruelties and barbarities of the Shiahs surpassing those of the Babis only from the fact that victory gave opportunity to the Shah's forces. The Babis massacred the captive soldiers and unarmed villagers at Dih-i-Nazar Khan ("New History," p. 362). They cut off the heads of the slain enemies and placed them on posts around the rampart of their fortress, by order of their leader, Janab-i-Kuddus (*Ibid.*, p. 73). Prisoners of war were put to death by them at Zenjan, the Shah's officer being skinned alive and then roasted (*Ibid.*, p. 155).

Meanwhile the government, thinking to bring the contest to a close by removing the cause, determined on the execution of the Bab. He was brought to Tabriz, and condemned to death by the clergy and government. In the Jabbar-khana, when he and one of his disciples were bound and placed for execution, a marvel occurred. After the soldiers had fired and the smoke had cleared away, the dead body of the disciple was seen but not that of the Bab. His followers were ready to shout, "A miracle! A miracle!" and the populace to acclaim him. But unfortunately for the cause, though the shots had freed him from the ropes, the shop into which he fled had no outlet. He was discovered, led back, and executed. The insurrection continued for a time, with fierce reprisals and barbaric cruelties on both sides. Finally the Babis were overcome and slain, many of them after they had surrendered. Later a plot by some Babis and an attempt to assassinate the Shah led to the execution of several score Babis in most cruel ways. Each one was separately allotted to a guild or class of the population of Teheran that all collectively might be liable to any revenge the Babis might see fit to devise. The repression and persecution failed to obliterate the sect. Some fled into exile. Many adopted the practice of dissimulation, which, under the name of *tagiya*, deems legitimate the denial of one's faith and conforming to the dominant religion for safety.

Babism as fully developed was intended to be a substitute for Islam. The Bab superseded Mohammed; and the Bayan, the Koran. The new law abrogated the old, and the Bab was rightful king entitled to supplant the Shah. As to his personality the Bab declared himself to be the manifestation and revelation of God—the Primal Will, the first and eternally created, the mirror of God, the Mukta or Point of Divinity. This Primal Will had been manifested in all the great prophets in an ascending scale of perfection and excellence. This manifestation said of himself: "I am God, and there is no other God than me, the Master of the Universe." In this theology the Babis resembled the Batinis or Ismielis. In teaching the eternity of matter, the emanation of the Primal Reason, giving esoteric meanings to the precepts of the Koran, declaring the resurrection to mean the Advent of a new Imam, they but followed Abdullah Ibn Maimun, the leader of the Batinis ("Spirit of Islam," pp. 489-92).

The Bab has been called a reformer, and he has, maybe, a slight claim to that title. In social matters he made scarcely an improvement, for while he taught, with the Sunnis and Sheikhis, that men of other religions could be associated with and were ceremonially clean, yet he ordained that no unbelievers should dwell in the five chief provinces of Persia, and this prohibition excluded Moslems as well as Armenians and Jews. He was illiberal, discouraging the acquirement of sciences and foreign or ancient languages, and prohibiting the study of grammar, philosophy, law, and logic, and ordering the destruction of books on these subjects. He looked with some favour on the elevation of women and maintained Kurrat-ul-Ayn, his celebrated disciple, when she at times threw aside the veil and instructed men in the religion. He enjoined marriage as obligatory, favoured monogamy, yet allowed bigamy. In practice the Babis continued polygamy. He allowed divorce for any cause, such as a quarrel; but the divorced should wait a year before seeking another partner. But a man should not divorce and marry more than nineteen times. A woman may go unveiled before the members of the family in which she grows up; she may even talk with a man outside of her own household, if necessary; but if the conversation is limited "to twenty-eight words it is better for the woman and the man." He prohibited alcohol, tobacco, opium, and begging, and enjoined the golden rule, with kindness to children and animals. It is remarkable how little he has to say about morals, yet how much about dress, baths, and burial. Moslem rites, as the prayer postures, fast and pilgrimage, are modified as to time and place but with no essential difference. The zikrs or vain repetitions of the name of God are continued. The symbolism of numbers and letters was greatly elaborated, and many doctrines were explained away by allegorical interpretations. Politically the Bab proposed no reform. Supposedly the substitution of himself and disciples or "Letters," as he called them, for the old Persian rulers would bring about a reign of righteousness. He had assigned governorships to different ones of his followers. That of Constantinople was promised to the Governor of Ispahan when he pretended to be a Babi. The value of the Babi movement for Persia lay not in its ideas, for neither theologically nor socially did it afford any panacea. But it shook and shattered the power of the Shiah Mujtahids. It helped to awaken modern Persia, to bring about independence of thought. It prepared some to break the bonds of traditions who were far from accepting Babism.

BAHAISM

The one outstanding result of Babism is Bahaism,[1] which sprang from it and won over almost the entire Babi community. The Bab taught that no revelation is final and that another dispensation was to be founded by "Him whom God would manifest." It is quite certain that the Bab expected an interval to elapse between himself and the next dispensation similar in extent to that which had passed between former dispensations. This interval is understood by Professor Browne to be either 1,511 or 2,001 years. It is irrational to suppose that the Bab delivered a revelation of several volumes and a detailed ritual to last only 19 years.

The Bab appointed, as his successor and head of the sect, Mirza Yahya, called Subh-i-Azal, the Dawn of the Eternal. At this time a number of the Babis laid claim to be "incarnations." A sort of hysteria or mania seized these men and led them to assert their deity and the divine inspiration of their words. Finally Azal, who had fled to Bagdad, was acknowledged as caliph of the religion. He had a half-brother,

[1] See writer's "Bahaism and Its Claims," Fleming H. Revell Co.

Mirza Husain Ali, called Baha Ullah. Both were sons of Mirza Buzurk, steward of the household of a vizier of the Shah. They were born in Nur, Mezanderan. Azal was son of the wife and Baha of the concubine. Baha Ullah acted as Azal's assistant for a time, but later repudiated his supremacy and announced that he himself was in reality "He whom God should manifest," and that by a secret arrangement with the Bab, they had put forward Azal to act as chief for a time that the risk and danger might come upon his brother, and he himself escape the persecution of the enemies. This rival claim resulted in a quarrel between the brothers which waxed hot at Bagdad, then at Adrianople, whither they were transferred at the request of the Persian Government to remove them from the frontier and from the pilgrim highway. At Adrianople the quarrel reached a climax. They even plotted to assassinate each other. So Azal was sent to Cyprus, and Baha Ullah and his party to Acca, Syria. Baha waxed stronger and his pretensions were accepted by the great majority of the Babis. A score of the leading Azalis who refused to follow him were assassinated. Azal became a negligible quantity, though his few followers in Persia have been rather conspicuous. Baha worked over the materials of Babism and evolved a system which he set forth as a new religion and universal dispensation. This is Bahaism. The two religions are essentially the same in theology, eschatology, hermeneutics, as well as in rites and ceremonies. They differ in some social and political principles and of course in substituting Baha for the Bab.

Bahaism is a dogmatic religion, imposed by authority as a "revelation" to be received unconditionally and without question. It claims to be rational, but has as much mystery as any religion, with elements of pantheism and mysticism. Baha Ullah is regarded as a manifestation of the Deity—a higher one than the Bab, possibly of the Divine Essence itself. As God, he is the former of the Universe from eternal matter and rules over it. He is worshipped as the supreme God, the Father, a dignity and degree which he himself assumed and which is granted him by his followers. The doctrine of incarnations is an old one among Persians. They regarded their ancient kings as divine and expected such an one in their deliverer, Saoshyant. They transferred their hopes and ideas to the line of Ali and the Imams. According to Makrisi, even in the lifetime of Ali there were those who exalted him to the divine rank. Afterwards Abdullah Ibn Wahab taught that "Ali was not dead but living, and that in him was a particle of the divinity" ("Asian Mystery," by Lyde, p. 31). The doctrine of *hulul* prevailed, that God descends into human form without ceasing to be a unity. Shahristani describes it as "a descent of God's essence or of the whole Deity, or of a partial descent or of a portion, according to the degree of preparedness of the person." This doctrine appeared all through Mohammedan history, among the Ismieliyahs, Fatimides, Druses, Assassins, and others called in general Ghulats or exceeders. One representative of these sects is the Ali Alahis of Persia, the same as the Alivi or Kuzul-Bashi of Asia Minor and the Nusairiyahs of Syria, who altogether number some two millions. The Catechism and Manual of the latter says: "Who created us?" "Ali, son of Abu Talib." "Is not Ali your God?" "He is the creator of heaven and earth. Besides him there is no God, the living, the self-existent" ("Asian Mystery," pp. 234-52). To Ali ascription is made as follows:

> "Mysterious Being! None can tell
> The attributes that in thee dwell;
> None can thine essence comprehend;
> To thee should every mortal bend."

The persistence and wide acceptance of this doctrine is interesting as showing that the cold Moslem creed which puts God at a distance as an inaccessible ruler did not suffice for the human heart. This doctrine, and that of the Trinity, counted among the Christian mysteries, are not foreign to the thought of Moslem races nor uncongenial to their minds. These sects, in some measure perhaps remnants of Christian peoples, are found not only in Persia and Turkey, but among the Kurds, Syrians, Arabs, and Egyptians. This doctrine is again emphasized in Bahaism. It teaches that divinity was manifested in Moses, Jesus, Mohammed, Zoroaster, and others, but in greater fulness in Baha Ullah, who is set forth to the Jews as the fulfilment of the prophecies of the Messiah; to the Christians as the Second Coming of Christ; to the Moslems as the Mahdi or Husain; to the Parsees as Shah Bahram; to Brahmans as the Avatar. He is "It" with a capital letter, as I have seen printed in their books.

Another doctrine emphasized by Bahais is "Rijat,"

the Return of the prominent believers of the former dispensation. It is akin to metempsychosis, but is explained to mean rather a reappearance in the spirit and power of the former Imam or apostle. Another aspect is allegorical interpretation. This method is said to have been first applied to Islam by Mohammed son of Ismiel, son of Imam Jafar-i-Sadik. It is called *tavil* or *elm-i-batin,* and its adepts were called Batinis. By setting forth the inner meaning they explain away the precepts and doctrines of Islam. In accordance with this, Baha, following closely the Bab and his predecessors, explained the general resurrection as the rising and appearance of a new manifestation, the judgment as condemnation or acquittal by the manifestation, and receiving spiritual life from him. The "Questioning by the angels in the tomb" is the summoning by the messengers of the manifestation to those in the tomb of ignorance to believe; and the return of the angels to God is the report of the missionaries; the "bridge of Sirat" is the testing at the call of faith; paradise is the condition of belief and hell is unbelief.

Bahaism makes much of the symbolism of numbers. It takes over the sacredness of 19 from Babism and establishes a new calendar of 19 months of 19 days each, abolishing the week. Baha also sanctifies the number 9 because the letters in Baha add to 9 in *abjad* counting. Much is made of the name Baha as a charm and talisman; it is inscribed on rings and breastpins.

The "Revelation" is contained in the "Ikan," "Kitab-ul-Akdas," and numerous other writings which surpass, it is claimed, all previous scriptures. Faith in Baha is now the supreme duty and the means of salvation. Baha condemned Sufiism and darvishes, yet his book, "The Seven Valleys," shows how to follow the Sufi Path; he commends the zikr or repetitions of the divine name and his messengers travel as darvishes in their rounds. The chief rites are the same as in Islam, with variations; prayer has similar ablutions, postures, and genuflections, with prescribed words, but is made with face towards Acca and addressed to Baha Ullah; the fast is for a month of nineteen days, with total abstinence from food during daylight; the pilgrimage to Acca includes bowing before Baha's image and kissing the shrines. There are imitations of baptism and of the Lord's Supper; ablutions of the dead are minutely prescribed. There is an effort to be different from Islam, but Bahaism has nothing new nor superior to it in regard to worship.

Baha also attempted to lay down laws, criminal, civil, and social. Among the punishments prescribed are execution for murder, branding on the face for theft, small fines for adultery, and burning alive for arson. Mohammed never prescribed punishment by fire, saying it was God's instrument. As to woman, she should be educated and more social freedom allowed her. Marriage is enjoined, monogamy recommended, bigamy allowed. Baha himself took two wives and a concubine, all of whom bore him children and survived him. Loose divorce is allowed. War, the jihad, slavery, wine, and opium are condemned. Baha's contact with the West at Adrianople and in Syria somewhat modified the theories he had learned in Babism. He revoked the condemnation of learning and travel, commended intercourse with all men, general education, and a universal language. The agitation connected with the great peace-movements of the first half of the nineteenth century influenced him to advocate peace and arbitration. He bound up the Bahai theocracy to a system of constitutional monarchy substituting local and national councils for one-man power. But he declared that all members of these councils should be Bahais and taxes collected and distributed according to Bahai law. It is quite evident that in such a newly constituted state Christians and Moslems alike would have few rights.

As a pensioner of the Turkish Government and restricted in residence to the neighbourhood of Acca, Baha spent the last twenty years of his life in a fine house and beautiful garden, surrounded by his disciples, receiving the pilgrims and their gifts and freely carrying on his propaganda by letters and messengers. His efforts at reconciliation with the Persian Government brought relief to his disciples, and their condition was rendered more secure by Baha's permission to practise *tagiya,* concealment or conformity to the Shiah religion.

Baha Ullah died in 1892. After his death a bitter quarrel occurred between his sons and wives regarding the succession. It was full of cursings and maledictions, anathemas and lawsuits. It resulted in a second schism and in both leaders being put under renewed restrictions by the Turkish Government. Finally Abbas, the oldest brother, became chief of the sect, with the title of Abdul Baha, the Servant of

Baha. He claimed to be the Centre of the covenant, the Interpreter and Expounder of the Faith and Lord of the New Dispensation. Under him Bahaism has begun a wide propaganda, and aspires to be the universal religion. The zeal of a Christian convert to Bahaism, a Syrian named Khairalla, who had come to America on business, gave an impetus to this idea. He was able in 1894-98 to make some eight hundred converts to Bahaism in Chicago and its neighbourhood. The credulity of Americans inspired great hopes of success. These American converts began to make pilgrimages to Acca, recognizing, in Abdul Baha, Christ Jesus in his Second Coming and worshipping and adoring him as Lord and Master. This is described by one of the pilgrims, Mrs. Getsinger, in the following words (Isaac Adams: "Persia by a Persian," p. 479): "I was waiting for the king to come. I reached Him first and knelt down before Him, kissing the hem of His robe. He helped me to my feet and keeping my hand walked with me into the house. He led me into the room where lies the most brilliant jewel that ever shone on the earth, Baha Ullah. . . . He led me down a flight of stairs and I pressed His hand to my lips." In another letter she describes the meeting with Abdul Baha: "My heart gave a great throb and I held out my arms, crying, 'My Lord! my Lord!' and rushed to Him, kneeling at His blessed feet, sobbing like a child. I sat down at His blessed feet, while He took my hand. . . . He allowed me to kiss His blessed hand." An Englishwoman, Mrs. Khairalla, of the same party wrote, "I threw myself on my knees before Him and sobbed aloud from the emotion that filled my soul. He gave me His dear hands to kiss, such fine delicate hands they are, and patted me tenderly on my cheeks and shoulders." But this party of pilgrims became affected by the schism. Khairalla became the leader of the sect of the younger brother, Mohammed Ali, in America. Though retarded by this, Bahaism has gained 2,000 or 3,000 converts in 17 States, comprising 27 congregations. It has a publication society, has issued Baha's "Revelations" in English, and has a monthly paper—i.e. published every 19 days. It has a missionary society called the Orient-Occident Unity, which sends missionaries to Persia and aids Bahai schools there.

In 1908 Abdul Baha was freed by the Turkish revolution from all restriction as to residence and spent several years in Egypt. Afterwards he made missionary journeys to Europe and America, being received to the pulpits and platforms of the United States with friendly cordiality as an honoured guest. His visit of eight months showed no special results. The propagandists have extended their journeys to India, Burma, South Africa, and Hawaii. They have gained small groups of believers in England and Germany. Though its success is very limited, and even in Persia its numbers have not reached beyond one or two hundred thousand, yet the fact that such a revolt from Islam has been able to establish itself among a Moslem people and to start a partially successful propaganda among Christian people constitutes it one of the interesting movements in the Moslem world of to-day. Its failure in Persia to cooperate with and assist the Constitutional movement and the struggle for the liberties of the people shows that expediency rather than the good of mankind guides its policy. In relation to Christian missions it is a hindrance. One aid that it has incidentally rendered is in breaking the solidarity of Persian Islam, and thus by its struggle to gain religious freedom for itself it has promoted freedom for converts to Christianity.

THE AHMADIYAS

A new religion, similar to Bahaism, was promulgated in India in the last quarter of the nineteenth century. Its founder was Mirza Gulam Ahmad, a moghul by lineage. He was chief of the village of Qadian in the Punjab. From him the sect is called Ahmadiya.[1] He was a man of some property and respectable family. His father was a physician of the old Greek school and Mirza Ahmad professed to be proficient in the same art. In religion they inclined to Sufiism. In his earlier years he was brought into contact and controversy with Christian preachers, and was perplexed by his inability to answer their arguments. He became a recluse and cogitated on reli-

[1] It has been investigated and described by Dr. H. D. Griswold, in a tract named "Mirza Gulam Ahmad." I have consulted also his article, "The Ahmadiya Movement" (*Moslem World*, 1912, pp. 373-79); Professor Siraf-ud-Din, "Mirza Gulam Ahmad" (*Missionary Review*, 1907, pp. 749-56); Dr. J. Murray Mitchell, "A New Sect in India" (*Missionary Review*, 1904, pp. 97-100); J. N. Farquhar, "Modern Religious Movements in India," pp. 137-48; Dr. E. M. Wherry, "Christianity and Islam, etc.," pp. 178-82.

gious themes, till he at last reached the conclusion that he himself was a "revelator." When about forty years of age Ahmad laid claim to being the Mahdi, according to Sunni traditions, and at the same time Jesus Christ who should accompany the Mahdi. In 1880 he issued his "Barahin-i-Ahmadiya," the Arguments of the Ahmadiya. Among his works is "The Teachings of Islam" in English. He seems to have identified the Mahdi with Mohammed, and thus he was the "return" of both Jesus and Mohammed, not literally, but exactly as has been explained in the teachings of Baha Ullah. He thus claimed to be the fulfilment of the hopes of these religions, professing to reform and unite them. He also claimed to be a manifestation of God in a certain sense. This he states thus: "The mantle of divinity is cast upon the person who is thus favoured of God, and he becomes a mirror for the image of the Divine Being. This is the secret of the words spoken by the holy prophet, 'He that hath seen me hath seen God.' . . . I shall be guilty of a great injustice if I hide the fact that I have been raised to this spiritual pre-eminence." (Quoted from "Teachings of Islam," *Moslem World*, 1912, p. 319.) As such he is the Lord of the Age, Mediator, Intercessor, Revealer, and Reformer.

Regarding Christ he taught that he was born of a virgin, that his miracles were not real but spiritual. He held to the swoon theory of Christ's death, declaring that he was crucified, seemed to be dead, was buried in a state of unconsciousness. He cited as proof of this the Gospel of Barnabas. The wounds of Jesus were quickly healed by a salve called the

Marham-i-Isa, the ointment of Jesus whose wondrous powers, he asserts, are extolled in a thousand medical books, Christian, Moslem, Jewish, and Persian. After coming out of the tomb and appearing to his disciples, Jesus went to Afghanistan and Kashmir. This departure is the ascension. The inhabitants of these lands were the lost ten tribes to whom Jesus preached. Finally he died a natural death and was buried in Srinagar, Kashmir. The tomb and shrine of a certain Yus Asaf is pointed out as that of Jesus. In reality it is the tomb of some obscure Moslem Pir of several centuries ago. In proof of his assertion he cites the fictitious story of the "Unknown Life of Christ," by N. Notovich, in which an imaginary account is given, ostensibly from a Buddhist manuscript, of a journey of Jesus to India before his ministry in Judea. Mirza Ahmad adds another imaginary journey after the crucifixion, and on it, as a basis, refutes the Christian religion. He is specially desirous to get rid of the doctrines of the atonement and the resurrection. In other ways he condemns Jesus, as for associating with evildoers. He denied his "power, wisdom, and moral perfection." He was extremely hostile to Christianity, and it was the progress of mission work that incited him. He declared Christianity to be corrupted. Its great errors were the deification of Christ and belief in his expiatory death and literal second coming; its corrupting practices are drunkenness, prostitution, and gambling. God has sent Gulam Ahmad to rebuke them and call them to a new faith. His message to Islam was that they receive him as a peaceful Mahdi. The traditions about a warrior

Mahdi are pronounced forgeries; he, the Mahdi-Messiah, had come to bring peace among nations and to reconcile religions. The jihad he abolished and declared it to have been a curse to Islam. His followers should be peace lovers and submit to British rule. One of the sect, writing in the *Review of Religions,* says: "I do not wish for any Islamic government or empire. What I do long for is this, that whoever be the ruler, the whole world may turn Moslem." He denounced the tomb-worship and immoralities of Islam; discountenanced polygamy, yet practised it himself. He excused Mohammed for allowing polygamy, divorce, and the seclusion of women, as a preventive of greater evils such as appear in Christendom. He explained the pleasures of Paradise figuratively. He claimed to be the exponent of true Islam and to propagate it. It is the true religion, as wide in its conception as humanity itself. It embraces all the inspired religions, and prompts us to love and reverence not only for Mohammed, Moses, and Jesus, but for Rama Chandra, Krishna, and Buddha. He appealed to the Hindus to accept him as an Avatar. Needless to say Moslems denounce him as a heretic and impostor.

The proofs of his mission submitted by Gulam Ahmad were from the former scriptures, from miracles, and from his own prophecies. For example from the analogy of John the Baptist being Elijah, from the teaching about the Second Adam, from the apocalyptic signs of the Millennium, and from the prophecy of the paraclete (John xvi, 7), which the Koran refers to in the words (Surah LXI): "Jesus the son of Mary said 'I . . . announce an apostle to come after me whose name is Ahmad.'" Gulam Ahmad's predictions frequently took the form of foretelling the death of the individual with whom he was displeased. When some of these died a violent death, suspicion was aroused. His followers were supposed to have helped to bring about the fulfilment. One of the men thus threatened, a prominent Christian, named Abdullah Atham, took precautions to have bodyguards, and the prophecy in his case failed. When these predictions of calamity had reached the number of one hundred and over, they merited the attention of the government and the Mahdi-Messiah gave his pledge to refrain from such imprecations. In view of these vindictive predictions, the Moslems composed a couplet, which I may paraphrase as follows:

The true Christ's power was such
He made the dead revive;
The false Christ's fatal touch
Brings death to those alive.

Ahmad had correspondence with Dowie, the Elijah of Zion City, Illinois, and challenged him to a discussion. He also proposed a test of the truth of their respective dispensations, namely, that whichever one of them died first should be proved a false prophet. Dowie, whether because he was much the senior in years or mistrusted Oriental providence, declined the test as irrelevant. In some cases where Ahmad predicted a son for his devoted follower, the advent of a daughter taxed his ingenuity for an explanation. One of his prophecies was that his village would be immune from plague without inoculation. He also prepared the marham-i-Isa "solely under the influence of divine inspiration" and set it forth in a pamphlet as "the Revealed Cure for Bubonic Plague." Neither prophecy nor ointment exempted his people from the scourge. The government also thought best to interfere with this divine quack-medicine. This latest Messiah was cut off in 1908 by the cholera.

Mirza Gulam Ahmad's method of propaganda was vigorous. He was well acquainted with Arabic, Persian, and Urdu. In words he was an aggressive disputant. He favoured education and established middle and high schools at Qadian. He made much use of the press, issuing more than fifty tracts, books, and memorials, and two magazines, one in Urdu called *Al Hakam* and one in English called *The Review of Religions.* He organized his congregations with weekly meetings and conferences and with the chief society at Qadian. The membership has increased in the last decade. The *Imperial Gazetteer* of India, which calls it "the wildest development of recent sectarianism," reported 10,000 in the Bombay Presidency in 1911; in the Punjab the census gave 18,695 as against 1,113 in 1901. There is a branch in the Deccan. Dr. Griswold of Lahore, a special authority on the sect, estimates the total at 50,000. Some of the members are men of respectability and intelligence, even university graduates. Nearly all are from the Moslems, and they regard it as a reform of Islam. It certainly works towards the disintegration of orthodox Islam. Some disciples are reported to be in Afghanistan, Persia, Arabia, and Egypt. An interesting phase of the movement is its propaganda in England. Mr. Khoja Kamal-ud-Din, an advocate, has established himself at Woking at the mosque erected by Dr. Leitner. By lectures and through a magazine called *The Islamic Review,* the doctrines are promulgated. A new translation of the Koran is being issued. Free literature is distributed. The mission has been encouraged by the conversion of Lord Headley to its faith.

In this effort to propagate itself in Christendom, it is like Bahaism. In not a few points there is a striking resemblance between these offshoots from Mohammedanism. Some of these may be accounted for by their springing up in a similar soil, a Mohammedan soil impregnated with Sufiism and Mahdiism, and in which some elements of nineteenth-century Christian thought had found lodgment. Both claim that a new revelation is needed because Christianity is dead and Islam needs reforming. Both claim to be in some sense divine manifestations, in another sense the " return " of Jesus, of Mohammed, and of Krishna. Both propose to unite all religions. Both do away with the jihad and advocate peace principles. Both, after the example of Mohammed, sent letters to kings announcing their coming and inviting them to faith. Both practised polygamy and praised Mohammed and the Koran. Both belittled Jesus Christ, denying his miracles, his resurrection, his ascension and literal Second Coming. Both have some followers in foreign lands even among Christians. Both failed to bring about moral reformation in the conduct of their disciples, who have divided into sects on the death of the founders. Both claimed as signs of their mission their eloquence in the Arabic tongue, the writing of spontaneous verses, fulfilled predictions, their success in winning converts, and the good effects as seen in the conduct of their followers. Both made large use of the press; Baha Ullah sent his books to Bombay to be published owing to lack of liberty in Turkey and Persia; Gulam Ahmad had a press of his own at Qadian. The teachings of Ahmad are free from some extravagances and inanities of Bahaism. Neither sect appears to have any great future before it. Their chief usefulness has been to help towards the breaking down of scholastic Islam—the one among the Shiahs, the other among the Sunnis of India. Bahaism has definitely broken with Islam, while the Ahmadiya movement continues within its fold.

THE MAHDI OF THE SUDAN

Exceedingly interesting is the Mahdiist movement of the Sudan. It has been a present-day example before our eyes of what has occurred many times in the centuries of Islam. It would undoubtedly have issued in success and triumph but for the terrible machine-gun of the Christians which turned the tide.

Mohammed Ahmad of Dongola, in 1878, proclaimed himself the long-expected Mahdi. He was descended from Mohammed through Husain and was of a family of successful boat-makers and worked at this trade in his youth. He received religious education at Khartum and at twelve is said to have been a *hafiz,* able to say the Koran from memory. He became a hermit at Abba, an island in the White Nile, and acquired a reputation for austerity and asceticism and was venerated as a saint. Moving about among the people, he described to them with thrilling eloquence their oppressions and their wrongs and recalled to them the promise of a deliverer who should bring in the reign of righteousness. This guide was at hand, he declared, right would triumph, and the accursed Turks and Egyptians be driven from the land; their cruelties would be brought to an end. His magnetic appeal to the people, giving hope of release from injustice, had a powerful effect. It is said (Colonel Wingate: "Mahdism," pp. 13-14) that "men wept and beat their breasts at his moving words; even his brother fakirs could not conceal their admiration. With rapid, earnest words he stirred their hearts and swayed their heads like corn beneath a storm. . . . In every hut and thicket echoed the longing for the coming saviour. At last a band said to him, 'You are the promised leader,' and in solemn secrecy he said, 'I am the Mahdi.'"

The time was ripe. Conditions facilitated the acceptance of such a claim. Half a century before, Mohammed Ali, Khedive of Egypt, after establishing his power in semi-independence of the Sultan, turned covetous eyes on the great south land of the Blacks—called the Sudan. He was urged on partly by greed of power, partly by the desire to extend the bounds of civilization. But instead of gold mines, the revenue to enrich him and his successors was from inhuman trade in human beings, and the grinding cruelties of unjust and oppressive taxgatherers. The rapacity and inhumanity of the slave-dealers cried out to God and became a stench in the nostrils of Europe. The Khedive Ismiel saw that to retain a reputation as a civilized ruler he must suppress the slave trade. Hence Colonel Baker and General Gordon and others were commissioned for this work. Their service, hampered while it lasted, was cut short, then the Sudan lapsed into a condition of oppression, corruption, rapacity, cruelty, and inhumanity,—creating in the hearts of the people a soil fit for the springing up of Mahdiism.

The suspicions and fears of the Egyptian governors were aroused by the claims of the new Mahdi. They made several unsuccessful attempts to seize him, but their forces were defeated. He retired to the Nuba mountains, Kordofan. This was called his *hegira* or flight. Here he enlisted the powerful Sheikhs of the Baggaras. The religious enthusiast declared to them: "God himself came near to me and said, 'Go, reform the Moslems and found a kingdom which shall be followed by everlasting peace.' The Prophet came to me, laid his sword in my hand, and said, 'With this sword conquer; for Azrael will go before thee and terror shall fall upon thy foes.'" The warlike Baggara professed their allegiance largely to secure power for themselves and the gain of the slave trade. They provided the Mahdi with wives and concubines from among their daughters. Abdullah of their tribe became his Khalifa. People flocked to his standard. The Mahdi subdued the forces of the Egyptians, bringing into subjection province after province. The defeat of Hicks Pasha and the annihilation of his ten thousand men carried conviction to all the land that this was the True Guide. Gordon was sent to withdraw the garrisons. He was entrapped in Khartum. Too late his rescue was attempted. The Mahdi did not wish the death of Gordon. He seems to have wished him to occupy the place of Jesus, who, according to tradition, should reign with him side by side. He sent Gordon the costume of a believer, and a command to accept the faith. But Gordon was formed in a more heroic mould and had a finer fibre to his character than Lupton Pasha, commander of Bahr-il-Ghazal, and Slatin Pasha, who denied their faith to save their lives. Gordon knew that he that loseth his life for the Truth's sake shall find it unto life eternal. So that peerless Christian knight, saint, and soldier of immortal fame fell in the final assault of Khartum.

Victory had certified the Mahdi. The predicted marks, the V-shaped space between the teeth, the possession of Abdullah for a father and Fatima for a mother, were not fortuitous; Mohammed Ahmad ruled over nearly a million square miles. Before him lay the assured conquest of the Turks, the Christians, all the world.

As a religious movement Mahdiism professed to be a reform. It was a pitiable attempt. The Mahdi gave revelations and laws of his own. The Koran was also retained. Belief in the Mahdi was the first duty; unbelief the greatest sin. He ruled with a rod of iron. A terrible inquisition held sway. Criticism of his administration was punishable with mutilation or death. Special emphasis was laid on asceticism in food and raiment. A costume was prescribed. All must wear this *jubba* or coat to avoid distinction between rich and poor. Feasts at funerals or weddings, and riding a horse, except in war, if able to walk, were not allowed. When riding a donkey, attendants must not walk in company. Wearing long hair, wailing for the dead, writing with cursive letters were prohibited. Three vices were to be avoided—envy, pride, and neglect of prayer: two virtues to be practised—poverty and the Holy War. Of ten commandments, five were specifically about women, that they should cover their heads and faces, should not go to the graves at funerals, not have a dowry above ten dollars, and that men should oblige them to pray. The old Islamic laws of mutilation for theft and beating for wine-drinking were retained, but the use of tobacco was punishable with a hundred lashes while the wine-bibber escaped with eighty. The two most remarkable aspects of the régime were a sort of communism of property and an abnormal indulgence of sensual passions. The property of all men had to be placed in the Bet-ul-Mal, the Community House, to be distributed by the Mahdi. To accomplish this the inquisition worked barbarously. Of this Colonel Wingate says: "The last Khalifate has been under European observation, its propaganda has been studied most carefully, and the whole may be summed up in the phrase, 'Your money or your life.' At Khartum the Mahdi changed into a sensuous voluptuary, luxurious and uxurious. He ate of all dainties, wore the finest materials, was profusely perfumed. Instead of the straw mat on which he had hitherto sat and slept, he had the finest Persian rugs and an imported bedstead. He changed to his former uncouth costume to appear in public as the leader of prayers, where seventy thousand men bowed before him on the grass and even stooped to kiss the dust he trod upon, and gathering it up kept it as a treasure. His bath water was carried away as a means of grace. Yet so great was his hypocrisy that, as Slatin says ("Fire and Sword in the Sudan"), "No man is more irreligious. I have never seen him say a prayer in his own house—only in public." Making a show of piety before the people, he was guilty of the wildest excesses in private. His haram consisted of four hundred wives and concubines. By divorce he changed his four legal wives as often as his fancy suggested. His concubines were booty captured in war, mostly from the tribes which at the point of the sword had been forced to acknowledge him as Mahdi. As the result of his voluptuous life, he became debauched and effeminate, and at last met the reward of his prodigal excesses. A girl who had lost family, property, and all in the siege, "submitted to outrage and obtained a terrible revenge. She gave the Mahdi a deadly poison, and after lingering in great agony, he died in 1885, but six months after the capture of Khartum. . . . The people stood round as though stunned. He could not die; he was immortal" ("Mahdism," p. 228). Thus perished this contemporaneous example of a Mohammedan prophet. The Khalifa Abdullah succeeded to power and crushed the people beneath a heavier yoke. If the Mahdi had beaten them with whips, the Khalifa chastised them with scorpions. They were reduced to such a degree of ruin that they might well long for the oppressions of the Egyptians. Their deliverance came by means of the Anglo-Egyptian force under Kitchener, at the battle of Omdurman in 1898. The bravery of the darvishes won the admiration and pity of their foes. Intrepid and undaunted, they charged again and again in the face of machine-guns, only to fall. Eleven thousand were killed, and 16,000 fell wounded out of 40,000 engaged in the battle. Sir Garnet Wolseley says: "I am sure our men would prefer to fight the best European troops rather than the same number of warriors who were under the influence of Mohammedan fanaticism." (Quoted from *Public Opinion,* Vol. VII, p. 210, in Atterbury's "Islam in Africa," p. 101.) In view of the devotion of these darvishes, Dr. C. R. Watson exclaims: "What magnificent Christians these men might have made! Why should they not be given the True Guide who will lead them not to death but to life?" The Mahdi's tomb had become a shrine as sacred as that at Mecca. It was said to be indestructible—a place of pilgrimage to last forever. The body was treasured as that of a deity. The tomb was destroyed, the body burnt, and the ashes cast into the Nile (Shoemaker: "Islam Lands").

The result of the Mahdi's rule was calamitous. The aspirations of the people for economic betterment were sadly disappointed. War, famine, and disease had wrought terrible havoc. Countless towns had been devastated, myriads of men and women had perished. Of a population of 8,500,000, three and a half millions were destroyed by famine and disease and three and a quarter millions by the wars. The country had diminished seventy-five per cent ("Encyclopedia Britannica," Article: "Mohammed Ahmad"). The battle of Omdurman is an important event in the history of Africa. Great Britain's defeat and withdrawal would have meant the throwing back of civilization in a large section of the Dark Continent. Gordon's death has been made fruitful in good for humanity in bringing the Sudan under the influence of European civilization, and the opening of the way sooner or later for the inculcation of Gordon's faith, even though at present the Memorial Gordon College has been perverted from that holy purpose.

CAUSES OF THESE MAHDIIST MOVEMENTS

What are the reasons for these Mahdiist developments in Islam? One reason is the condition of degeneracy, corruption, injustice, and weakness. The Bab inveighed against the corruptions: the Sudanese Mahdi against the injustice. One sign of the Mahdi's coming was decadence in Islam. Decline is not to them a proof of its falsehood, for traditions clearly state that this is to be expected before the coming of the Imam Mahdi. Thus the Bahar-ul-anvar of Majlisi (quoted in "Crusades of the Twentieth Century," W. A. Rice, p. 424) has a tradition that Mohammed said: "A time will come upon my people when nothing will remain of Islam except its name and naught of the Koran except its writing," and "the mosques of Mussulmans will be destitute of knowledge and worship and the Ulema will be the worst people under the heavens, and contention and strife will issue from them and return upon them." This will precede the triumph of the Mahdi and Islam will be revived and strengthened. To read "The Bahai Proofs" and its description of the mullahs one would suppose that such a time had come upon Islam. There is no doubt that Islam feels its weakness even more than it appears to us, for the decline of political power and the prosperity of the Christians weigh on their hearts. A writer in the *Moayad* of Cairo (*Missionary Review*, 1914, p. 163) says: "Where are our Ulema? Where are our leaders? Where are those who are able to donate funds for us to follow the example of the Christians? Things are in a bad condition. Oh God! send us some one to collect together our scattered forces!" This cry for a Mahdi was noticed by Keane, who under the name of Haj Haji Mohammed Amin made the pilgrimage to Mecca. He says ("Six Months in Mecca," p. 33): "The old ideas of the near approach of the end of the world are very prevalent in the East just now, which all in all is about as ready for the reception of some darvish Peter the Hermit as it well could be."

SIGNIFICANCE OF MAHDIISM

Some have asked: "What is the dynamic of these movements?" It is the belief that these hopes are about to be fulfilled and that the glorious results which have been promised and long anticipated are now to be realized under the present Leader. But they come and go—the Mahdi of the Sudan,—the Mahdi-Messiah of India,—the Bab,—Baha Ullah—and still the Moslem world awakes to disappointment and hope deferred. These all show the sense of need, the unsatisfied longings of heart in the Moslem world. Is it not significant that two or three of these latest prophets have proclaimed themselves the advent of Christ, and preached "peace on earth" and not the jihad? These new religions have failed, the hopes of reform and world regeneration through them have not reached fruition. The high aspirations and enthusiasms of our fellow-men have fed on husks. The Church must make known to them Him who is the Desire of all nations, the True Guide.

V

MODERNISM IN ISLAM

MODERNISM in Islam is a tendency and a movement to bring the thought and life of Moslem peoples into harmony with the present age. Its object, in the words of one of its advocates, is "to dispel the illusory traditions of the past, which have hindered our progress, to reconcile Oriental learning with Western literature and science, to preach the gospel of free inquiry, of large-hearted toleration, and of pure morality." The movement affects not only the religion but the life and customs as well. Though some new influences have undoubtedly originated in Islam itself or been resuscitated from its past, yet the chief cause is the impact of the West on the East. It is the effect of Western civilization and Christian thought and life on Islam. This impact has been continuous and strong during the last century. Contact with Europe has been through various channels. Governments, diplomacy, jurisprudence, commerce, travel, education, languages, science, arts, industries, literature, missions have each made its impression. A chief influence has been education. The going of young men to France and the prevalence of French language and literature have been large factors. Wider and deeper has been the effect of

British thought because brought to bear more directly and on the greater number in India and Egypt. The influence of America, through its missionaries and their schools and the atmosphere they create, has not been small. The "spirit of the age" has affected Moslem peoples, and philosophical and scientific principles, social and economic truths have awakened a response in their minds and consciences. Modernism as an intellectual system or a manifestation of open protest or aspiration is not fully in evidence in literature and the press. But extensive modification in thought and desires is evident to one who has lived among Moslems for some years. He recognizes that there is a great, a wondrous change in mental attitudes, in social ideals, in prejudices regarding theological conceptions. The reality cannot be set forth by statistics, nor by the examination of public or printed utterances of Moslems, for on matters pertaining to religion and the Sacred Law expediency often prevents expression of views, even if there is no actual repression. My conviction is that there is a marvellous change in the intellectual attitude and conceptions of intelligent Moslems. Islam for a thousand years has been traditional and under dogmatic authority. Reason had its place, which was to expound and enforce that which was accepted on authority. Logic and metaphysics were highly valued, but nothing contrary to the Traditions must be set forth. Now thought is being liberalized, moral conceptions and customs are being modified, and this is coming to pass through the infiltration, penetration, the direct impact and impress of Western or Christian civilization. This trend is toward Christian ideals and away from traditional Moslem conceptions. Islam is in ferment. I do not believe there are signs of religious disintegration, but there is demand for large modifications. There is a definite trend, partly conscious, largely unconscious, to adapt itself to the modern age. The reason is the conviction which has sunk into the minds of many that they are behindhand, retrograde, non-progressive. This consciousness of inferiority has aroused a desire for improvement, a spirit of emulation. It is accompanied at times with a feeling of inability to proceed without guidance from those who are known to be in a superior status, in spite of a prejudice which wishes to deny such superiority. The full effects of the leaven of modern ideas in Islam are not yet evident, and only the initial stage of the movement can be described. I shall present Neo-Islam in relation to religious thought, to the intellectual revival, and to social amelioration,—in other words, to theology, education, and the family.

NEO-ISLAM IN TURKEY

In regard to theological thought, if I begin at the seat of the caliphate, it is evident that new interpretations of doctrine could not be made the subject of public discussion in Turkey, in the time of Abdul Hamid. There was no liberty of the press. There was expressed some sympathy with the reactionary doctrines of Wahabism; Pan-Islamism was maintained, but liberalism in theology had no opportunity to find expression. Sheikh Jamal-ud-Din's book regarding the caliphate was suppressed. Yet it is plain that Western thought was continuing to permeate the minds of the educated classes of Constantinople and of the port-cities such as Smyrna, Beirut, and Salonica. Those who received the modern education, whether at home or abroad, became tinged with liberalism in theology. They have broken in many points with the old creed and ceased the observance of the fast of Ramazan and such rites. Secularism and scepticism often have taken the place of faith. Some of the Young Turks, in exile, even drifted away from all religion and became scoffers. Religion with many persons is but an outward cloak, kept on for the sake of popular opinion. They have zeal for Islam traditionally as against any other creed, partly from pride, partly from race prejudice, or as the embodiment of national aspirations because it is a bond of popular unity. These modifications in practice and in mental attitude are evident to all. The report on the "Preparation of Missionaries to the Near East" (p. 14) emphasizes the fact that the Mohammedanism of Constantinople differs materially from that of other regions, due to Europeanizing influences and the "inroads of Western scientific, philosophical, and religious teachings." These influences have been felt, though in a less degree, in smaller cities and in Anatolia and Irak, but even there they have found deep lodgment and borne fruit. Even the wilds of Kurdistan have been penetrated by the modern ideas.

Since the establishment of the Constitution, liberty has increased and reforms in Islamic social life have been advocated, but the stormy years have not invited men to the discussion of theological themes. The Sheikh-ul-Islam, the State Minister of Religion in Turkey, has made many decisions which do not coincide with traditional views and has expressed many liberal and modern opinions. In them he has followed the habit of attributing to Mohammed traditional sayings or finding in the Koran the basis for modern political and social reforms. The Sheikh-ul-Islam declared to Sir Edwin Pears that it was in accordance with the teaching of Mohammed and his example that Christians be treated as the equals of Mohammedans (" Turkey, etc.," p. 330), that Mohammed had proclaimed unity and equality and that all who accepted the Unity of God were to be treated as brothers. Some Turkish Ulema have come to the point of admitting the right to examine and investigate matters of religion and to criticise and investigate the Koran and the Law. New explanations and new expositions are made possible by emphasizing a verse or tradition which may have been passed over previously but is now seized hold of because it suits the new purpose. The further consideration of modern influences in Turkey I defer till the discussion of political movements, as they are closely associated.

MODERNISM IN PERSIA

In Persia liberty of thought and writing has been much restricted. The assumption by Babism of a political and revolutionary attitude probably increased the restrictions. The publication of criticisms of the faith has not been permitted. A pamphlet describing the mullahs, their faults and opposition to progress, was published in Baku, Russia. When copies of it were distributed through the book-room of the school of Mirza Husain Kamal in Tabriz, the antagonism to him was so fierce as to close the school and drive him from the city. The illustrated weekly *Mullah Nasr-ud Din,* published at Tiflis, which cleverly criticised, often with striking cartoons, the foibles of the clergy and state in Persia, was excluded from distribution through the mail. Even after Constitutional government was established, Sayid Hasan, editor of the *Hablul Matin,* who with his brother, the editor of the prominent paper of the same name in Calcutta, had given strong support to the Constitution, was adjudged guilty of a serious offence because he referred with pride and regret to the condition of Persia before Islam and spoke of the Arabs as "lizard-eaters," using this expression of the poet Fardusi. For this offence he was brought to trial and sentenced to prison (Browne's "Persian Revolution," pp. 244, 234). In Tabriz, at the same time, Mirza Husain Khan, an editor, referred to the tradition of Mohammed in which he said that "Woman was made out of a crooked rib of Adam. If you try to straighten it, it will break; if you leave it alone, it will remain crooked." He semi-humorously advocated freedom for woman and the amelioration of her condition, even an attempt to straighten the crooked rib. So much excitement was caused by the article that the editor was in danger, and was called to Teheran ostensibly to answer for his offence, really for his protection.

Modernism among the Shiahs may be said to have its rise with Mullah Sadra of Shiraz, Mohammed bin Ibrahim, an eminent theologian of the time of Shah Abbas the second. He revived the study of philosophy and science. He maintained liberal principles of the interpretation of the Koran and of judging traditions rationally. His system strove to reconcile philosophy, Sufiism, and the Shariat. He and Abdu Razzak revived the study of Avicenna and his philosophy and set in motion currents of liberal thought. He no doubt had influence on Sheikh Ahmad of Ahsa, the founder of Sheikhism—which is an example of modernism among the Shiahs. He was the source of the influence which led on to Babism and Bahaism, but while the latter both broke with Islam, the Sheikhis remained within the fold and strenuously opposed the Babis as anti-Islamite. The Sheikhis themselves suffered from the suspicion and hatred of the more orthodox Mutasharis. Their views have the virtue or taint of Neo-Islam. Sheikh Ahmad explained away the miracles of Mohammed. The two mentioned in the Koran,—namely, the cleaving of the moon and the miraj or ascent to heaven,—he did not deem supernatural. The latter he regarded as a dream or vision of the night, not a real journey. He denied the resurrection of the body, teaching that man has an astral or spiritual body which accompanies the soul into the other world, and this is the resurrection. He directed his disciples to regard Christians as clean and not as a contamination ceremonially. He taught that there is always in the world a "perfect Shiah," the representative of the Imam and his medium of communication. Through him is given the opportunity for the modification of interpretations. This overcomes the chief difficulty to the renovation of the creed in accordance with modern ideas and needs. The liberality of the Sheikhis is noticeable in their relation to Christians. The Sheikhi Mujtahids of Azerbaijan mantained social relations with the missionaries, and even sent their children to Europe and to the schools of the mission for education. One of these was the Sigat-ul-Islam. He would visit us, drink tea with us, discuss questions of science with us. He had a library of considerable size, received magazines from various countries, and was engaged in preparing an historical chronology. He did not express himself freely on religious themes and rather avoided discussion. I remember on one occasion when, seated in my parlour, I was discussing certain points with one of the mullahs who accompanied him, the Sigat-ul-Islam finally said: "Won't you two stop trying to convert one another?" He was an open and sincere friend of the Constitution and did much to further the cause of popular liberties. He tried to bring about peaceful settlement with Mohammed Ali Shah, holding telephonic conversations with him at Teheran to settle Tabriz troubles. Those were indeed troublous times. He fell under the suspicion of instigating and abetting the riot in Tabriz against the Russian garrison, and was hanged on the tenth of Muharram, by order of the court-martial, in the *mashk-madan*—the drill grounds. His last words were: "I have done my duty. I have tried to serve my country. Long live the Constitution."

Another modernist Mujtahid of Persia was Haji Sheikh Hadi, Nazmabadi (Browne's "Persian Revolution," p. 406). He was of first rank among the Ulema of Teheran, learned, incorruptible, a counsellor and instructor of all. He was somewhat of a recluse and ascetic, sat on the ground outside of his house, and was visited by high and low. Viziers and princes were received by him without ostentation. He rose to receive no one save Nasr-ud-Din Shah. Sheikh Hadi's influence was very great. He, a liberal-minded thinker, was branded as a heretic, but his influence was rather increased by this. He opposed popular superstitions, denounced prevailing abuses, led the minds of his hearers away from old beliefs. He had some of Tolstoi's conviction of the dignity and necessity of manual labour and insisted on his sons and disciples working at a trade. His influence was very great in bringing about what is called the awakening of Persia. Men of all classes and creeds were helped to break with the traditional past through his criticism and instruction.

Though many mullahs were held in high repute and honour both for their learning and their faithfulness to their religion, yet it may be said that one characteristic of the age in Persia has been the contempt and obloquy heaped upon the mullahs. Dissatisfaction with the condition of religion has been great and has voiced itself in denunciation of the mullahs as the cause of the degeneracy of the times and of religious life. One cause of this was that many of them opposed progress. Another and greater cause was that many of the Mujtahids are large landlords and were supposed to look kindly upon if not to assist in cornering wheat.

MODERNISM IN EGYPT

In Egypt, modernism has come in as a result of Western education as well as from the influence of certain progressive mullahs. Among these was Sheikh Jamal-ud-Din, who has been described in the chapter on "The Revival in Islam." He had much influence on the Egyptians by applying philosophy to theological discussions. From 1871 to 1879 he was lecturer-extraordinary with a salary from the government. He influenced young writers who became eminent in the presentation of modern thought in new literary style. His most conspicuous pupil was Sheikh Mohammed Abdu, afterwards Grand Mufti (1875-1905). The latter is called the founder of Neo-Islam in Egypt (Browne, *Ibid.*, pp. 3, 7, and Cromer's "Modern Egypt," pp. 174-77). He steered a middle course between the Europeanized Egyptians and the conservatives. He wrote books such as the "Amud-ul-Muslimin," in which he protested against various laws and usages of Islam. He tried to reform divorce laws and the corrupt practices of the courts as well as the system of education. His freedom in dealing with traditional theology and law left him under the ban of the orthodox. His opposition to the extravagances of the Court of the Khedive and his sympathy with the aspirations of his own people made him at times unacceptable to the authorities. Lord Cromer describes another of these modern Sheikhs, El Bakri, who "boasted of his acquaintance with

Gladstone and Salisbury, quoted Rousseau on the Rights of Man in excellent French; indulged in platitudes about the blessings of parliamentary government, and borrowed books to study the French Revolution,—a compound of Mecca and the Paris Boulevard, the latest development of Islam" ("Modern Egypt," Vol. II, p. 177).

With the Grand Mufti and the reformers who have succeeded him the cry is "Back to the Koran." This cry, says Rev. F. Wurz, "is heard in addresses, read in books, pamphlets, and daily papers, and has become rather universal" ("Islam and Missions," p. 58). With some "Back to the Koran" and "Back to Mohammed" mean the same thing, namely, a desire to get away from the traditional law. S. H. Leeder ("Veiled Mysteries of Egypt"), a friend of Islam, expresses Sheikh Mohammed Abdu's position as follows: "Back to the Koran and the simple godliness of the Prophet; away from the superstitious inventions and fables of later men; let Islam be true to the spirit of its great founder and his friends." Some who are saying "Back to Mohammed" are meaning rather to an idealized Mohammed, a prophet with the incarnated divine Light—not the prophet of history. Some there are who make a distinction, rejecting Mohammed as an example and simply accepting him as the revealer of the Koran. A young reformer said to Mr. Gairdner ("Vital Forces," p. 23): "The important thing is to accept the Koran; it is no part of the mission of the Prophet to give a moral ideal. Accept the Koran and then let Jesus, if you like, be better than Mohammed." These quote the Ulema as saying, "The Koran contains all that is necessary to salvation." In this movement the Koran is being made more use of for ethical study. It is also being examined and commented on as literature and its finest selections published separately for devotional uses ("Vital Forces," p. 136).

This modernist call to go back to primitive Islam means a different thing from what it did as the cry of the Wahabis. The latter wished a puritanical reformation, rejecting all foreign influences. With the New Moslems it is a method of discarding antiquated customs and laws and bringing Islam into harmony with Western thought. They feel the necessity of appearing to be good Moslems and have a desire to maintain such a position with their own people. By a loose exegesis they hope to hold what they wish and discard what is unacceptable to them. They think thus to revitalize Islam and inspire it with a spirit of progress. They nominally stand in the orthodox position and cannot be classed as Mutazalites, as the New Moslems in India can. Lately some actual reforms have been brought about in Egypt, through the efforts of Sayid Ahmad Al Bakri and the heads of the darvish orders. They have regulated and limited the zikrs of the darvishes, their extreme gesticulations, hypnotic rites, and excitement. The ceremony, called Dozeh, at Cairo, in which the Sheikh of the Saadiyah on horseback rode over the prostrate bodies of the devotees, has been abolished. The attributing of supernatural powers to the tombs of the Sheikhs is being discouraged. (See Dr. J. Giffin: "Islam and

Missions," p. 295; Dr. C. R. Watson: "In the Valley of the Nile," p. 219; Professor Macdonald: *International Review of Missions,* 1913, p. 596.)

IN MALAYSIA

In Malaysia the influence of New Islam has been felt. Moslems in Java, conscious of their backwardness, have inaugurated a movement looking towards progress and education. The "Society of Islam," sympathetic with modernism, held a congress in Java attended by thirty thousand people. Among the questions discussed were the education of women, the freedom of the press, and self-government. A resident reports that "Within the past year greater changes have come into the minds of the Javanese than in the past twenty-five years." (Quoted by Dr. Zwemer: *Missionary Review,* 1914, p. 182.)

NEW ISLAM IN RUSSIA

Modernism is represented among the forty-two races of Moslems in Russia. This may be noted in external things. Men and women, too, are adopting Christian modes of dress, living in the Christian quarters of the cities, and conforming to their customs. Some of the women no longer live in seclusion nor wear the veil. Mullahs complain that the people are lax in their religious duties, even increasing their use of alcoholic drinks. Boys and even girls are attending Russian government schools. The young Moslems enter the army and civil service as officers. In the Caucasus the movement is advanced. In Tiflis, *Mullah Nasr-ud-Din,* the journal already referred to, makes sport of the foibles of the mullahs, holds up to ridicule old notions and customs and does effective work by its bright cartoons. There is a weekly journal for Moslem women, edited by a Moslem woman. Besides these there are two dailies, the *Hakikat* and the *Shariat,* and a monthly called the *Mak.tab.* In Baku, Tagief, a petroleum millionaire has built a large school for girls. A society carries on other schools. Tracts and books have been published advocating reforms, and especially inveighing against the mullahs. Liberal education is progressing in Kazan and the interior of Russia. A prominent leader in Neo-Islam is Ismiel Bey Gasparinski. His organ, the *Tarjuman,* circulates through Russia and Central Asia. At Tomsk in Siberia a Moslem society for reform and progress has been organized (*Missionary Review,* 1910, p. 738). In 1904 Mohammed Fatah Gilmani published a book in the Tartar language (Professor Vambery: *Nineteenth Century,* February, 1905), called "A Travel to the Crimea," in which he commends to the Tartars the acquisition of European science, laments their backwardness, blames it on the mullahs and the old education, demands a vernacular version of the Koran, and that polygamy and divorce be discouraged, that women be allowed freedom, permitted to attend school, become teachers, preachers, and authors, and participate in public life. He declares that this desire for awakening is a national feeling, born and fostered by their societies. Professor Vambery affirms that the movement has extended its influence to Eastern Turkistan and to many of the nomadic tribes of Central Asia, and that it has a political and revolutionary side as well as literary and religious. It is certainly a notable fact that Tartars have developed their language, are preparing a modern scientific and general literature, and giving a corresponding education. A congress of Moslems met at Petrograd in 1914 with forty-two delegates, representing all parts of the Russian empire, even Tartary and Central Asia. They discussed the care of schools, the maintenance of high schools and colleges for Moslems, the need of women doctors, and general amelioration of moral and economic conditions of their co-religionists in Russia. They also formulated demands for equal rights with Christians. Concerning this, the Moslem members of the Duma are also alert to seek action.

NEO-ISLAM IN INDIA

It remains to consider Moslems in India with reference to the influence of modernism among them. Here the movement has been more open and more widely extended, and from there has influenced other lands.

Neo-Islam in India received its great impulse from Sayid Ahmad Khan of Aligarh, 1818-98. He was distinguished in the Indian civil service, served the Crown well in the mutiny, was received in royal audience in 1870 on his visit to England and knighted. His aim was to bring his co-religionists into harmony in doctrine and life with the modern age. To this end he encouraged English education, especially by founding Aligarh College, edited a magazine called *The Reform of Morals,* wrote a Commentary on the

Bible, admitting its truth and authenticity and trying to reconcile it with the Koran. He interpreted Islam according to rationalism and denied miracles. He recognized a human element in the Koran and admitted the fallibility of both it and Mohammed. He declared that Islam in its traditional and exclusive mould had no future and strove to bring it into conformity with the times and so strengthen it. Because he wrote much in regard to natural religion his followers were called Naturis. He started conferences among Moslems and was the founder of the Moslem League, which had for its aim social, economic, educational, and religious reforms.

His influence was increased still further by his successors, who developed the same policy. One of these is Sayid Amir Ali, a graduate-in-law in London and a Justice in the Indian Courts. He is the author of "The Life of Mohammed," "Mohammedan Law," "The Legal Position of Woman in Islam," "The Spirit of Islam," etc. His attitude is that of a special pleader. He would explain away and gloss over the defects of Mohammed's character and by strained interpretations show that the Sacred Law is in conformity with twentieth-century ideals. His teaching in regard to inspiration is evident from his saying ("Life of Mohammed," 1873, p. 25) that Mohammed's knowledge of Jesus was received from floating traditions in Arabia, prevalent in his time, part of the folklore of the country, and that the law regarding spoils in war was promulgated by Mohammed and incorporated in the Koran. He knows nothing of revelation from eternal tablets preserved in heaven. The Koran comes by a lower form of inspiration. He suppresses the supernatural and miraculous in the *miraj*, in the flight to Medina, or angelic action at Bedr (p. 83), rejects a personal devil and the jinns (p. 86). As to the facts of Mohammed's history, he utterly disregards all that the ancient Moslem historians tell against his character, so that Dr. W. St.C. Tisdall is led to say: "A great modern discovery of the Neo-Mohammedan is that no reliance is to be placed on the earliest and most celebrated Muslim historians, traditionalists, and commentators, when they relate anything which a modern apologist deems discreditable to Mohammed, but that the very same writers are thoroughly reliable when they state anything in his favour" (*Moslem World*, 1913, p. 408).

As to the Shariat, Amir Ali states his far-reaching principle in the following words: "Commands and prohibitions have invariably been in consonance with the progress of humanity, and the law has always grown with the growth of the human mind" ("Mohammedan Law," p. 13). "The elasticity of laws is their great test, and this test is pre-eminently possessed by those of Islam. Their compatibility with every stage of progress shows their founder's wisdom. Inquiry will evince the temporary character of such rules as appear scarcely consonant with the requirements or prejudices of modern times" ("Life of Mohammed," pp. 227, 157). Many sumptuary regulations, precepts, and prohibitions of Mohammed were called forth by temporary circumstances. With the disappearance of the circumstances, the need for those laws has also disappeared. The people, whether Moslem or not, who suppose that every Islamic precept is necessarily immutable do injustice (p. 194). With such views he relegates to a secondary position verses and passages of the Koran and Traditions which have held the field, and gives emphasis to other verses. He claims the right to ignore verses and to change interpretations, as he says the Christians have done. And further, as Bosworth Smith says ("Mohammed and Mohammedanism," p. 257), "There are some among the New Moslems who see now, and there will be more who will soon see, that there will soon be an appeal to the Mohammed of Mecca from the Mohammed of Medina." Amir Ali affirms the right of private judgment and, with special interpretations, rejects from the Koran all that does not accord with his own ideas. He shows, to his own satisfaction at least, that Mohammedan "law itself may be considered a prohibition of the plurality of wives," and that slavery, intolerance, and war for the propagation of the Faith are not parts of Islam. It is at least a gratification to find an expounder of Islam who repudiates such practices. He does not accept the decisions of the Imams on traditional law as unchangeable nor exempt them from criticism. The Imams have injured Islam by making it fixed, reactionary, and unable to adapt itself. Their decisions must be disregarded. The fatvas of the Ulema, too, are without authority. Even the Koran can be criticised. All provisions of the Shariat not suited to the present age can be discarded. Reason is to be the judge and contemporary sense of fitness the criterion. The Imams have rejected five hundred thousand traditions and only found eight thousand authentic. Let us throw all overboard that do not suit us. Such is the attitude of this representative reformer.

Another writer of Neo-Islam is Maulvie Chiragh Ali, an officer of the Nizam's government. He has published "Reform Under Moslem Rule" and "Critical Exposition of the Jihad." Another of the group, Ali Hasan, has published a life of Mohammed, "The Last Prophet," in which he discards the miraculous. The Light of Mohammed is simply the light of conscience with inspiration; the miraj or midnight journey was in vision only, jinns are but bad men, jihad is only to be in self-defence. Mohammed's intercession, sinlessness, and miracle-working are not mentioned. The example of the Prophet has not the binding force of law on his followers.

Controversy has occurred among the Hanifites over the use of the vernacular in prayer and of translations of the Koran. The modern party take the ground that worship should be in a language understood by the participants. Besides the arguments of reason, they appeal to the tradition that Mohammed allowed his Persian converts to make their prayers in their own tongue ("Spirit of Islam," p. 522).

Another New Moslem is S. Khuda Bakhsh. In his "Essays Indian and Islamic" he quotes with approval the teachings of Von Kremer and Goldziher regarding the relation of Roman law to the Shariat. He cites Nawaur as saying: "By far the greatest portion of the Muslim law is the outcome of true inquiry, for the actual passages of the Koran and Sunna have not contributed a hundredth part of it. The Board of Nazar-ul-Mazalim had to decide not according to the letter of the law, but according to the principles of equity." "Islam, stripped of its theology, is a perfectly simple religion. The Koran is a spiritual guide, not a body of civil laws. It was never the intention of the Prophet to lay down immutable rules or to set up a system of laws which was to be binding apart from changed conditions." He laid down rules of marriage, etc., intended to meet the then existing conditions. Muslim jurisprudence grew by the adoption of foreign rules ("Essays Indian and Islamic," pp. 284-86). These principles give scope for a complete modernizing of Islam.

Another Indian reformer is Mulvi Abdullah of Chakrel, somewhat of an ascetic and a voluminous writer. His teachings are described by Canon Sell as a wide departure from orthodox Islam. He would return to the Koran, rejecting all traditions. Polygamy and the jihad are declared to be against the Koran, the *azan* or call to prayer and the rosary are rejected, as well as all pilgrimages except the one to Mecca, which must be limited to simple ceremonies and be without the kissing of the black stone. Neither Mohammed nor any other man can be mediator at the Day of Judgment. The intermediate state is one of unconsciousness.

Another new sect is the Ahli Koran, the People of the Koran, who have some following in the Punjab. They reject traditions entirely, denounce polygamy, and affirm that neither Mohammed nor any other of the prophets had more than one wife

("Vital Forces," p. 173).[1] In general it may be said of these Indian Moslem reformers, in the pertinent words of Mr. Gairdner ("Reproach of Islam," p. 206): "They read into the Koran almost everything they have come to like, and out of it almost everything they have come to dislike."

Such are the principles of Neo-Islam. Have its expounders forsaken the Faith? By no means. They are strenuous Moslems. They proclaim the greatness and glory of Mohammed, whitewash his record, expurgate from Islam all blemishes, and make it the possessor of every excellency demanded by public opinion of the twentieth century. Justice Amir Ali[2] is bitterly and scornfully anti-Christian and scours the history of Christendom from age to age to find crimes to set against those of Mohammed and

[1] It is curious how the reformers of Islam cling to some of the old Oriental ideas. This is noticeable in regard to assassination. Sheikh Jamal-ud-Din said in an interview with Professor Browne ("Persian Revol.," p. 45): "No reform can be hoped for until six or seven heads are cut off," and specified Nasr-ud-Din and Amin-i-Sultan. Both these were afterwards assassinated. Jamal-ud-Din also proposed that Khedive Ismiel should be assassinated and Sheikh Mohammed Abdu says (quoted by Lord Cromer, Vol. III, p. 181, from W. S. Blunt's "Secret History," p. 489): "I strongly approved of it, but we lacked a person capable of taking lead in the affair." We are reminded of the assassination of the Azali Babis by the Bahais. The attempts to assassinate the new Sultan of Egypt are also instigated and applauded by high religious authorities of Constantinople. See Chapter V.

[2] The historical attitude of this learned representative of New Islam may be seen in his lament over three things (p. 342): 1. The failure of the Persians to conquer Greece. 2. The failure of the Arabs to conquer Constantinople in the eighth century. 3. The unfortunate results of the battle of Tours. "Each of these has prevented the growth and progress of civilization."

primitive Islam. (See "Life of Mohammed," last chapter.) Principal Morrison of Aligarh College says: "They believe that in their Faith are enshrined the great truths of religion and morality; but that in the past they have misread the word of God, and that the narrow-minded mullahs have expounded it amiss." (Quoted in "Crusaders of the Twentieth Century," p. 49.)

It must be borne in mind that this rationalistic method of interpreting Islam is not new. This Indian school of thought is a revival of the Mutazalis, who existed under the Abbaside caliphate of Bagdad. Then Persian thought and influence were prevalent and exercised a strong tendency to free Islam from the fetters which were fast being bound upon it. Victory was apparently with this party of free thought. Orthodoxy seemed to have lost the adhesion of the learned. But Al Askari, using as his weapon the dialectics of Aristotle and teaching Greek logic to the orthodox, gave them the victory and established rigid legalism and traditionalism in Islam (Stanley Lane-Poole: "Studies in a Mosque," pp. 171-74; Geden's "Studies in the Religions of the East," p. 831). Again the disciples of free thought take the same name. Amir Ali says (preface to "Mohammedan Law," p. x): "Belonging myself to the little known but not unimportant philosophical and legal school of the Mutazalis, and thus occupying a vantage ground of observation, I cannot but observe the movement that has been going on for some time among them. The advancement of culture and the growth of new ideas have begun to exercise the same influence on them as on other races and peoples. The young generation is tending unconsciously to Mutazalite doctrines. It must not be supposed, however, that this movement results from a weakening of the Islamic faith. It originates more from the desire to revert to the pristine purity of Islam and to cast off the excrescences which have marred its glory in later times. To me it appears that great changes are imminent in the social institutions and personal laws of Indian Mussulmans." But we need not expect much to result in the way of uplift to Islam from rationalizing and intellectual defence and pruning. No Erasmus can set on fire a genuine reform. Still as Persian influence had great results in the old time, the foreign civilization in India will show effects on Islamic thought and conscience.

VI

THE NEW EDUCATION IN ISLAM

MOSLEMS, especially in the Near East, have had considerable intellectual life. But education long ago became stereotyped. For centuries it has been clerical. Its centre was the mosque, its teacher the mullah or mudarris. Generally there is a mullah in each village and a mud-walled, adobe mosque, unceiled and unfloored, without furniture save the *membar* or pulpit and a bastinado in the corner for refractory boys. The father on bringing his boy into view of this instrument of torture, would say to the mullah, "The bones are mine, the skin and flesh are yours, only teach him letters." The pupils gave fees and presents to the mullah. These were not large nor abundant, as is evidenced by the story of a father who brought his boy to the mullah and said: "Ay, mullah, what will you take to teach my boy to read?" "I want ten tomans," answered the mullah. "That's too much," exclaimed the father; "I can buy a donkey for that sum." "Buy," retorted the mullah, "and then you will have two." (See author's "Persia; Western Missions.") The income of the mullah was supplemented by writing deeds, contracts, letters, and charms for the people. The pupils sit on reed matting without desks. They are unclassified, and when one recites alone the rest of the pupils learn their lessons aloud in a singsong tone. In cities these schools are in different wards, and some of them in the bazaars, separate from the mosques.

The basis of the curriculum is learning to read the Koran. In countries in which Arabic is not the vernacular, this is injurious to the pupils. Many of them spend all of the few years which it is their lot to attend school learning to read Arabic by rote and often very imperfectly. This schooling is of no practical use to them. Many who read fluently do not understand its meaning, yet they have their reward in the great merit of simply reading the holy words. This has been a great hindrance to popular education even in Persia and Turkey. In less civilized lands it has been nothing short of a calamity. In Sierra Leone and Central Africa, Moslem education is described as an unintelligible learning by rote of the Koran and committing to memory of a few prayers, to which is added a course in witchcraft, making charms and fetishes. In Malaysia the instruction has a stupefying rather than an enlightening effect. It is mechanical and parrotlike. They learn neither the tribal language nor the Malay. Mr. Simon says: "They acquire a number of Arabic formulæ and facility in rattling off a few Malay phrases of which they practically do not understand a word." Fortunately common sense and race pride asserted themselves in Persia. So after some time spent in reading Arabic, the pupil is permitted to learn his vernacular, and a course in Saadi, Hafiz, and other poets has developed many Persians of good literary ability.

Private instruction at home has been a substitute for good schooling for the nobles and the scribes. Even in Arabic-speaking lands the old system hampers education by confining education to the dialect of the Koran and not using the modern dialect.

Higher education, under the old system, was confined to training for the Ulema. The course of instruction included theology and law, the Koran and the Traditions and their exposition, with grammar, rhetoric, and logic, and possibly some mathematics. It excludes modern sciences and languages. These madressas are supported by tithes and *vakf,* endowments. They develop acute and well-trained faculties, and have served their purpose through the medieval period of Islam. But a spirit of narrowness and bigotry rules in them. Many of them are hotbeds of fanaticism. They train up their talabas or softas to be reactionary, not only hard-bound to traditionalism in the sphere of religion, but adverse to the progress which modern science brings to mankind.

THEOLOGICAL SCHOOLS

The theological-law schools of Islam have continued on the ancient basis. Shiah madressas at Kerbala and Najef, Sunni ones at Mecca and chief cities of Turkey and Central Asia, have changed but little. One of the most celebrated of these is Al Azhar at Cairo. Time was when a Christian was not even permitted to enter its precincts, but fortunately for the members of the Cairo Missionary Conference that rule no longer holds. I was greatly interested in walking through its crowded cloisters, and seeing its multitude of students, sitting on the floor, in circles around their Sheikhs and Muftis. As we passed from group to group I kept imagining what ones might be from Kazan or Bukhara, what ones from Morocco or Java, from Cape Town or Peking, and where they will be scattered after years of training in the lore of Islam. This famous theological school was founded by the Fatimide Jowhar, vizier of Sultan Muiz, A.D. 969, at the time Cairo was laid out. It has as high as 325 professors and 11,095 students from many lands. Each nation has its section or dormitory. The Italian Government lately established a hostel with 150 students from Erithrea and Tripoli "to train students to teach the coming generation in Tripoli the Islamic doctrine, the Arabic tongue, and love of Italy." Al Azhar has large endowment from which a daily dole of bread is given to the students. It is noted specially for instruction in theology and Arabic. Rev. F. Wurz points out that it is a mistake to refer to Al Azhar as a great foreign missionary centre, for it does not send out missionaries to non-Moslem lands. It is rather an international theological seminary. It is intensely conservative. The Grand Mufti, Mohammed Abdu, tried to modernize its curriculum by introducing some secular learning into the preparation—for example, geography and history. The necessity for this may be seen from an incident related by Dr. Watson ("Egypt and the Christian Crusade," p. 48). A graduate of Al Azhar was teaching Arabic to a missionary and came upon the word Asia. He asked, "Where is Asia? Is it a part of Europe?" The

Mufti's plan was not accepted by the professors, caused difficulty, and the Khedive secured his resignation. Al Azhar continued to illustrate the stagnation of Moslem conservatism. The Khedive tried his hand at reforming it, and as an inducement increased its revenues from forty to two hundred thousand pounds. But owing to dissatisfaction with its spirit and management, he ceased to patronize it. A ninth attempt to modernize it failed in 1910. A new regulation was that all students who had been in the university more than seventeen years should leave if they failed in the coming examinations. I believe that it still teaches the Copernican system. A similar school in Constantinople, used, until a few years ago, a textbook for physical science which was a thousand years old. There is much dissatisfaction with such institutions. This is voiced by a Moslem, Mushir Husain Kidwal, who wrote in the *Hindustan Review:* "Even the educational institutions stink of the old decaying smell."

The old system of education reached only a small proportion even of the boys. Illiteracy prevailed in all Moslem lands. For example, take the Persians—a people with a literary classic tongue and masterpieces which have merited the admiration of the world. Travellers who report about the proportion of the population who can read fail to consider the village and nomad people. In many villages scarcely one in a hundred can read. Probably the estimate made about Moslem lands for the Cairo Conference is approximately correct,—namely, that ten to fifteen per cent are literate, though in India, where the census gives the correct figure, not more than five in a hundred of the men can read and only four in a thousand of the women.

Discontent with these conditions has led to a movement for modern education. The desire is to do away with this antiquated system, and to substitute modern methods and curricula. This is one of the significant movements—one that is having large influence on their lives and religious conceptions. The new education is Western and carries with it a large element of Christian truth.

In the Near East the modern ferment of ideas began at the time of Napoleon. After his invasion of Egypt and Syria, those lands continued in closer and more constant contact with Europe. After that time European influence is continually evident. It was at the same time that ambassadors from France, Britain, and Russia began special efforts to influence the Shah of Persia; and the people of Persia began to know something definite about Christian civilization. A powerful influence was exerted by Europe on the Near East during the nineteenth century by the coming of young men in considerable number from Turkey, Syria, Egypt, and Persia for education. They returned much changed in religious belief and practice and with ideas and purposes out of harmony with the old conditions. They especially felt the need for their own people of the literary and scientific culture which they had seen in Europe. This need was made more prominent and a general impulse was given to new education among Moslems by the mission schools and by those of the Oriental churches among their own people as well as in some countries, as India, by the government schools.

NEW EDUCATION IN PERSIA

I shall begin a review of this educational movement with Persia. The first Persian students who returned from Europe to Persia about the middle of the nineteenth century were not well received and were viewed with suspicion (Markham's "History," p. 19). But in the subsequent period, many of the most enlightened men have had the benefit of European training. Such was Hasan Ali Khan, Amir-i-Nizam, the able though unscrupulous governor of Azerbaijan, who did so much to overthrow the tobacco monopoly. The late regent Abul Kasim Khan, Nasir-ul-Mulk, a graduate of Oxford, and different members of the family of Riza Kuli Khan, Lala Bashi, were prepared by it to take a prominent part in organizing the Constitutional government. Many members of the medical profession were of the modern school, and not a few of them received the foreign training. What is true of Persia is more the case with reference to other countries of the Near East. The visit of the Shah Nasr-ud-Din to Europe led him to encourage Western learning. He founded the Shah's College, with a curriculum on European models. When I visited it in 1881 it was doing fairly good work, but it did not develop rapidly in standard and efficiency. A few other schools were established in the chief cities of the country. The teachers and graduates of these schools were, for the most part, liberal-minded and progressive, with a lighter sense of the obligation of the Shariat and a less bigoted attitude towards Christians. There was a tendency towards secularism and scepticism which seemed to endanger religious character, and threatened to bring about a condition where young men of culture would be freed from the restraints of Islam and have no faith in Christ to take its place. A term, *Frangi mahab,* was applied to a class of men who were imitators of foreign ways and often without substantial character back of it. Spasmodic but for the most part unsuccessful efforts were made to establish schools. The Constitutional movement gave a vigorous impetus to new effort, but no systems could be organized owing to disturbed conditions. Within a year twenty schools were opened in Tabriz and a correspondingly larger number in Teheran, where the education of girls took a good start. But all these schools only accommodated a few hundreds in the smaller cities and a few thousands in the larger places. The reactionaries under Mohammed Ali Shah showed their attitude towards the new education by looting and burning the schools, the libraries, and breaking in pieces the printing-presses. A remarkable opportunity came to the Missions to educate the Moslem youth. They came by the hundreds to their schools, taking the religious lessons because of their desire for the science and languages. Impetus was given to plans for higher education and projects were initiated to develop colleges for Moslem students in Teheran, Tabriz, and Ispahan.

EDUCATION IN TURKEY

On Turkey the influence of Western education has been marvellous. Many young men have gone to France and some to England and Germany. French to a great extent became in the nineteenth century the language of diplomacy and business. It became also a means of literary culture. A European movement set in strongly, especially from 1850 to 1870. Literature took on new life and developed under the stimulus. The literary style and taste of Osmanli scholars were transformed. Of Turkish poetry previous to that time Gibbs says ("Turkish Poetry," Vol. V, pp. 1-21): "It was Persian in its inception, Persian in substance it remained." Thereafter the literature of Turkey no longer followed the Persian models but those of France. The intellectual life of the educated was changed as were their political ideals. Remarkable modifications are noticeable in their ideals and forms. The language itself was remodelled and a new prose created by Shanasi Effendi, Namik Kamal Bey, and Ziya Effendi. Abd ul Hak Hamid Bey acquired fame as a vernacular poet, though the Sultan prohibited his works from circulation. Literature ceased to be an adjunct of the work of the clergy. The drama was introduced. French drama and Shakespeare were translated. Ideas of patriotism and liberty permeated literature.

The reforming Sultans favoured popular education as a means of bringing Turkey into accord with European life. About the middle of the nineteenth century schools were established in which children of all races were to be educated without distinction. These were elementary, middle or *rushdiya,* and lyceums or colleges, including normal, agricultural, technical, medical, law, military, and naval schools. The primary schools were fairly numerous in the provinces, and high schools in the cities. Some few were for girls. The School of Commerce did not prosper, because the Turks do not take to business life. After a score of years it has only a handful of students.

The Christian population did not take kindly to these mixed schools, preferring to have schools distinctive for their own language, literature, and religion. Nor were they acceptable to the Moslems. They were changed in 1870 to schools for Moslems only, in which their religion was specially taught and foreign languages abandoned. Of this period Charles Dudley Warner wrote: "Signs enough are visible in the Levant of a transition period, extraordinary but hopeful; with the existence of poverty, oppression, superstition, and ignorance, are mingled Occidental and Christian influences, the faint beginnings of a revival of learning and the strong pulsations of awaking commercial and industrial life." Later Abdul Hamid restricted the schools, for he would have kept the people in ignorance, and especially would have prevented the spread of liberal ideas. But he knew the necessity of education for officers, so he supported some good military and medical schools. He even let some students go to Europe to learn military science, but prevented all others even from travel, as much as he could. He allowed more freedom for the education of girls, not apparently dreading their influence on politics or perhaps despising it as of no account. Yet many young men escaped to Europe, and were educated there and the Young Turks are largely men of this class. Since the Constitution was established, Turkey has talked much about promoting education. Indeed, some of them attributed their defeat by the Balkan states to their lack of education. The *Ikdam* (quoted in *The Orient*) says: "Why have we been beaten? Because our adversaries have even in their villages primary schools." They have given liberty to scientific and philosophic study. They have planned much, but accomplished little. One reason is that the prosecution of or preparation for war has exhausted their funds. The appropriation for public instruction is 65,000,000 piastres, about $3,000,000, while that for war, navy, and pensions is 1,400,000,000 piastres (more than $60,000,000) in time of peace. Even the schools with a religious endowment, or *avkaf*, are in a pitiable condition and have been decreased from 325 to 250. Another difficulty has arisen from mixing politics with the educational plans, and pursuing the policy of Turkifying the subject races, and compelling the Albanians, Arabs, and others to learn the Turkish. In spite of all, some progress is being made. Female education is being encouraged. Girls are being prepared as teachers; some have been placed by the government in the normal course of the (American) Constantinople College and others sent to Europe. A significant incident occurred at Nicomedia in February, 1914. Moslem boys and girls took part in school exercises together. Girls of twelve and thirteen made recitations and addresses before an audience of two thousand people. The governor made a stirring appeal for general education and especially for the culture of the future mothers. Another significant event was the inception by the Sheikh-ul-Islam, Hairi Bey, of a new "Theological Madressa of the Great Khalifate," at Constantinople,—to be a training-place for the Ulema of the whole Islamic world, to rival and eclipse Al Azhar. Its distinctive feature is that it will give instruction in all modern science and philosophy, and turn out Ulema who shall be progressive leaders in intellectual life (*The Orient*, October 7, 1914). A Moslem university has been started at Medina. The cornerstone was laid November 29, 1913. An address was made by Sheikh Abdul Aziz Shawish. The *irade* of the Sultan declares that its object is the teaching and spread of the eminent truths of Islam; all Christian influence is to be excluded. It will also teach agriculture and engineering. Its central committee will be in Constantinople, but superintendence in the hands of a committee at Medina.

At Jerusalem, the Madressa-i-Kulliyah has been founded to prepare religious leaders in theology, with scientific and sociological training. It is under the direction of Sheikh Shawish, who says it is a restoration of an institution founded by Salah-ud-Din, but which became a Roman Catholic school, but now reverts to the Turkish Government. Its programme is broad. It starts with one hundred boarders, free instruction, and government endowment. Secular universities are announced for Bagdad and Damascus.

The Committee of Union and Progress is at least in some respects true to its name.

Since the increase of liberty, Moslems showed a desire to attend the mission colleges. The largest representation has been at the Syrian Protestant College at Beirut, but there has been a disposition to shirk the religious instruction.

A curious development has been the organization of Turkish Boy Scouts. It was initiated at the War Office, with Enver Pasha as Chief Scout. It has a definite military object, to draw the wealthy Turks into military life, and secondly to promote a Neo-Turanian spirit,—to develop Turkish nationalism, to use the Turkish language by discarding Persian and Arabic words. For example, in the oath Allah is not used, but Tengri, not Sultan or Padishah, but Khakan. It is an attempt to link themselves with the great Turkish race which extends to the border of China. Maybe it is prophetic of the fact that Byzantine and Arabian connections are about to cease.

IN EGYPT

In Egypt the influence of Europeanized Moslems has been specially felt. Even Khedives and the present Sultan of Egypt were educated in Europe. The Khedives opened schools, normal, polytechnic, medical and military, and for girls. They had in 1880, before British occupation, 5,000 schools with 111,800 pupils. Under British superintendence the system has been enlarged on European methods. The traditional religious teaching is given to the classes. Some Moslems are held firm by it, others tend to scepticism.

Some Coptic pupils under the influence of the lessons have accepted Islam (Gairdner: "Methods, etc.," pp. 62-63). To crown the system the National University has been founded on Western models. It has considerable grants of land and endowments from Princess Fatima Khanum. The cornerstone was laid April 10, 1914. It is without a religious foundation. Schools of engineering and agriculture have been opened at Giza. At Tanta success seems to have been attained in modernizing the Sheikh's Mosque School. There 3,400 students have the benefit of a course of study including geography, history, physics, drawing, and hygiene (S. A. Leeder, in "Veiled Mysteries of Egypt"). Young men seem to care little for higher education except as a means to official appointment. Six hundred youths are in Europe for education at their own expense, the majority of them in England. They do not seem to attend to study, and a committee has been appointed to have oversight of them.

Striking progress has been made in female education. Lord Kitchener wrote in 1912: "There is nothing more remarkable than the growth of public opinion among all classes of Egyptians in favour of the education of their daughters. The girls' schools are crowded, and fresh schools are to be constructed. In 1900 there were 1,640 girls in Kutabs (common schools); in 1910, 22,000." (Quoted by Dr. Sailer in *Woman's Work.*) In 1899 no girl presented herself for the primary certificate, in 1911 there were 43. A Woman's Educational Union was founded under the patronage of the Khedive's mother and with the co-operation of the ladies of Cairo, with the aim of developing education among married women. Special lectures for them were given in the University. In 1907, in order to start a certain school, the government enjoined its employees to send their daughters. Now the attendance is over three hundred, and six women teach unveiled in the presence of the male principal (Sailer: *Ibid.*). But all this is only a beginning, for as yet only three Moslem women in a thousand can read in Egypt.

NORTH AFRICA

In the French possessions in Africa primary schools have been opened in which French and Arabic are taught, with the usual course of European schools. A Frenchwoman conducts a school largely attended by wealthy Moslem girls, in which nothing is said of religion. A significant incident was a strike of the students of the Mosque of the Olive Tree at Tunis against lazy professors and a demand for a scientific course with geography, physics, chemistry, and like studies. Regarding the education of Moslems in Russia I have spoken in a former section.

IN INDIA

Moslems under these Christian governments have come more directly and without their own initiative under the influence of the new education. This is especially so in India. But there the Moslems for a long period failed to take advantage of government schools and consequently fell behind in culture and preparation for life. They clung to the Arabic and

Persian learning and were distanced by the Hindus. Now they have awakened and acknowledge the value of Western science and learning, but they are trying to obtain the benefits without departing from Islam. They would separate the civilization of the Christians from their religion, take the former and repudiate the latter. They are entering into the educational competition with some eagerness with regard to boys, but with lukewarmness with regard to girls. Female education is advocated by them in conferences, but no efficient system has been organized by them, while they still hesitate to patronize government or missionary schools "as not fit places for the training of Moslem girls" (*The Comrade,* quoted in the *Moslem World,* 1914, p. 310). Among the schools opened for girls is one at Lucknow in charge of a Canadian woman, a convert to Islam. The Anjuman at Lahore has nine girls' schools and shows some zeal for female education. The Moslem Educational Conference for Southern India passed a resolution requesting the government to start schools "with *purdah* or curtained conveyances for pupils." In India but four women in a thousand can read. Ninety-five per cent of Indian Mohammedans are illiterate. What a commentary on a "Religion of a Book" that sixty million Indian believers cannot read the Koran!

ANGLO-MOHAMMEDAN COLLEGE

I have already referred to the one notable attempt of Moslems in India to promote modern learning, the Anglo-Mohammedan College at Aligarh. It was founded by Sayid Ahmad Khan, the promoter of

Neo-Islam, with the avowed object of "reconciling Oriental with Western literature and science and to make the Mussulmans of India worthy and useful subjects of the British Crown." Lord Lytton, viceroy, laid the foundation in 1877 and the government aided it. Its principal and some of its teachers are Englishmen, its courses in Western sciences and languages are standard. It gives instruction in both Sunni and Shiah law and theology. The attendance is eight hundred. Its influence on the students is liberalizing. Dr. Murray Mitchell says ("The Great Religions of India," p. 240): "Under the instructions they receive, the pupils cannot long retain their intense bigotry and narrowness. If the college continues to prosper an immense change must gradually take place in the Mohammedans of India." The college has been successful in having a succession of intelligent and forceful men who have elevated its position. With headquarters here, there has been organized the All-India Moslem Students' Brotherhood. A project was set on foot to develop the college into a great Moslem university with affiliated colleges in other provinces. Much enthusiasm was manifested. Generous subscriptions were made towards the fifty *lakhs* of rupees desired, of which Agha Khan of Bombay gave one lakh. Some dissensions arose as to the place religious instruction should have. Some claimed that "the function of a Mohammedan university should be to make a Mohammedan a genuine one, well grounded in the doctrine and principles of Islam." Others claimed that "the comparative study of other religions could be safely introduced into the university."

While they disputed and planned, the British Government vetoed the scheme as likely to aid Pan-Islamism without benefiting education. Subscriptions were in part sent to the Turkish war fund. Among other advances made by Moslems is a scientific college at Karachi, to give technical and industrial training. The attempt has also been made to modernize theological education. A Mohammedan Educational Conference aims to promote the cause of learning. Of Indian Mohammedans, Professor Siraj-ud-Din says ("Vital Forces," p. 160) that "through their political and educational condition, they have been more thoroughly leavened by Western civilization than the Mohammedans of any other community in the world, not excepting even Turkey in Europe."

Of Afghanistan it may be noticed that the Habibiya or Chiefs' College has been established in spite of the opposition of the mullahs, and a modern hospital opened, following the introduction of the telegraph and telephone.

MODERN MOSLEM PRESS

Islam had and continues to have considerable intellectual life of its own kind. Its old presses issue many books by the lithographic process. Bookstores are in all large cities, with general literature, but with a special output of theological books. The Mujtahids have good-sized libraries and considerable general intelligence. All over the Moslem world the press is taking on new life. In Persia after the Constitution was established, newspapers sprang up like mushrooms. A similar manifestation occurred in Turkey, where 747 newspapers were started after the new régime. In Constantinople there still exist eleven dailies. The circulation of the chief ones is the *Sabah* (Morning), 20,000; the *Tanin* (Echo), 15,000; the *Ikdam* (Progress), 13,000; the *Yani* (New Gazette), 10,000. In India Moslem newspapers abound and many of them have a strong reform tendency. Monthly magazines, literary and religious reviews, and even novels are widely circulated. Egypt has 39 dailies in Arabic, 17 literary reviews, 3 law magazines, 3 of medicine, 2 for women, 11 for religion specially. Yearly 2,500,000 Moslem newspapers were posted from Egypt to other Moslem lands (Zwemer). In Russia, Moslems have journals in their various dialects as they have in Algeria. Even Tunis has its daily and an organ for the Young Tunis or Nationalist party. In South Africa and in South America likewise they have their journals. The press of Islam has a powerful influence,—anti-Christian of course, often anti-government, so that even India and Egypt have their regulative press laws. But on the whole the papers are instrumental in spreading new modern ideas of life, of civilization, of science, of social and political reform. They have a great deal of fanaticism, but they carry to all Islam convincing news of Moslem defeats and increasing weakness; their accusations against their enemies and their laments telling the tale.

TRANSLATIONS OF THE KORAN

Of some significance is the desire of the New Moslems to have the Koran in the language of the people.

Mr. Farquhar says ("Modern Religious Movements in India," p. 439): "The Christian contention that sacred books can be of no value unless understood by the people has led all the movements, Jain, Sikh, Parsee, and Moslem, as well as Hindu, to produce translations of the sacred books they use and to write all fresh books in the vernacular." It is true that the Koran has been translated in the past by Moslems into their own tongues, though objected to by the Hanafi School. These are interlinear translations of a literal, non-idiomatic kind, in Persian, Urdu, Pushto, Javanese, Malayan, Turkish, and other tongues. Now the effort is being made to have freer popular vernacular translations. One of these has been made in Urdu by a well-known novelist, Mulvi Nazir Ahmad (Canon Weitbrecht: "Moslem World of To-day," p. 197). A new version in Turkish was in part published in Constantinople lately, but it was quickly suppressed, as likely to lead to unbelief. A similar fate overtook the Turkish translation forty years ago.

Regarding this educational and literary movement, several things are worthy of attention. It is caused by the example of the Christian world. The stimulus is the knowledge of the benefits accruing to Christian lands and even to the Christian subjects of Moslem rulers. Not a little of the latter is due to missionary institutions. Another fact is that the new education is out of the hands of the mullahs and ignores their dicta. As to method, it grounds primary training on the plain vernacular,—on the modern Persian, not on that of Saadi and Hafiz, on the Turkish of the people, Osmanli, Azerbaijani, Tekki as the region may require. It teaches the colloquial Arabic, using even the readers of the Beirut Mission Press. It strives to reform the chirography and make correspondence and business easy. It teaches European languages, disregarding the old saying of the mullahs that "he who learns the language of the Frank is an infidel." It gives the enlightening benefit of physical science. It quotes approvingly a tradition attributed to Mohammed: "Go forth in search of learning, even if you have to go as far as China." It is founded on the belief that knowledge is power and that they should share with the Christians the secret of this power. Their eagerness makes them apt pupils. The effect on their condition and religious attitude is marked. It results in discontent with their social and political environment and almost as certainly in a modification in their religious thought. Young Moslems are liberalized. The bonds of religious tradition are loosened. Yet some Moslems scorn the possibility of any injurious effect as far as their faith is concerned. M. T. Kadirbhoy writes: "It is possible that religious enthusiasts may cry that science, and especially Western science, may exercise a sceptic influence on the Moslem mind. The possibility is too remote to cause any apprehension. So fast does the Moslem hold to the word of the Prophet and the Koran that no amount of sceptical influence will ever serve to lessen his devotion to his religion and to his God. Youths may put the new wine of the West into the old bottles of the East, keeping the colour and quality of the bottle unimpaired" (*Moslem World,* 1912, p. 304). Of more weight is the opinion of Lord Cromer ("Modern Egypt," Vol. II, p. 230), who declares that the Europeanized Moslem loses his Islamism, cuts adrift from his creed while retaining its lax morality, does not approach Christianity, is intolerant, hates Christians as rivals and because those who are in contact with him deserve to be hated. "European civilization destroys one religion without substituting another." What a strong argument this is that the Church should give them the truth of Christ along with our civilization. Dr. J. A. Oldham, in a review of the condition of the Islamic world (*International Review of Missions,* 1914, p. 46), says: "The disintegration of Islam and the growth of unbelief among the educated classes are proceeding at an accelerated rate and are likely to increase with the growth of foreign influence."

VII

NEO-ISLAM AND SOCIETY

BY general agreement Islam is a failure as a social system. Those familiar with the conditions it has brought about, and especially with the low position of woman and the estimate put upon her, are frankly hopeless of any true reform unless these conditions are changed. Stanley Lane-Poole says ("Studies in a Mosque," p. 101): "As a social system Islam is a complete failure. The degradation of woman is a canker which has eaten into the whole system; it has misunderstood the relation of the sexes, and by degrading woman has degraded each successive generation of their children down an increasing scale of infamy and corruption." Lord Cromer asks: "Can any one conceive of the existence of true European civilization, on the assumption that the position which woman occupies in Europe be deducted from the general plan? As well can a man blind from his birth be made to conceive the existence of colour. The position of woman in Mohammedan countries is therefore a fatal obstacle to the attainment of that elevation of thought and character." Intelligent Moslems have arrived at the same judgment. An educated Turk said to Sir Edwin Pears ("Turkey and Its People," p. 57): "No reform is possible, because we have no family life. You may believe in the possibility of Turkish reforms when you see Turkish husbands and wives, arm in arm, on Galata bridge,—that is, when we Turks respect and trust our women."

The hopelessness of the case lies in this, that this dark blot has been indelibly stamped on Islam by the Koran and the example of the Prophet. He has fixed the standard. It is a man-made religion for man.

WOMAN'S POSITION BEFORE ISLAM

There is much to show that Islam brought woman into a more degraded and debased condition. Her social status under the Arabs in the "time of ignorance" was higher than after Mohammed. Prof. Robertson Smith says ("Kinship and Marriage in Ancient Arabia," p. 100): "It is very remarkable that the place of woman in the family and in society has steadily declined under his [Mohammed's] law. . . . The Arabs themselves recognize that the position of woman has fallen." Similarly Stanley Lane-Poole testifies ("Studies in a Mosque," p. 23): "In the desert woman was regarded as she has never since been viewed by Moslems. The modern haram system was undreamt of; the maid of the desert was unfettered by the ruinous restrictions of modern life in the East. She was free to choose her husband and to bind him to have no other wife than herself. She might receive male visitors, even strangers, without suspicion." Dr. Zwemer corroborates this, saying ("Islam, etc.," p. 6): "The use of the veil was almost unknown in Arabia before Islam, nor did the haram system prevail." At the present time the same fact is seen. In the East Indies and some parts of Africa the advent of Islam brings further degradation to woman. Professor Westermann says: "The position of woman among the Shilluks [heathen of the Sudan] is no doubt a higher one than with most Mohammedan people of the Sudan. She is shown remarkable respect. Women sometimes take part in public assemblies with the men, discuss affairs, share in the dances and religious ceremonies." In these the young men and girls meet each other face to face and eye to eye, dancing in harmony. Dr. C. R. Watson testifies that the position of woman seems invariably to be lowered ("The Sorrow and Hope of the Sudan," p. 189): "In pagan communities a woman, especially an unmarried woman, may go about and be quite safe from all molestation. Not so after the introduction of Islam . . . her person is safer under paganism than under Islam." In the Dutch East Indies woman was held in higher esteem in pre-Islamic days. This is evident among the recent converts. It has lowered the privileges of women and disintegrated family life. Where tribal customs punished adultery, frowned on divorce, and confined polygamy to the higher classes, Islam has relaxed these beneficial customs. Especially loose divorce has injured the position of woman. "Contempt for woman has fallen to a point even below the zero of moral esteem for woman in heathenism" (Simon, p. 184). Another witness is Sir William Ramsay. He says ("Impressions of Turkey, etc.," p. 49): "The Turkish tribes originally did not practise the seclusion of women. They learned the custom from the Arabs and the Koran."

POLYGAMY AND DIVORCE UNDER ISLAM

What is the position of woman under orthodox Islam? What is the attitude of the New Moslems? The orthodox claim superiority for their law in this as in all matters. The *Muslim Review* asserts that Islam "sets a purer and more divine standard of domestic life" than any other. Specifically it is claimed that Mohammed limited polygamy, prohibited marriages within certain degrees, made women heirs, prohibited widows from being regarded as part of the estate to be disposed of as chattels, gave them power over their own property brought at the time of marriage, provided for the maintenance of children and abolished infanticide.[1] Allowing due credit for whatever good it wrought, the facts are that Islam perpetuated and sanctioned the degradation of women and increased it. It allows a man four wives and as many concubines and slave women as he can obtain. The wives can be divorced at the whim or caprice of the man on condition of paying over a dowry, usually small. According to his desire he may take the divorced wife back twice without condition, but after the third divorce he cannot take her back until she has been married and divorced by another man. Loose divorce works more evil than polygamy. In the street near me in Tabriz lived two men, one rich,

[1] Stanley Lane-Poole ("Studies in a Mosque," p. 24) says, "Infanticide, which is commonly attributed to the whole Arab race, before Islam was exceedingly rare in the desert."

the other poor. The former, a sayid, was in the habit of marrying pretty young girls and sending them away with their dowry, when his fancy tired of them. He had reached the thirtieth when I left Persia. The poor young man astonished us more by the facility with which he yearly took and divorced a new wife. He only kept one at a time and apparently most of the time had to go in debt to pay the dowry. Of this feature of Islam, Lane in his "Modern Egyptians" says (chap. vi): "While no more than one husband in twenty has two wives at the same time, there are many men who in the course of ten years have married as many as twenty, thirty, or more wives; and women not far advanced in age who have been wives of a dozen or more men successively." A Moslem of prominence has affirmed that ninety-five per cent. of Mohammedan wives in Egypt are sooner or later divorced; in other words, only five women in a hundred remain with their first husband. In that same country there is one divorce to three marriages, even though a man may keep the wife and take three others. There is a Moslem saying that "a woman is like an old pair of shoes; a man throws her away and buys another as long as his money lasts." One youth divorced his twenty-eighth wife. He justified himself by saying, "Why not? My father divorced thirty-eight."

A disgrace of Shiahism is the temporary marriage, *mutaa*. Under the sanction of religion and with the blessing of the mullah the contract wife is taken for a day or for a year. (See author's "Persian Life and Customs," p. 263.) Mrs. Major Sykes, who lived at

Meshed, brings new testimony to the prevalence of this abomination at the Holy Shrine of the Imam Reza, where many temporary wives are kept for the pilgrims. She adds: "This is common throughout the country and is a potent factor in the degradation of the womanhood of Persia."

This disgrace of Shiahism is surpassed by the black stain of forcible concubinage which lies against the Sunnis.[1] Hear these vigorous words of Lane-Poole ("Studies in a Mosque," p. 105): "One cannot forget the unutterable brutalities inflicted on the conquered nations in the taking of slaves. The Moslem soldier was allowed to do as he pleased with any 'infidel' woman he might meet in his victorious march. When one thinks of the thousands of women, mothers, and daughters who must have suffered untold shame and dishonour by this license, he cannot find words to express his horror." Such, sanctioned by the example of Mohammed, has been the record since the conquest of Persia, when slave girls were a drug in the markets of Arabia, till the days of the Armenian Massacres and the Holy War of 1915.

THE SECLUSION OF WOMEN

Another element in the degraded condition of the Moslem woman is her seclusion. She is confined in the haram, behind walls and lattices, and, if means permit, in a separate court-yard. She is veiled when she appears on the street. This veiling is in varying

[1] The disgraceful conduct of Persian Shiahs in Urumia in abducting Christian women in January, 1915, makes it necessary to include them in this condemnation also.

degrees, reaching its extreme in Persia, where the whole person is absolutely covered, and neither the hands, head, nor even the flash of the eye can be seen. The jealousy of Mohammed caused the command of the Koran which requires the seclusion of women and his example enforced it (Surah XXXIII, 55). Dr. Watson writes: "Where faith in chastity ended, the seclusion of women began." Mohammed's order for veiling is sometimes attributed to the Zaid-Zainab incident. Persians say that one day Mohammed was seated with Ayesha, when a passing Arab, admiring her beauty, offered Mohammed a camel in exchange for her, and this produced the order for veiling. He formed into law customs which pertained previously to kings and grandees, so that they became as the will of God. Only Kurds, Beduins, and wild tribes among Moslems have disregarded the law. In India many women never leaves their harams. One caliph in Egypt even prohibited the making of shoes for women, that they might not be able to go out of doors. A man does not allude to his wife in conversation nor inquire for yours. If under some necessity to mention her, he uses a euphemism as "the mother of Zaid" or "the children." The effect of this seclusion is to limit the mental development of women, to cramp and crush their lives. The inviolability of the haram is even made a plea to prevent proper sanitation and quarantine in case of cholera and plague. It has an injurious effect on the children and is answerable for the lower intelligence and slow progress of the men. The mothers are incapable of the best training of the children. Sir William Ramsay (" Impressions, etc., p. 41) says: "In the condition of the Turkish women lies the reason for the steady degeneration of the Turkish people. They are poorer both in physique and mind than the Christians, —a stunted and impoverished motherhood produces a poor and diminishing people."

Some Moslems maintain that the seclusion of their women is an advantage—that it conduces to their happiness, the continuance of the marriage union, removes causes of jealousy, and protects females from insult. One of them said in jocose vein, " No Moslem sees any woman save his own wife, so he thinks her the prettiest one that lives."

NEO-ISLAM ON WOMAN

What is the attitude of New Moslems to woman and her position in the family and in society? It is truly remarkable and is a radical departure from traditional Islam. The movement advocates freedom for women. I will first notice modern interpretations and opinions with reference to woman and then some changes which are evident in her condition in Moslem lands.

The position of Neo-Islam in India is strongly stated by Sayid Amir Ali in his books, " Mohammedan Law" (Preface, and pp. 21, 159, 226) and the " Legal Position of Woman in Islam." He declares that polygamy is not a part of Islam, that " the law forbids a second union during the subsistence of the former contract." He argues that since the Koran requires that the husband should deal justly and equally with his several wives, and since fulfilment of this requirement is an impossibility, it amounts to a prohibition. He pronounces polygamy an unendurable and unmitigated evil, which must necessarily cease to exist. He says ("Spirit of Islam," p. 365): "I look upon polygamy in the present day as an adulterous connection and contrary to the spirit of Islam —an opinion which is shared by a large number of Moslems." He and other modernists deny the law of divorce or repudiation as held and practised by Moslems, and argue that Mohammed meant that divorce should be founded on the charge of adultery and should be carried out only by granting a regular bill of divorcement and also that the seclusion of women was a recommendation, not a law obligatory and perpetual. A modified view is taken by Sheikh Abdul Kadir, who says: "The Koran recommends the man to restrict himself to one wife and imposes on the polygamous the obligation of treating his alike and equitably. By these difficulties which the law throws in his way very rarely can a man venture to do it, unless he is drawn to it by extreme necessity such as barrenness or sickness of his wife, or his absence from home or unless he is a voluptuary or, like the holy patriarch, through a desire to multiply the human species. Another learned Mohammedan leader put on the title-page of his book the words, "Listen to me, if your ears are not deaf; on no account marry two wives, for a man has not two hearts in his breast" ("Vital Forces," p. 173).

A Moslem writer in the *Journal of Reformed Islam* strenuously combats the use of the veil and presents many reasons for its abolition (Margoliouth's

"Mohammedanism," p. 136). In the female educational section of the Moslem League in India, Maulvi Shibli maintained from an Islamic point of view equality of rights and opportunity for woman; and others agreed with him. Some held that seclusion in the haram is a custom, not a command of religion; that the Koran commanded the Prophet's wives only should be veiled and secluded. Though the Koran says (Surah IV, 8): "Men are superior to women on account of the qualities with which God has gifted the one above the other," yet Justice Abdur Rahim of India says: "God has endowed women with intellectual gifts as much as men. Islamic laws accord the same status to women as men," and that Moslems "are proud of the liberal spirit of their religion and laws."

These modernist interpretations do not change our conception of what real Islamic law is. Their casuistry does not alter the historic Shariat nor convince us contrary to facts. But it is deeply significant that this effort is made to reconcile the Shariat with modern ideas. It indicates progress of thought in Islam.

MOSLEM WOMEN'S POSITION IMPROVING

Significant also is the modification in practice with regard to woman. Her day of emancipation is perceptibly nearer. Regarding polygamy, testimony is practically unanimous that it is declining. Combined with the growing feeling that it is unlawful or inexpedient, many extraneous circumstances are tending to root it out from among Moslems. "Large numbers place in the marriage contract a formal renunciation on the part of the husband of any right to contract a second contemporaneous marriage."

In India not more than three per cent of the Moslems are polygamous. In Egypt monogamy has been gaining ground (Cromer: "Modern Egypt;" Giffen: "Islam and Missions," p. 297). Ismiel Khedive had many wives and concubines. His successor Tewfik had but one. The last Khedive had but one for many years, but later took a second, a Christian woman whom he turned into a Moslem. The Khedive Tewfik said to De Guerville: "The custom of having several wives is rapidly disappearing. The principal reasons are the abolition of slavery and the increased cost of living." Of Turkey Sir Edwin Pears declares (p. 68): "The habit of having more wives than one is decreasing. The influence of the West is having its effect." The Young Turks are almost all monogamists. In Persia no doubt the same tendency is at work, though I can hardly endorse the opinion of Mrs. Major Sykes ("Persia and Its People," p. 75), that "polygamy is becoming rare in Iran. Persians speak of it as unfashionable." This is to be attributed partly to poverty and partly to the worry of rival wives; according to the proverb, "Two tigresses in a house are better than two mistresses."

Woman is also being released from her seclusion, slowly but surely. Fortunately in certain outlying countries of Islam, it has not yet succeeded in shutting up woman in the haram. This is true in Malaysia. There primitive customs continue and woman is permitted to go about freely and unveiled, and to converse with men who are not relatives. In China, too, women do not live in seclusion nor wear the veil. Yet they do not go to the mosque. They bind their feet like the Chinese heathen women. In Russia Moslem women have greater freedom than under their own rulers. Some have adopted certain Christian social customs, like receiving men visitors, riding about and travelling with their husbands. They are trained in the Russian gymnasia and normal schools and universities, teach school, practise medicine, are admitted to the bar, hold conventions, and have the temerity to request the ballot in the Communes. This movement is widely extended, on the Volga, in the Crimea and Caucasus, and even among the Kirghiz (*International Review of Missions,* 1915, p. 39; *Moslem World,* 1914, p. 264). In India a society of young men has been organized with the object of doing away with the veil. They are making a propaganda to this end. A bride and groom lately drove off in a vehicle together, the bride with her face uncovered. Freedom, which has become common among Hindu and Parsee women, is scarcely allowed among Moslems, who have been largely responsible for much of the seclusion which has existed among the others. Yet a Conference of Moslem ladies has met at the same time and place as the men's Educational Conference, to promote the education of girls.

In Egypt agitation for the freedom of woman is active. A leader in this movement was the late Kasim Bey Amin, whose books, "The Emancipation of Woman," "The New Woman," and "The Veil," have been eagerly read by men and women alike. In these writings twentieth-century ideas of woman are advocated and the evil effects of Moslem customs are set forth. A society for the abolition of the veil is working. The debate in the press, pro and con, is active and full of vim. The old and the new are clashing in discussion. But as yet even those women who have been educated in Europe must conform to custom and live in seclusion. An exception was the Princess Nazli Fazil Khanum, a descendant of Mohammed Ali Pasha, who refused to be bound by the restrictions of the haram and mixed freely in the society of men and women, yet retained the respect of the devotees of Islam. She was very proficient in Arabic, Turkish, English, and French. She resided in Paris and other European capitals as wife of the Turkish Ambassador Khallil Pasha Sherif. After his death her house in Cairo became a celebrated salon, where many great men and ladies were received with honour. Her conversational powers were of a high order and her influence on politics elevating. She was an ardent advocate of freedom and her words had power in Turkey as well as in Egypt.

In Persia discussion prevails, but with little change as yet. A woman who, some years ago in Tabriz, ventured in the street with the semi-veil of Constantinople, was promptly warned by the Mujtahid that if she did so again, she would be beaten. The girls' schools, either native or mission, are scarcely securely established outside of the Capital. Girls do not attend with boys as in Turkey. For a girl to appear on the platform of the Mission School, even thickly veiled, to receive her diploma, was a great innovation in Teheran. The contrast with the Christian girls caused some comment in the Persian newspapers showing that they had aspirations for freedom for their girls. During the Revolution, Persian women organized patriotic clubs and secret societies, a dozen or more of them, in the Capital, and watched keenly, even with veiled eyes, the course of events. They were ardent supporters of liberty, acting as informants for Mr. Morgan Shuster, intriguing for the Constitutional party. At the final crisis the veiled women invaded the House of Parliament, daggers in hand, and threatened the deputies if they yielded the liberties of their country.

In Turkey the movement for the emancipation of woman has made definite progress. Sultan Abdul Hamid did not repress female education, evidently thinking woman a negligible factor. In Constantinople and the coast cities, the education of girls made considerable progress. Until they are eight or ten years of age they are allowed to go with the boys. Some families have had European governesses from whom the girls learned European languages and imbibed European ideals. For some this was a means of excellent culture, for others the result was a mimicry of French styles in dress and a taste for reading of romances. One of these governesses afterwards opened up a private school for Moslem girls in Beirut. It was patronized by the well-to-do of the city. The result of the Christian spirit in the school was so great upon the girls and their training so effective in character, that during the period of several score years, in which many of the girls becames wives of Moslems, not one of them was divorced and not one of them had the humiliation of having a companion wife brought to vex her. Constantinople (American) College was not permitted to receive Moslem girls in Abdul Hamid's time. One, however, Halidah Salih, daughter of the Sultan's treasurer, finished her course of study. She is proficient in French and English, and has become a writer of distinction and the "leading woman in Turkey in popularity and influence." For her first book, a translation of "The Mother in the Home," she was decorated by the Sultan. Her articles frequently appear in the press. She wears a veil in public, but is unveiled before men in her own house. She is a member of the Young Turk Committee of Union and Progress, and was marked as a victim in the counter-revolution, but was not found by the assassins. Another advanced Turkish woman is Balkis Shevket Khanum, up-to-date editor of the *Kadinlar Dunyasi* (The Woman's World) of Constantinople. To be up with man in everything, she took a flight in an aeroplane with Fathi Bey. The paper had in one issue a front-page illustration of a group of unveiled Moslem women. Later the paper was suppressed. The educated Turkish women took a special part in the Revolution. Their reading had led them to deep sympathy with liberty and progress. Being largely exempted from the espionage from which men suffered so much, they were able to aid the cause greatly. After the downfall of despotism, the women had a taste of freedom. Some appeared unveiled, rode with open face in carriages and walked about at the watering places and parks, made speeches in the hall of the University, formed clubs and circles for discussion and enlightenment, corresponded with the newspapers, and even organized two feminist journals. Yet, according to the best testimony (Sir Edwin Pears, p. 66), they acted with modesty and discretion and their speech showed remarkable culture and wisdom. Yet the shock to the conservatism of Islam was too great, and a handle was given the reactionaries to work against Constitutionalism. An order was therefore issued by the Commandant of the city: "Whereas women are forbidden to go in public places in costumes unbecoming with reference to national customs and Moslem morals, those who infringe this regulation will be arrested by detective agents and severely punished, according to the laws." So restraint was put upon the women but not successfully, as appears from the journal *Tasfiri Efkiar* (Orient), September 6, 1914. It says: "Certain of our women, not appreciating the situation, and in spite of reiterated orders from the military authorities, dress themselves in an unsuitable way and one calculated to seriously offend the religious sentiments and national customs. In the name of the well-being of the country we call upon the military authorities to make a few exemplary punishments." Professor Cheyne ("Reconciliation of Races and Religions," p. 116) mentions that forty of the boldest women were arrested and exiled to Acca. I have seen no confirmation of this report. When telephones were introduced, of one hundred or more operators, seven were Moslem girls. It is said they became clerks, not because of necessity, for they were daughters of officials, but to open the way for Moslem women to engage in honest labour. They do not wear the *char-shab*. During the Balkan war the women held and addressed large mass-meetings, and acted as nurses of the Red Crescent. The establishment of homes on Christian or Western models is set before them as a desideratum. The old haram life is no longer considered praiseworthy nor commendable. In Syria, too, much the same condition prevails. Men are no longer willing to marry a bride unseen. It has become the habit to advocate the elevation of women and to strive for the amelioration of social life. The injunction of the Koran to scourge refractory wives, interpreted by the Shariat to mean that he shall not give her less than three nor more than thirty lashes, is one of which the modern Moslem is somewhat ashamed. Already the switch has replaced the bastinado—the switch itself has dry rot. Effort is also being made in Turkey to put down the white-slave traffic. A Turkish newspaper says (*The Moslem World*, 1914, p. 268): "The East will not be elevated until woman is elevated and restored to the position she once occupied. The fall of Moslem womanhood has been the great reason for the fall of the whole nation, and her education and uplift are necessary if the nation is to regain its lost position."

THE ABOLITION OF SLAVERY AMONG MOSLEMS

The Koran and the Shariat definitely ordain and regulate slavery, yet the abolition of slavery and the slave trade is going steadily forward in Islam. This is largely due to the influence of Christian governments. But the effort commends itself to the conscience of modern Moslems. In those lands directly under Christian rule the abolition has been accomplished. An act of the Indian Legislature abolished slavery in 1843. In 1877 Lord Vivian entered into a convention with the Egyptian Government forbidding the slave trade or the sale of slaves from family to family, providing for the gradual manumission of slaves and for the right of the slave to claim his liberty through the government. Slave-trade in the Egyptian Sudan was suppressed after many years of effort; slavery is being superseded by paid service. It was ended in Zanzibar in 1897 and nominally in Afghanistan in 1895 by treaty. Persia has entered into treaty for its abolition. Russia has accomplished the same among her Moslem subjects and, by treaty, in Khiva and Bukhara. The Osmanlis enslaved many from the Christian races of the Balkans, of the Greeks and Armenians. Less than two hundred years ago they carried off one hundred thousand German and Magyar woman in a single campaign. By the Constitution of 1876 slavery was abolished in Turkey. In 1890 the Sultan signed the declaration of the Antislavery Conference, held at Brussels, by seventeen nations, "of a firm intention to put an end to the crimes and devastation engendered by traffic in African slaves." Renewal of the Constitution in 1908 brought the abolition again into effect. Though slavery still exists, both of concubines and eunuchs, it is gradually being brought to an end. The auction of slaves still continues in the public square of Mecca and existed in Morocco till French occupation. To supply these marts and the secret traffic the trade still goes on in Central Africa (Professor Westermann, *International Review of Missions,* 1913, p. 481). In 1909, pilgrim caravans via Molfi, Western Sudan, carried through nearly three thousand women and children to be sold as slaves. It appears, however, that slavery will be brought to a close in Islam. There will be no modification of the Shariat, but the expense, the cessation of war captives, the force of moral sentiment are all working with the influence of Christian governments to accomplish its complete abolition.

MODERNISM AND RELIGIOUS LIBERTY

Neo-Islam professes to stand for religious liberty and it is no doubt more liberal than the orthodox party. But the words of its expounders are far from the ideal. Justice Amir Ali, after a long defence of Mohammedanism in an historical view, concludes: "We deny altogether that Islam ever grasped the sword for the purpose of proselyting. Islam never persecuted" ("Life of Mohammed," pp. 212-15). If such is the decision of an enlightened, anglicized High Justice of British India—a reformer—we may well despair of any appeal to history in reasoning with a Moslem. Yet notwithstanding this, there is undoubtedly among the New Moslems a modification of the fanatical spirit. Practically they do have a more friendly feeling to Christians. Not only in India, but in Teheran, in Beirut, in Constantinople, in Cairo, there are tens of thousands who do not believe in injuring the Moslem converted to Christianity, who would not lift a finger to execute the law which decrees death to the apostate. There is a wide prevalence of the spirit of toleration. There has been a marked change, a change encouraging to Christian missions. The mental attitude of intelligent Moslems has been modified. This change may be due partly to indifference, partly to the relaxing of his own faith, partly to his enlightenment and a real appreciation of the right of the individual conscience to decide its belief. Many Young Turks and Persian Nationalists have personally clear conceptions of and belief in liberty of conscience, did not questions of politics and national aspirations get inextricably mixed up with religion. Persian Sufis are natural friends of religious liberty. There are many forces working in Islam bringing about freedom of conscience. Even the Ulema of Turkey, says Sir Edwin Pears (p. 395), "are beginning to be under the influence of Western ideas, and the day is coming when even the ignorant Moslem will not consider it meritorious to kill a Christian. . . . There is promise of continued though slow improvement."

THE FUTURE OF NEO-ISLAM

I have considered Neo-Islam in detail,—a movement which aims to adopt Western science and education, change the status of woman, and bring Moslem law into conformity to Western civilization. What will be the effect of this movement? Will Islam be changed? Will it be freed from the shackles of tradition and brought into conformity to modern thought? It is impossible to reach an absolute conclusion. Undoubtedly there is a trend towards transformation. Regarding many Islamic peoples, this opinion rests upon impressions made upon observers. Even in India, where there is much more public discussion and publication of views, competent witnesses differ as to the conditions. Rev. W. A. Wilson declares ("Islam and Missions," p. 149), that the New Islam largely moulds Mohammedan thought. On the other hand, Canon Sell thinks that the influence of the movement is waning and conservatism is reviving.

Lord Cromer expresses strong doubts of the possibility of Islam reforming. The difficulty of bringing Islam and its ways into harmony with modern society is comparable to squaring the circle, in his judgment. He says ("Modern Egypt," Vol. II, p. 184): "Let no practical politician think that he has a plan capable of resuscitating a body which is not indeed dead, and which may yet linger on for centuries, but which is nevertheless politically and socially moribund, and whose decay cannot be arrested by any modern palliatives however skilfully they may be applied." "One could not make the Egyptian horse drink of the waters of civilization, albeit the most limpid streams of reform were turned into the trough before him. It has yet to be proved that Islam can assimilate civilization without succumbing in the process. It is not improbable that in its passage through the European crucible, many of the distinctive features of Islam, the good and the bad alike, may be volatilized, and that it will eventually issue forth in a form scarcely capable of recognition." Thus after wavering, he reaches the conclusion that Islam will probably change, but he adds: "It should never be forgotten that Islam cannot be reformed, that is to say, that Islam reformed is Islam no longer. It is something else, and we cannot tell yet what it eventually will be" (pp. 175, 161). Professor Macdonald expects modifications in Islam, and says (*International Review of Missions,* 1913, p. 597): "It is never well to underestimate the strange power that a religion has of transforming itself in adaptation to new situations." Similarly Professor Margoliouth says ("Mohammedanism," p. 224): "What is to be expected is not the supersession nor the abolition of Islam, but its accommodation to the conditions imposed upon the world by European science." May we not suppose that a reformed Islam will bear such a relation to the Koran and the Traditions as Reformed Judaism bears to the Torah and the Talmud? It will bear the name and heritage of Islam, acknowledge its creed and book, and have an anti-Christian spirit, whatever may be its change of methods and weapons. Christianity can expect no spiritual victory by the forces of civilization. As Islam opened its doors to take in and take on Greco-Syrian and Persian civilizations and showed itself capable of adapting itself to the higher condition in Bagdad and Spain and bearing fruit by this grafted culture, so it may do again. Whether Islam is being changed or not, it is certain that Moslems are changing. Numbers of them have broken away from the old traditions and practices. They stoutly maintain that they are Moslems, and will likely continue to do so. But their old adherence to Islam as a body of laws for the state, as a hard-and-fast rule for social life, is passing. The universal sway of fanaticism, the belief in the obligation to persecute, is going. There are few signs of the rejection of Islam as an outward profession. But more and more a condition is being reached in which the community will divide into religious, indifferent, and irreligious—a condition in which those who wish to, can openly neglect the rites of religion and be unmolested, when those who allegorize or rationalize the Koran and its system shall be held accountable to no court or judge and physical penalties shall not be inflicted for unbelief nor a new belief. There will be open toleration within Islam, to be followed by open acquiescence in apostasy from Islam. Popular opinion has accepted this in many places under Christian rule, and is not far from accepting it in some communities under Moslem rule. New Islam in practice has wider acceptance than as a system of doctrines. Dr. Young of Aden takes a most hopeful view ("Islam and Missions," p. 126): "The time has come," he says, "for a general advance, and when that advance begins, the cleavage in Islam will widen and a new form of Islam will arise with subtler doctrines and purer life," but, he adds with missionary vision, "even that must finally give way before the higher life of true Christianity." Expecting this consummation, we must sow the seed of Christian truth. It is a critical time for Islamic peoples. The call is for strenuous effort to direct the thought and conscience of Moslems to the Source of true reform.

VIII

POLITICAL MOVEMENTS AMONG MOSLEMS

IN the political world of Islam the most striking fact is the subjection of Moslem lands to Christian rule. The phrase "the disintegration of Islam" is sometimes used, but whether Islam is disintegrating may be questioned, yet of the disintegration of the empire of Islam there is no doubt. This movement had begun before the last century in the freeing of Spain, Hungary, and Russia from Moslem dominion, yet this was rather an escape of Christian countries from subjection. This latter period has been characterized not only by further liberation of Christian peoples, but by the conquest and subjection of Moslem peoples (see table on p. 219) by Christian governments. Moslem lands in Africa have passed under Christian sway; its vast territory is divided. Its European empire has decreased to a small strip, and the present war will likely result in pulling down the Star and the Crescent from the last stronghold of Islam in Europe—the beautiful, the unique city of Constantinople. Even Persia is but semi-independent, being divided into spheres of influence between Russia and Great Britain. The rapidity of this decline may be seen in the striking contrast between the present condition and that existing when I went to

Persia. At that time Rev. Dr. H. H. Jessup stated before the General Assembly that 50 millions out of the 175 millions of Moslems, or twenty-nine per cent, were under Christian rule. Now there are 170 millions, or eighty-five per cent, under Christian rule, and only seventeen per cent under Moslem rule. Russia, France, and Holland each rule over many more Moslems than does the Sultan of Turkey, and Great Britain over five times as many. Islamic rulers hold sway over but one twenty-second part of the earth's surface, while Christian Powers rule over nineteen twenty-seconds. The sword-arm of Islam is withered, its mighty empire has faded away. Pan-Islamism cannot save it; the jihad cannot save it; the old battle-cry, "Allah Akbar" ("God is Great"), cannot save it, for God wills that its intolerant, despotic sway should cease.

ADJUSTMENT OF MOSLEMS TO CHRISTIAN RULE

How has this condition been brought about? By fierce and bloody wars of conquest. In this we cannot see the spirit of Christ. Moslems have made heroic resistance under such leaders as Sheikh Abdul Kadir in Algeria and Schamyl in Daghestan, or of mad mullahs and Mahdis. But they meet in vain the modern armour of the European Powers. Everywhere machine-guns have been victorious against the poorly equipped troops of Islam. Their courageous leaders, undaunted by defeat, have either fallen in vain attack or languished in exile as pensioners of the conquerors. Sometimes these conquests have been made in ruthless disregard of the rights of humanity and with too

TABLE OF TERRITORY FREED FROM ISLAMIC RULE SINCE 1800

DATE	COUNTRY OR PROVINCE	TO WHOM CEDED
	I. Caucasus and Transcaucasus	
1800.	Georgia from Persia	Russia
1813.	Darband, Shirwan, Baku, Karadagh from Persia	"
1813.	Sovereignty of Caspian Sea from Persia	"
1828.	Erivan, Nakhejevan, etc., from Persia	"
1829.	Poti, Anapa, and Circassian coast from Turkey	"
1878.	Batum, Kars, Ardahan from Turkey	"
	II. Central Asia	
1844.	Kirghiz	"
1864.	Samarcand	"
1868.	Khohand and Bukhara	"
1873.	Khiva	"
1881.	Merv	"
1891.	Part of Khorassan from Persia	"
	III. Southern Asia	
1799.	Nizam's Dominions, India	Great Britain
1803.	Mogul Empire, India	" "
1824.	Straits Settlements	" "
1830.	Dutch Rule consolidated	Holland
1839.	Aden and Arabian Coast	Great Britain
1843.	Sinde, India	" "
1849.	Punjab and Kashmere	" "
1856.	Oudh	" "
1876.	Baluchistan Protectorate	" "
	IV. Europe	
1829.	Greece and Servia granted independence.	
1858.	Wallachia and Moldavia from Turkey	Rumania
1878.	Bessarabia from Turkey	Russia
1878.	Cyprus	Great Britain
1878.	Bosnia and Herzegovina (annexed 1908)	Austria
1878.	Greece, Servia, Montenegro, and Rumania enlarged.	
1878.	Bulgaria formed from Turkey	Bulgaria
1885.	East Rumelia " "	"
1898.	Crete autonomous " "	
1912.	Crete annexed	Greece
1912.	Ægean Islands from Turkey	Italy
1913.	Parts of Macedonia, Albania, and Islands	Greece
1913.	" " " "	Servia
1913.	" " " and Thrace	Bulgaria
1913.	" " Albania	Montenegro
1913.	Albania made independent.	
	V. Africa	
1830.	Algeria	France
1882.	Tunis	"
1882.	Egypt (annexed 1914)	Great Britain
1884–89.	British East Africa	" "
1884–89.	German East Africa	Germany
1880–90.	Eritrea, Somali coast	Italy
1884–98.	Sahara and Western Sudan	France
1898.	Eastern Sudan	Great Britain
1909.	Zanzibar	" "
1910.	Wadai	France
1912.	Morocco	"
1912.	" part to	Spain
1912.	Tripoli and Cyrenaica	Italy

much imitation of the barbarous warfare of the Moslems themselves. Neither the motives nor the methods of the conquests nor the morals of the diplomacy which preceded, nor the frequent disregard of plighted word given at the time of occupation or annexation, have commended the religion of the Christians. Some of the wars, as those against the Turks for the liberation of the oppressed Christian races; of Italy in Tripoli, blessed by the Pope; of the Balkan allies proclaimed by King Ferdinand as one of the Cross against the Crescent; or when accompanied by the destruction of a Mahdi's tomb or the bombardment of the shrine of an Imam, have seemed like religious crusades, and the results have made the impression of a triumph of Christianity over Islam rather than that of Bulgaria or Italy or other European Power over the Osmanlis. The result has been the increase of century-long hatred and bitterness and of zeal and fanaticism among Moslem races. It is a significant fact that under Moslem rulers, Sultan and Shah, Khedive and Amir, large sections of the population are dissatisfied with the government and hostile to the mullahs, who are oftentimes bribe-taking and unscrupulous administrators of the Shariat. The people denounce them and are apparently ready to renounce them. But when political power passes into the hands of the Christian, taxation and policing become the function of the foreign infidels, the powers of judging, bastinadoing, and fleecing pass from the hands of the mullahs; then people and priest are soon reconciled, there is a drawing together in the common dislike of the Frangis, religion becomes a bond of union, and, reinforced by a nascent patriotism, issues in a strong and zealous Islamic spirit. This was strikingly seen in the contrast between the Caucasus and Persia before the late change. Under the rule of the Shah and the Shari, the people were cursing king and mullahs alike; whereas in the Caucasus the relation between the mullahs and the Moslem people was cordial.

Dislike to living under Christian rule has led to the expatriation of large populations who, forsaking land and property even in the winter's cold, have voluntarily exiled themselves rather than continue to live comfortably under the rule of the Christian. Thousands of Circassians, Abkhasians, Bosnians, and Macedonians have thus followed the trail to Turkey. Not a few Sayids have abandoned their North African homes for Syria and Arabia.

The adjustment of Moslems to Christian rule has legal difficulties. For Islam never anticipated such a condition. It was to be a triumphant empire, always to rule, and extending its sway further and further till it became universal. All lands which had not submitted to its law were Dar-ul-Harb, lands of warfare, against which the jiḥad was not only lawful but obligatory. Its attitude towards Christian governments ought always to be one of hostility. But the laws of Islam have yielded to major force. Moslems have learned to live under Christian rule, either secretly biding their time, though still rebellious in heart or satisfying their consciences by bringing in new legal definitions to justify their loyalty to infidel governments. With this purpose, explanation is made that

India is still a "land of Islam" because the rites and laws of Islam can still be fulfilled with liberty; and that the jihad is unlawful because there is not a reasonable assurance of success. Even where part of the law cannot be obeyed, necessity becomes a higher law, as under the Austrian regulations for Bosnia and Herzegovina, which forbid polygamy and slavery. But undoubtedly the spirit and law of Islam demand that the sole allegiance of the Moslem should be to a ruler of his own faith, and only expediency or necessity makes him submissive to any other rule. To him race is secondary; the Cretan who has become a Moslem is no longer a Greek, the Pomak Bulgar is not a lover of Bulgaria.

PARTIALITY OF COLONIAL GOVERNMENTS TO ISLAM

The utmost care is taken by the governments not to offend the religious sensibilities nor to contravene the customs and laws of Moslems—in vain as far as winning their loyalty. Indeed, the steps of the colonial governors have been so carefully ordered that they have assisted Islam both in Asia and in Africa. Kafiristan (Abode of Infidels) resisted all the efforts of the Afghans to bring them to Islam, till a political agreement with Great Britain consigned them to the tender mercies of their old enemies and they were forced to accept the yoke of Mohammed. Similarly in Russia, Father Macary went to Altai to begin a mission among the Kirghiz. He was turned away by Russian officials on the plea that they were too wild and savage to be accessible to the Gospel. Moslem mullahs were not forbidden to approach them and were able to convert them to Islam. The care taken not to offend Moslem susceptibilities has been interpreted by Africans and Malays as a sign of fear on the part of Europeans and led them to believe in the great power of Islam. This partiality was made the subject of a special report and remonstrance in the Edinburgh Conference. The attitude of colonial officials may be shown by some examples. Lord Curzon voiced the mind of some in his advice to the students of Aligarh College: "Adhere to your own religion." A British resident officer in the Sudan said: "My influence is exerted to make the region Mohammedan" (Dr. A. P. Sterritt, of Sudan Interior Mission). Pagan chiefs are installed by putting on a turban, a part of the Moslem dress, and this gives the impression that the government wishes the pagans to become Moslems. At times the heathen soldiers are circumcised, contrary to their desires, to make them acceptable to their Moslem comrades. Assistants and subalterns are allowed free privilege of converting the people to Islam, while the commander or governor from a Christian land preserves neutrality supposedly. At Lagos, at the dedication of an expensive mosque, the headmaster of the government school expressed the satisfaction of the Moslems in these words: "The British is the star in the heavens which guided Islam to the shores of liberty. . . . By British protection Islam has increased in numbers by thousands and thousands with miraculous rapidity" (*International Review of Missions,* 1914, p. 54). Another Moslem has said: "God raised up the British Government for the progress of Islam." Heathen tribes which withstood Islam and refused to admit its propaganda have been overcome by European Powers and so opened up to Moslem inroads. In Egypt government offices and schools are open on Sunday and closed on Friday. In Turkey, at Constantinople and Smyrna, Christians are excused from work on Sunday; they are kept at work in Egypt. More Moslems are heads of villages under British rule than were under Turkish rule and more Christians were in the civil service under the old régime (C. R. Watson, "Egypt, etc.," pp. 92-93). A Moslem magazine, *Arafate*, says (C. R. Watson, "The Valley of the Nile," p. 208): "Moslems will not wish to be under other than this government which has shown itself determined to put the law of the Koran into force. Who knows? It will perhaps be the glory of Lord Cromer . . . to resurrect the Moslem Law, which the majority of our leaders declare without blinking to be utterly out of date." A journal in Constantinople notes the fact that the "French have established nine hundred Koran schools in which reading and recitation of passages from the Koran are the only occupation of the pupils, and negro fetish worshippers are being converted in great numbers." Islam is bolstered up and its intolerance in Egypt and its pride throughout Africa is increased by the partiality shown by the European conquerors to Moslems over heathen and Christians. Let me quote the finding of the great Edinburgh Missionary Conference (Vol. I, p. 209): "The lamentable fact is that the tendency in the local representatives of these foreign governments, not excepting the British Government (all of them professedly Christian), is to facilitate and encourage the acceptance of the Mohammedan religion, and to restrict and in some cases to prevent the propagation of Christianity."

In the Dutch East Indies there has been a change of policy in late years. Formerly the spread of Islam was aided greatly by the officials, whose clerks, interpreters, policemen, and other assistants were Malay Moslems. Through the influence of this corps, and the government schools, and the exclusive use of the Malay language, Islam made great strides and most of the forty millions who were heathen when the Dutch took possession are now Moslems. A report says (*Missionary Review of the World,* 1898, p. 360): "The Mohammedans of Sumatra themselves believe that Allah has given the rule to the Dutch in order that all heathen tribes may become Mohammedan." No government official in Java was allowed to become a Christian. The government built magnificent mosques in Sumatra and Borneo, and allows rest-day for Moslems on Friday but refuses it for Christians on Sunday. Now, however, fair opportunity is being given to the Christian propaganda. Graf von Lunberg-Sturm told the Dutch officials that "for years the policy of the Dutch Government had been influenced by the fear that the spread of Christianity might arouse the fanaticism of the Mohammedans, but that short-sighted fear is gradually vanishing in influential circles and is being more and more replaced by the very opposite opinion, that for purely political reasons no obstacle should be placed in the path of missions" (Simon: "Progress, etc.," p. 286). There seems, moreover, to be an awakening among governments to the danger of the Moslem advance in Africa. The German Colonial Conference warned of the danger and Emperor William spoke strongly of the necessity of promoting Christianity and of hindering the spread of Islam in Africa. It is to be hoped that after this war and the humbling of Turkey and the death of political Pan-Islamism, the fear of Moslems will pass away, the attitude of truckling to them disappear, and an open door and real neutrality to Christian missions prevail.

DISLOYALTY OF MOSLEM SUBJECTS

Notwithstanding the care exercised not to give offence, it is impossible for European governments to win the Moslems, their confidence, and their heart loyalty. I do not mean that individuals may not be sincerely loyal and devoted. The ignorant populace still believes that Islam is invincible and irresistible. God in His own good time will put to naught the power of its enemies. The fellahs of Turkey and Persia are not convinced to the contrary. The Javanese believe that the Sultan is all-powerful and that the Christian rulers are under his sovereignty. This accounts in the eyes of the negro heathen for the way the European honours the Moslem. Educated Moslems are opposed to Christian governments, for their education has brought in its train other aspirations. Even though weaned from their bigotry, they have ideas of independence and self-government, with an increased jealousy of the rulers both as foreigners and as anti-Moslem. There is a tendency among Africans and Malays to look upon Islam as the religion of the black and the brown men, and to put hope in it as the power which in its future development may free them from the dominion of the white men. The Moslems in Africa are fellow-subjects with the heathen, and both are now drawing near each other in sympathy. The old-time enmities are passing away. They intermarry and are bound together socially. Mr. Simon says ("Progress, etc.," pp. 39, 44-45): "There is an idea of far-reaching significance in the modern Moslem movement. It means the organization in the face of the European nations —the rallying of the oppressed proletariat among the nations in the face of the ruling Christian Powers. . . . Islam parades before the people as the power that can turn against the Europeans: it embodies the hope of the brown race for freedom from European supremacy." He says that anti-European feeling is so strong that the Malay fears to become a Christian lest he be a Dutchman in the next world.

NATIONALISM AMONG MOSLEMS

Among the more cultured Moslem races there has developed recently a spirit of Nationalism. The genius of Islam, maybe, would merge all races in one great people under one caliph, but that dream has long since passed. It was natural that the spirit of Nationalism which has shown itself so markedly in Europe and has led to the renaissance of the Italians, Greeks, and Balkan peoples should communicate itself to Asiatics. The national aspirations of these subject Christian races have deserved our sympathy and encouragement. We can sympathize with the aspirations of subject Moslem races as soon as they learn to treat other religions on an equality. The Christian can sincerely wish well to all rightly directed efforts for liberty. Patriotism, too, the love of country and people as distinct from love of Islam, is a growing feeling fostered by the new education and the permeation of Western ideas. The awakening of Asia is a marked characteristic of the age. The movement which has so marvellously affected Japan and which has aroused China is evident among Moslem peoples.

The victory of Japan over Russia had a far-reaching and marked effect on Asiatic peoples. Its demonstration of the fact that the Orient could face the Occident and win, sank deep into their consciousness, inspired them with hope, and roused them with determination to throw off the domination of Europe. The impression on Moslem peoples was specially marked, for they have regarded Russia as their inveterate and irresistible enemy. The press and pulpits of Islam took up an anti-Christian, anti-foreign propaganda with new hopefulness. The modernists emphasized the fact that Western science, military skill, and political institutions could be acquired and utilized entirely apart from the Christian religion. "What heathen Japan had done, could they not do with the help of Allah?" This interest was universal. Battak Moslems discussed how they could now expel the Dutch. Those of India addressed the Emperor of Japan and asked him to take the headship of Asia and expel the Europeans. It may be remembered in this connection that Japan, when it began to seek modern civilization, sent a commission of investigation around the world. They travelled through Persia and Turkey, but saw nothing in the Moslem capitals of Teheran and Constantinople which they need tarry to learn. On the other hand, Japan has given a startling lesson to the Moslem world.

MOSLEM NATIONALISM IN INDIA

In passing in review political movements among Moslems in the present day I will begin with the people under the rule of Christian governments. In India Moslems continued for a long while in sullen and inactive subjection to the British crown. They refused, as I have already indicated, to take advantage of the modern education, by means of which the Hindus forged ahead. Jealousy of the Hindus and their predominance led the Moslems to give steady support to the British Government, that by its aid they might be able to hold their own against the encroachments of the Hindus. The first Mohammedan leaders adhered to a programme of loyalty to the British and development under their ægis. The leaders following Sayid Ahmad Khan were Justice Amir Ali, president of the London-All India Moslem League; Ali Khan, president of the Central League; His Highness Aga Khan, chief of the Bohrah sect of Ismieliyahs of Bombay; and the Prince of Arcot in Southern India. This All-India Moslem League, intended to include all sects, has provincial leagues and a council in London designed to act upon the Imperial Government. It has developed ardour and enthusiasm and manifested considerable activity. It wishes to make a common language for all Indian Moslems, possibly the

Urdu. The government, in a reform scheme, gave representation to the people in the Legislative Council and in other official bodies. Moslems took advantage of these privileges and became members of the High Councils. In order to be prepared for their new status, they are seriously seeking modern education and making progress. Of late many influences have combined to arouse the political aspirations of the Moslem people. The Pan-Islamic influences of the Sultan, hajis and darvishes, the active press, the critical condition of the Moslem world, and the rapid influx of new political ideas have caused a sudden change. A new party has been formed which is strongly nationalistic. It is composed, for the most part, of lawyers, editors, and teachers of the younger generation. They have forced the adoption by the Moslem Leagues of a programme calling for "political and religious unity with Turkey and the outer Islamic world," and for the freedom of Islamic races and countries from the rule of alien and Christian governments. This thesis is one upon which theoretically modernists and Pan-Islamists, politicians and darvishes, editors and Ulema can agree. But later the Nationalists, undeterred by the resignation of their old leaders, and by the anarchistic tendencies and outbreaks of the Hindus, reached an understanding with the Hindu National Congress, sinking their religious differences and giving adhesion to the motto, "India for the Indians" (*International Review of Missions,* 1914, p. 34). The newly organized League passed resolutions severely disapproving of the course of the British Government concerning Turkey and

Persia in 1910. The state of feeling was becoming more embittered. Everything was critically regarded. An example of this was seen just before the war. In order to open a new street, a fountain which was used for ablutions was removed. This was declared to be an insult to Islam and was made the occasion of riot and loss of life. The fountain was rebuilt by the government on a new level. The *rapprochement* of Moslems and Hindus and adjustment of their programmes does not indicate any widening of religious outlook, but simply a temporary sinking of them for political purposes. Indeed, the attitude of both races is reactionary, rejecting the idea of the superiority of Christian civilization, except in physical science and its applications, and exalting the worth of all things Indian. It opposes the movement of Neo-Islam to graft European law and ideas on Islam, but rather would renew confidence in the old religion as in all things of their own. At present all expression of criticism is under the ban of the censor and the police, and what amounts to martial law.

NATIONALISM IN EGYPT

Among those who withstood Napoleon in Egypt was Mehemet Ali Bey, an Albanian. He became Pasha of Egypt, subdued and massacred the Mamelukes, and established a hereditary vice-royalty, called the Khedivate. His fourth successor, Ismiel, 1863, followed his example in favouring the introduction of European civilization. He established public utilities, railways, telegraphs, manufactories, developed resources, adorned the capital with parks and palaces, and inaugurated a new system of education, including medical institutions. His was the good fortune to open the Suez Canal. With these externals of civilization, there was no real reform. All the splendour caused enormous debts, so that he was not a real blessing to his country. For the bondholders a commission of investigation was ordered. Finances fell under the control of French and British administrators. Economies were enforced. The notables were restrained. Jealousy and dissatisfaction became prevalent. A nationalist party began to form to oppose foreign control. The Khedive dismissed the Controllers, and was himself deposed. Tewfik Khedive, his successor, was unable to maintain political equilibrium. The Nationalist movement increased in power, taking in various classes. Its cry was "Egypt for the Egyptians," directed against Turkish officers as well as against Europeans, for the army was under Circassian or Osmanli officers who were as distasteful as the European tax-collectors, who represented foreign bondholders. The movement culminated in a revolt led by Ahmad Arabi Pasha, who stirred up popular fanaticism to make demonstrations against the British and French. He became a popular hero and Minister of War. Riots took place in Alexandria. The French and English fleets were fired on, and in return bombarded the forts. Mob violence massacred two thousand people, including Europeans. Great Britain retaliated by bombarding the city, and quelled the revolt at Tel-el-Kebir, July, 1882. Arabi Pasha was exiled to Ceylon. Great Britain occupied Egypt as temporary administrator. The British Government strove, as Lord Cromer, its able representative, says ("Modern Egypt," Vol. II, p. 197), "to let the rays of true civilization lighten with their sunshine even the mud hut of the Egyptian fellah; to deliver them from the thraldom of their oppressors; teach them that they might be treated like human beings and have opened to them the path that leads to moral progress and elevation of thought." British officials succeeded in freeing the Egyptians from the three C-s, courbash, corvée, and corruption, which may be paraphrased as the three F-s, flogging, forcing, and fleecing. Great material prosperity and vast internal improvements followed the Occupation. Egypt was fortunate to have justice, security, and light taxation. I noticed when I visited Cairo after leaving Constantinople the difference between the conditions of the people. Constantinople, under the repression of Abdul Hamid, was gloomy in spirit, silent, fearful, requiring a caution of speech which made it difficult for one accustomed to the freedom of speech of Persia. Cairo, in contrast with the Sultan's capital, was light, gay, and free. The people moved about, spoke, and acted without restraint or fear. Popular amusements, assemblies, literary activities, political theorizings were freely indulged in. During the threatened invasion of the Mahdi and the efforts for the reconquest of the Sudan, agitation was in abeyance. But Britain's sincere efforts to be fair, even to the point of partiality to the Moslem, did not succeed in winning their loyalty. The Nationalist movement broke out again after a time. For the Moslem prefers oppression from one of his own faith and race to justice and progress under the infidel foreigner. Pan-Islamic agitation from Turkey helped to revive Nationalism in Egypt and the new spirit moving upon Asiatic peoples was felt there also. Discontent and dissatisfaction grew apace; partly from the agitation of those shut out from former emoluments; partly from the exclusion of Egyptians from high civil and military offices; partly from the injustice of the capitulations which favoured foreigners even when criminals; partly from hostility to Christianity itself. This hostility was kept alive not only by the Ulema, but by the Europeanized Egyptians, who, often sceptical themselves, regarded Islam as the rallying cry for nationalism. The demand was, "Cessation of British occupation and Home-Rule." Khedive Abbas Hilmi was anti-English and the Council was manipulated by the Nationalists. The Sardar, Sir Eldon Gorst, tried a policy of accommodation and conciliation.

Two parties, at least, existed among the Nationalists. The first and oldest was led by Ali Pasha Yusuf. They advocated reforms and the gradual withdrawal of Great Britain. Their newspaper was *Al Moayad.* The other party was led by Kamil Pasha. He had been educated in France, loudly denounced everything British, and strenuously advocated immediate withdrawal, saying, "Rather an unreformed Egypt than one reformed by the British; rather the Turks, for they at least are Moslems." He was supported by the Sultan of Turkey. Their organ was the *Lewa.* The newspapers had great influence in exciting patriotic feeling, for while few of the people can read, story-tellers in the villages read and re-read the papers to groups. The movement was directly encouraged by the Minister of Education. Anglophobia was rampant in the schools, especially the School of Law. The Club of High Schools, founded for educational purposes, was turned into an organization of the Nationalist party. Students were continually involved in criminal investigations. Of the graduate Nationalist, W. N. Willis gives the following description (quoted in *The Near East,* from "Anti-Christ in Egypt"): "He is half-educated and wholly superficial. He is a nuisance to himself and a worry to everybody else. Many of the foreign consuls play upon his vanity by sympathizing with him—with their tongues well planted in their cheeks. They simply make a tool of him in order to breed trouble and discontent."

Nationalist agitation reached a climax when, in February, 1910, Boudros Pasha, the Prime Minister and a Copt, an able supporter of British administration, was assassinated by Wardani. The power of Moslem fanaticism appears in the fatva or decree of the Grand Mufti, that Wardani should not be executed—(1) because he killed with a revolver, and Moslem law has said nothing about such a murder, (2) because the government entered process, and by Moslem law it should have been done by the relatives, (3) because it is not a capital crime for a Moslem to kill a Christian. Wide sympathy for the assassin existed among the Egyptians. It was at this time that Former President Roosevelt passed through Egypt on returning from Central Africa. In an address at the University in Cairo he strongly condemned the murder. The Nationalists were greatly enraged, and hundreds of them made a demonstration against him, shouting, "Down with Roosevelt!" "Down with the Occupation!" The Copts have been alienated from the Nationalist party, whose cry, "Egypt for the Egyptians," is more truly, Egypt for the Moslems. The Nationalism attaches itself to Islam and does not include in its scope the real Egyptians, the Copts, who are six hundred thousand, or one-tenth of the people, and proportionately the more intelligent. Indeed, it is said that a large proportion of the Nationalists were of Turkish, Kurdish, Circassian, and Syrian extraction. Moslem fanaticism has even awakened in the Christians a fear for their personal safety. The British Government awoke to the necessity of action and sent Lord Kitchener to be Sardar with an iron policy. A press law was enforced with severe penalties. Offending editors were dealt with. Among these was Sheikh Abdul Aziz Shawish. He was a graduate of Al Azhar, lecturer on Arabic at Oxford, Inspector in the Egyptian Ministry of Education, an able writer and editor and a contributor to Nationalist journals. He was fiercely anti-English, and was for a while imprisoned for libel and sedition. Some editors fled to Geneva and Paris. There they published a paper called *El Kisas* ("The Punishment"). Its spirit is shown in its exalting the assassin of Boudros Pasha to the rank of hero and patriot.

The Turkish Revolution of 1908 strengthened Nationalism in Egypt. The Young Turks actively promoted it, and the Ottoman High Commissioner, who represented the Sultan, had no occupation but to carry on intrigues and to try to inflame the spirit. Though Egypt was neutral in the war in Tripoli, yet Egyptians helped the Turks. A significance incident showed that Nationalism is not love for the Turks. Among those who assisted Turkey in Cyrenaica was the Egyptian Aziz Ali Bey. After the war he was court-martialled in Constantinople through the jealousy of Enver Pasha and Sheikh Shawish and condemned to death. The unjust sentence was protested against by the united voice of the Egyptian press and people, seconding the efforts of the two governments, and was accompanied by a vehement outburst of anger against the Turks until he was freed. Lord Kitchener, with severity, combined efforts to satisfy the people. He specially strove to relieve the condition of the fellahs by just laws, by supervision and restraint of the landlords, and by postal savings banks freeing them from usurers. A delegation of Egyptians presented in London a petition for increase of rights. Shortly afterwards the powers of self-government were enlarged. In lieu of the Legislative Council, established in 1883, a Legislative Assembly was inaugurated in 1914. It consisted of 66 members elected by the people and 23 nominated by the government, including 6 ministers and representatives of the Beduins, Copts, Jews, and special classes. It has power of initiating legislation.

When the present war began, opinion was divided. Some feared that they might fall into the hands of Germany if England were defeated. When Turkey proclaimed a Holy War a wave of sympathy passed over the people. The Khedive Abbas Hilmi was in Constantinople. He had been anti-British. He had even refused to preside at cabinet meetings, and through his intrigues had involved many princes, so that they exiled themselves. His attempt to sell the Mariut Railway to foreigners had almost brought about his deposition. He remained in Constantinople and accepted appointment to go with the Turkish army against the British. In consequence of all this, Great Britain, on December 18, 1914, declared Egypt a British protectorate, repudiating Turkish sovereignty. Prince Husain Kamil, second son of Ismiel Pasha, was proclaimed ruler of Egypt, with the title of Sultan. Martial law was declared, and the arrival of British armies made further Nationalist manifestations inopportune. Only the students of the High School have dared to show their spirit by "cutting" attendance when Sultan Husain visited their institution, and some anarchists by twice attempting his assassination.

ARABS AND ALBANIANS

Concerning the spirit of Nationalism in other countries of North Africa or in Russia and Central Asia, all that is necessary has been said under the Pan-Islamic movement. Political agitation has not been permitted to show itself so openly in those countries. Even Moslem countries under Moslem rulers of a different race have strongly manifested Nationalism. The Arabs have been in a continual ferment against Turkish domination and have made many revolts. The Kurds, under Sheikh Obeidullah, in 1880, formulated a programme of independence. The Albanians have shown a strenuous resistance to Ottomanization, even the Moslem Albanians (1,500,000) appearing to put race before religion. It is possible some of them are secret Christians, both men and women, and that they maintain Christian practices secretly (Pears: "Turkey and Its People," p. 173). They say that they were made Mohammedans by compulsion and have no loyalty to Mohammed. Rev. C. T. Erickson says (*Missionary Review*, 1913, p. 322): "I am convinced, having it from the people themselves, that once they are free from the Turkish yoke, off goes the Moslem yoke also." Dr. J. L. Barton testifies to the same effect: "When an Albanian chief was asked if he was not a Mohammedan, he denied the fact with great emphasis. He said Albanians had no love for the Turks nor for Mohammedanism, and that no reason exists why they should not accept Christianity." But it seems doubtful whether the national spirit will unite the Roman Catholic, Orthodox, and Moslem Albanians in political solidarity.

HOW CHRISTIAN CIVILIZATION AFFECTS MOSLEM LANDS

I turn now to consider Moslem lands which are politically independent. It is remarkable how they are under the influence of Christian civilization. Their economical dependence has been a prelude to their absorption of social and political ideas. Just a paragraph about this economic relation. Turkey and Persia look to Europe for public utilities, as railways, tramways, telephones, telegraphs; for internal development, as mining, irrigation, and engineering; for weapons for the jihads—cannon, muskets, cruisers, and aeroplanes; for gold and silver for their money, for machines to mint it, safes to hold it, purses to carry it, loans to replenish it; for window glass, lamps and matches to light their mosques, compasses to show the kibla of prayer, and watches to tell their times of worship, and for paper on which their Korans and prayers and charms are written, and for stamps to send their letters; for their spectacles and teeth and drugs and hardware and dishes and knives and forks and an indefinite supply of their needs. For much the Islamic world is indebted to the Christian. It is even adopting the style of dress, the shoes, the brushes, the kaloshes, the umbrellas of the Christian, and the Sherif of Mecca rides on the day of pilgrimage on a saddle, made in Europe, of pig-skin (Keane: "Six Months in Mecca").

In all departments of science the Moslems are borrowers from the Christian world, and very profitably in medicine. But more remarkable is their readiness to learn in politics, law, and statecraft, in which they have a Koran, a Shariat, and a Khalifa to guide them. Nothing has more surprised the world than the Constitutional movements in Persia and Turkey. Even Afghanistan is undergoing remarkable changes in thought and "Young Afghans" are ambitious for a liberal government. Amir Habib Ullah is inclined to reforms in the administration. His visit to India increased his desire for progress.

POLITICAL REFORMS IN PERSIA

Political reforms in modern Persia were first attempted by Mirza Taki Khan, the celebrated vizier of Nasr-ud-Din Shah (1848-52). This man, sprung from the common people, was of sterling integrity, scorning bribes and flattery. He succeeded for a time in bringing about a reform of abuses and of the corruption of official life. The sale of offices was abolished, the absurd civil pension roll cut down, oppression of the peasants restrained, the use of bombastic titles discountenanced, the sea slave trade prohibited, the interference of foreign legations in the internal affairs of Persia was discountenanced. The power of the mullahs in political affairs was restrained, the right of asylum was taken away from the Mujtahids, popular fanaticism was frowned upon, especially as exhibited and incited by the Muharram ceremonies. But the jealousy and opposition of the reactionaries was too much for him. He was dismissed and executed. Yet the indignation caused by his death brought about at least this reform that the custom of executing exviziers ceased. Though he had no thought of consulting the people and continued the old method of autocratic rule, yet "the short period of his administration is now looked back upon as having been the golden age of modern Persia" and he is regarded as the "only man who possessed the ability, the patriotism, the energy, and the integrity" to regenerate the country (Watson's "History of Persia," pp. 366-404).

Next in time comes the advocacy of reform by

Prince Malcom Khan, Minister to Great Britain. I had the pleasure of calling on this intelligent and progressive man in Tabriz. When Minister and afterwards when under the ban of the Shah, he set forth a programme of reforms and Constitutional government for Persia. He established a magazine, called *Kanun* (Rule), which, published in London, circulated in Persia, and set forth liberal ideas of government and discoursed on the faults of the administration, especially of the Vizier Ali Askar Khan, Amin-i-Sultan. He organized a society called the "World of Humanity" and also, from its secrecy, "Faramush Khana," through which liberalism was propagated.

Other preachers of reform in Persia were Sheikh Hadi of Teheran and Sheikh Jamal-ud-Din, of whom I have spoken. The latter, before his work for Pan-Islamism, associated himself with Malcom Khan in advocating a Constitution for Persia. He expressed regret that he had spent so much of his effort in trying to influence sovereigns. "Would that I had sown all the seeds of my ideas in the receptive ground of the people's thoughts. The sword of unrighteousness has not suffered me to see awakening of the peoples of the East and the hand of ignorance has not granted me the opportunity to hear the call of freedom. The stream of renovation flows quickly towards the East. The edifice of despotic government totters to its fall. Strive as far as you can to destroy the foundations of despotism, not to pluck up and cast out its individual members" (Browne's "Persian Revolution," p. 29).

These agitations were a preparation for the crisis which came in 1891, on the occasion of the Shah granting a monopoly of the tobacco trade to a British company. Abetted by Russia, the liberals, the mullahs, and the governors who had been overlooked in the distribution of bribes combined to overthrow this concession. (See writer's "Persian Life and Customs," pp. 290-96.) The *Akhtar,* the Persian journal at Constantinople, denounced it and was suppressed. Sheikh Jamal-ud-Din, who had been acting as a Minister, was arrested and expelled. Malcom Khan telegraphed his disapproval. He was dismissed and remained in exile. Thus he escaped the fate of his friend, M. Yusuf Khan, Mustashar-ud-Doulah, Foreign Agent—my next-door neighbour at Tabriz. His correspondence was inspected. He was called to Teheran, but at Kasvin was met by a royal cup of coffee which terminated his journey. Tracts were circulated through the country demanding the suppression of the monopoly, reform of the finances, religious freedom, and a representative government. Finally a fatva of the chief Mujtahids of Kerbala and Najef interdicted the use of tobacco. The people ceased to use the weed. Strikes and riots threatened; the monopoly was rescinded. The royal power by this defeat received a great check. Priests and people had learned their power when united. Of those who took an active part in these riots was one Mirza Riza, a disciple of Sheikh Jamal-ud-Din. He was imprisoned and maltreated. He wreaked his vengeance by assassinating the Shah in 1896, no doubt instigated thereto by the Sheikh,[1] and possibly by the Babis (Azalis).

[1] See chapter on Neo-Islam. The assassin in his examination said: "Those who share my view are many, but no one, save

Agitation was kept up during the reign of Muzaffar-ud-Din Shah. In 1901 pamphlets, placards, and protests were distributed and even delivered on the table of the Shah himself, directed against him and the Amin-i-Sultan and the new loans and mortgages which were being made for the Shah's journeys to Europe. Some of these agitators were arrested, imprisoned, and exiled. Discontent grew apace during the following years. The people felt that their situation was desperate. They were suffering grievously from injustice and oppression. Their ancient country was weak, its government corrupt, its independence threatened. The people, rich and poor alike, were groaning on account of their pitiable lot. Their Kismat was ill-fortune. Bribes weighed down the scales of justice. Security of property was at the caprice of venal judges, both civil and religious. Men cursed their rulers with a

myself and Sayid Jamal-ud-Din, was aware of the idea of mine to kill the Shah" (Browne's "Persian Revolution," p. 67). He also said: "A tree,—meaning the Shah,—whereof the fruits after all these years are such low-down rogues and scoundrels . . . who are the plagues of the lives of the Moslem community, such a tree, bearing such fruits, ought to be cut down." Some suspected that the Babis had part in the crime, for the two men who visited Mirza Riza at Shah Abdul Azim, the scene of the murder, were Babis, i.e. Azalis, and the two men whom he visited in the prison at Trebizond, en route for Teheran, were of the same sect. These two were extradited and executed at Tabriz on the charge of complicity. One of them, M. Hasan Khan, Mukhbir-ul-Mulk, I had conversed with at the Mustashar-ud-Doulah's in Tabriz. Another of these Babis was an editor of the *Akhtar* and a son-in-law of Subh-i-Azal (Ibid., pp. 78, 92-95, 405, 415). The reform movement was not, however, a Babi movement. Those who took part did so with other Persians of all sects desiring the good of the country.

vim and a vindictiveness which were startling. For several decades the city people had lived on the verge of famine, though the crops were fairly good. They exclaimed: "Allah gives us our daily bread, but greedy men starve us." Princes and nobles, mullahs and other capitalists, had their hands on the throat of the people as effectively as if they had been a landlords' trust. They doubled and trebled the price of bread in the cities. The labourer was obliged to work ten days for a bushel of wheat. This high price scarcely benefited the farmer, for he had little wheat or barley to sell after feeding his family. The rent and taxes he paid in kind, by measure not by value. The Crown Prince, Mohammed Ali Mirza, was the most avaricious grain merchant. The people bitterly resented it, saying: "Our Prince should be our Protector and Shepherd; he devours us like a hungry wolf." It cost him his crown. The officials, the farmers of taxes, and the mullahs whose stipends were collected by them from the villages in produce, were waxing richer and the mass of the people grew poorer and poorer. The Mujtahids are among the greatest landlords, and wealthy because recipients of the tithes and because in their capacity as judges they have been corrupt. Bitterness against them was intensified because, while as representatives of religion they were expected to manifest justice and mercy, they have so often shown avarice and hardheartedness. Men with fair earnings were under the necessity of pawning their household goods. Bread riots of men and even of women failed to bring relief. With heart and lip they cursed both priest and prince.

The corruption of the government was causing intense dissatisfaction. Ministers were quarrelling, possibly poisoning one another. Loans had been contracted from Russia, making possible royal jaunts in Europe and lining the pockets of viziers and court favourites, but with no result in public utilities. For these loans the customs duties were hypothecated. Foreign (Belgian) controllers were put in charge of customs, post, and passports. Road concessions gave control of highways into the hand of foreigners. Bridges which from time immemorial had been public property became toll-bridges through the connivance of bribe-taking officials. Patriotic anger was aroused by these circumstances and by the threatened danger to the independent regulation of religion should foreign control increase. The conviction that the country, and with it the religion, was endangered by concessions, loans, and the foreigners, had the deepest influence. Sheikh Jamal-ud-Din wrote to the principal Ulema, "By God's life, folly and greed are allied to destroy religion, abrogate the Holy Law, and to hand over the home of Islam to foreigners!"

Under these conditions the outcome of the Russo-Japanese war made a profound impression. The invincible Russians were humbled. Persians began to hope. The Constitutional struggle in Russia had a great influence, especially in its effect on the Persians and Shiahs of the Caucasus, who imbibed Constitutional and socialistic ideas and were initiated into revolutionary methods. Other Persians were influenced in Turkey. In Persia secret agitators were working and planning. The relation between the mullahs and the government became more and more strained. Prudence seemed to have forsaken the officials. Sayids, mullahs, and even Mujtahids were bastinadoed. The killing of a Sayid finally inflamed the embers of discontent. A great popular demonstration occurred. People to the number of twelve thousand took refuge at the British Legation. There the demand for a Constitution was formulated as the panacea for their ills. Muzaffar-ud-Din bowed to the will of the people and granted a Constitution August 5, 1906. His successor Mohammed Ali Shah abrogated it and dispersed parliament at the cannon's mouth, hanging the editors, June, 1908. Civil war ensued, and he was forced to abdicate, by the Nationalists, July, 1909. Ahmad Sultan Shah succeeded him at the age of thirteen. Mr. Morgan Shuster was called in to regulate the finances as Treasurer-General, but his plans were incompatible with the purposes of Russia, which forced his retirement and continued to hold parts of Northern Persia with the army of occupation. The Constitution continues nominally in force; the new Shah was crowned before the reassembled second parliament, and the third one assembled in December, 1914.[1]

[1] Outline of the Constitutional Movement in Persia.

(1) Merchants and mullahs protest against oppression, take refuge at Shah Abdul Azim, force Ayn-ud-Doulah's resignation, 1905.

(2) Petition for reforms, leaders exiled, April, 1906.

(3) Killing of Sayid and fifteen others by soldiers. Mullahs and people take refuge at Kum, June 21, 1906.

(4) Great political demonstration. Twelve thousand people take refuge at British Legation, July 19-August 5.

(5) Constitution granted by Muzaffar-ud-Din Shah August 5, 1906.

PERSIAN CONSTITUTION AND RELIGION

The adoption of a Constitution did not put much of a strain on the relation of Persians to their religion because they had long been under the *urfi* or civil law, which was largely the decisions of the Shah and his Ministers. This urfi had often crossed the will of the mullahs. Between them and the civil authorities there had been much rivalry and jealousy. This accounts in a measure for the fact that the mullahs had such a conspicuous part in the Persian revolution. Whereas in Turkey the movement was carried on largely by young scholars, educated in Europe,

(6) First National Assembly inaugurated, Teheran, October 7, 1906.

(7) Shah died, Mohammed Ali crowned, January 19, 1907.

(8) Vizier Amin-i-Sultan (Atabeg) assassinated August 13.

(9) Russian-British agreement, dividing Persia into spheres of influence, published September, 1907.

(10) Coup-d'état June 23, 1908.

(11) Civil war. First siege of Tabriz, June-October. Royal troops withdrew, vanquished.

(12) Second siege of Tabriz, January-April, 1909. Relieved by Russian troops.

(13) Nationalist troops occupy Teheran, July 6th. Shah abdicated. Ahmad Sultan made Shah.

(14) Second National Assembly convened November, 1909.

(15) Mr. Morgan Shuster made Treasurer-General May 12, 1911.

(16) Ex-Shah's raid and defeat, summer of 1911.

(17) Dissolution of Parliament. Shuster dismissed on demand of Russia.

(18) Third siege of Tabriz ends, December 25, 1911. Shuja-ud-Doulah begins reign of terror in Tabriz.

(19) Ahmad Shah crowned,   , 1914. Third parliament assembles, December, 1914. Neutrality of Persia proclaimed in the Great War.

often irreligious and with reliance on the army, in Persia the mullahs were the force that broke the government in the first place, though they were influenced more than they knew by men who had drunk from the streams of liberal and revolutionary thought. Another class which was strong and influential were the Sayids, the descendants of Mohammed, who are supposed to be a fanatical class. From first to last they were prominent in the liberal ranks and many of them suffered death for the cause of liberty and progress. They demonstrated that the religious class of Islam contains a good proportion of liberal-minded men. Because of this, the Nationalists were constrained to allow the mullahs large influence in drafting the written Constitution, especially as without their aid the Shah could not be forced to accept and sign it. Some provisions favour clerical domination and provide for the continuance of their power. Article I establishes Islam according to the Shiah sect of the twelve Imams as the religion of Persia, to which the Shah must belong and to the spread of which he must contribute. Article II declares that the National Assembly has been founded by the help of the Twelfth Imam, and it must never to all ages pass laws contrary to the Shariat; and a commission of five Mujtahids shall have power to reject all bills which their judgment decides to be contrary to the Law. Articles LXXI and LXXXVI seem to limit the power of the Mujtahids' courts by giving the final decision to a tribunal established by the government. There is no doubt that the principles of the Nationalist party really tended to undermine the Islamic courts and the traditions. It was not long before most of their strict religionists turned to the reactionary side. When the contest of arms came on, mullahs and Mujtahids were generally against the Nationalists. In Tabriz they organized a society called the Islamia, which used all the weapons of bigotry and religious hate in their efforts to overthrow the cause of freedom. They branded the supporters of the Constitution as Babis or heretics, disloyal to Islam and worthy of extermination in a jihad. To convince the royal army of besiegers that they were good Shiahs, a unique demonstration was made—one that will never fade from memory. Mounting the flat roofs of Tabriz, the people repeated with the mighty sound of ten thousand voices the creed, calling out: "Allah akbar! Allah akbar! God is great! There is no God but God; Mohammed is the Apostle of God; Ali is the vicegerent of God." Times without number this creed rang out, testifying to the besieging army that the city were true Shiahs. There arose an intense feeling of bitterness against the mullahs, who were denounced with hatred and contempt. Among the few houses looted and destroyed by the Nationalist mob were those of the Mujtahids, and they did not venture to return to Tabriz even when it was under guard of the Russian troops. For the time the power of the mullahs was broken and freedom of speech and action regarding religion was increased.

PERSIAN REFORMS AND LIBERTY

The provisions of the new law are a series of compromises. People shall enjoy equal rights except where it contravenes the Shari. The study and teaching of arts, letters, and science are free except as forbidden by the Shari. Publications are permitted except when harmful to the religion of Islam. Other articles disqualify from voting or being a candidate any apostates from the Shiah faith and those living in open sin, and declare that only a Mohammedan Persian can be a Minister of State. While the banner "Liberty, Equality, Fraternity, and Justice" was widely displayed, the question of giving real equality to Christians and Jews was scarcely mooted. The smallness of their number precludes the question becoming one of active politics, but for this reason the Moslems could without endangering their supremacy in any particular have applied the principles of liberty. Non-Moslems were not regarded as regular citizens. As exceptional populations, the Armenians, Nestorians, Zoroastrians, and Jews were each allowed one representative in parliament, and these must be sound in their respective faiths.

Civil rights were guaranteed, reforms projected, popular education advocated, the adoption of Western civilization decided upon, under a Constitutional régime. But many difficulties hindered the carrying out of these purposes. First there were the schemes of the reactionaries, including several insurrections by the ex-Shah and Kajar Princes. These were successfully put down. Two difficulties proved insurmountable, one internal, the other external.

CAUSES OF FAILURE OF CONSTITUTIONAL MOVEMENT

What was the internal cause of the failure of the new régime? An Oriental story seems apropos. The wise man said that three things were necessary for the progress of the kingdom: an army, money, and the trust of the people. He was asked which could be most easily dispensed with. "The army," he said, "for with the other two, prosperity could still exist." "Which of these two?" "Money," he replied, "for the trust and confidence of the people would give success." But what shall we say of a country where the army is untrained and divided under tribal leaders and factional chiefs, united by no common patriotic purpose nor aspiration; where money is lacking and financial administration inadequate; in which distrust of the leaders is keenly felt and that righteousness which exalteth a nation is absent? Why did the Constitutional movement fail? It failed for lack of men, men of character and integrity. The old royalist officials were corrupt and venal; the new men, the would-be reformers, for the most part proved deficient in the same way. Let me call some independent witnesses. Mr. Arthur Moore came to Persia as a representative of the Persian Committee of the British Parliament. He sympathized with and aided the Constitutionalists, even drilling their troops, and joined in the sortie in which the devoted Mr. Baskerville was sacrificed. After much experience, Mr. Moore said to me: "This movement must fail. The men lack moral stamina." Take, for example, the hero of Tabriz, Sattar Khan. When Mohammed Ali Shah abolished the Constitution, he sent an army of freebooters against Tabriz to punish it for its stubborn advocacy of liberty. These mountaineers began to loot, burn, and destroy the homes and bazaars of the defenceless inhabitants. Then up rose an unknown man, mounted his horse, gathered some comrades, and rode through the streets calling on the citizens to arm and resist. They seized the armoury, organized the butchers and bakers and candlestick-makers, endured two sieges, and caused the final triumph of the Constitution. Sattar Khan was the hero of this fight for freedom. Shall we honour his name as a Washington or a Garibaldi? No! He was conquered by greed and graft, wine and women. His name became a by-word and a reproach.

How was it when Mr. Shuster tried to put Persia's finances to rights? He dealt with the cabinet ministers of the Constitutional government. What kind of men did he find them to be? He describes them as selfish, self-seeking, greedy, looking out for their own interests and not for those of their country (Shuster's "Strangling of Persia," pp. 239, 200). A member of the British Boundary Commission voiced the same verdict: "We have lost hope of Persia on account of the lack of men of character and ability to lead it."

The external factor which controls the situation in Persia is Russia. For many years its influence has been gradually on the increase. It received legal sanction when the Shah solicited loans and hypothecated the custom duties as security. Its position was rendered impregnable when the agreement with Great Britain acknowledged its sphere of influence as extending over the largest and best part of Persia, as far south as Ispahan and Yezd inclusive. The British sphere extends over a much smaller section, including Kerman and Bandar Abbas. Between these spheres a considerable area is left as a buffer. By this arrangement the Lion and the Bear lay down together, and the Persian lamb within them. Later Russia's position was strengthened by stationing troops and consular guards at various points. In the present war the invasion of Azerbaijan by Turks and Kurds has brought dire calamity upon the Christian population, adding another full chapter of untold horrors to the story of Moslem cruelty, savagery, and lust. Russia later drove them from Persian soil, which, though neutral territory, has suffered terribly.

IX

POLITICAL REFORMS IN THE TURKISH EMPIRE

I HAVE already referred to the gradual weakening and dismemberment of the Turkish empire. This disintegration impressed upon the government and people the necessity of finding a remedy. European civilization had gone forward by leaps and bounds; the Turks were distanced in the race. The consciousness of this condition aroused the Sultans, who began to act partly on their own initiative, and partly at the instigation of Europeans like the British Ambassador, Lord Stratford de Redcliffe, and not at all in response to any popular demand or agitation. Mahmud II, Abdul Mejid, and Abdul Aziz are called the Reforming Sultans. Mahmud II paved the way for reforms by abolishing the Janissaries, who, on mutinying, were destroyed at the cannon's mouth. He strove to placate European States by bringing Turkey into the line of progress. Some of his projects were external and did not touch the root of the matter. He discarded long robes and the turban, donned the European dress, and adopted the fez as a national headdress—an article which had previously been used by some Greeks in Turkey. His assistant in organizing the new administration was Raif Mahmud Effendi, who as secretary to the Ottoman Embassy in

England had imbibed some principles of free government. Some of the changes affected in this and the following reigns were as follows: A new Sultan should not on his accession, openly at least, slaughter all his brothers, nor cut off the head of a Grand Vizier on his deposition, nor imprison ambassadors in case of war. The Vizier thereafter deigned to rise to a foreign ambassador; even the Sultan might grasp the hand of such an infidel or become his guest. One Sultan, Abdul Aziz, even visited European capitals, 1875. Politeness to foreigners became the custom. Torture of criminals was prohibited, slavery was mitigated, the slave-trade and public slave-markets were abolished, the poll-tax on *zimmis* or Christian *rayats* was for a time removed and the evidence of Christians was to be admitted in court. Though done, for the most part, under the pressure of Christian governments, yet all this was encouraging. Reforms were summed up in two celebrated decrees issued by Abdul Mejid. One in 1839 was the Hatti Sherif of Gulkhana, called the Magna Charta of Turkey, which systematized taxation and military service, and guaranteed security of life, honour, and property to all subjects, irrespective of race or religion. The other, in 1856, called the Hatti Humayun, guaranteed religious freedom and abolished the death penalty for apostasy from Islam. This was issued at the demand of the Christian ambassadors, following the public and shameful execution of an Armenian youth who through fear and in intoxication had professed Islam and had afterwards recanted. The decree caused great rejoicing in Christian lands, but this interpretation was subsequently repudiated by the Porte (William Goodell: "Forty Years in the Turkish Empire," pp. 240, 292, 385, 481, 486). It stated that "every distinction and designation tending to make any class whatever of the subjects of my empire inferior to another class on account of their religion, language, and race shall be forever effaced. . . . No subject shall be hindered in the exercise of the religion he professes, nor shall be in any way annoyed on that account. No one shall be compelled to change his religion."

About the same time, following the Crimean War (1855), the Turkish army was reorganized and the Sultan was able to confirm his rule in the borders of Kurdistan, Syria and Arak Arabi, and to a certain extent over Nejd and the Persian Gulf littoral. European codes of law were introduced. The laws of landed property were changed. At the conquest one-third of the land had been assigned to the Ulema. Donations and endowments, *vakf,* had increased these properties greatly. The darvish orders also held large endowments. The State took over the administration of these vakfs. The privileges of the nobles and beys as landlords were revoked. These measures caused great discontent. These powerful elements were alienated and the salaries assigned in lieu of the former incomes did not satisfy them. Their spirit is seen in the act of a darvish who came before Rashid Pasha at a public audience, reviled him, called him dog and infidel, and invoked the vengeance of heaven and the dagger of the Moslem upon him for introducing reforms. Because of such a spirit, an eminent

Turk remarked: "Our Ministers labour in vain, for civilization will never enter Turkey so long as the *turbeh,* shrines, of the darvishes are in existence." Mr. Ubicini (quoted in Browne's "Dervishes," p. 349) says: "The two bodies of which religious society is composed, the Ulema and the darvishes, are the enemies of all reform. There is conservatism in the Ulema, who speaks in the name of Law, saying, 'Touch nothing that is established, borrow nothing from the infidels, because the Law forbids it.' The darvish Sheikh says: 'I am the Law; all is good that I commend, all is evil that I forbid. My sentence is the sentence of God.' The government may hope from the Ulema, but not from the darvishes."

Towards the end of his reign, Abdul Aziz became reactionary, and persecuted, and exiled the reformers. The Palace and the Porte contended. The reformers, led by Midhat Pasha, prevailed. Abdul Aziz was deposed and murdered. Murad V became insane. Abdul Hamid was made Sultan, 1876. Shortly afterwards he proclaimed a Constitution and assembled a Parliament. Maybe he did this with no serious purpose, but to throw dust in the eyes of Europe. At any rate, in the midst of the war with Russia, 1878, he suspended the Constitution. Crushed and humiliated as the result of the war, by the loss of large territories in the Balkans, Abdul Hamid entered upon a career of autocratic oppression and tyrannic repression, with firm purpose to thwart reforms among Moslems and with a fierce fanaticism against Christians. He threw himself heart and soul in with the reactionaries, ruled as a despot through the Palace junta, suppressing the Viziers at the Sublime Porte. By means of the telegraph he kept in personal touch with every corner of his empire. His system of espionage was most terrible; forty thousand spies, maintained at an expense of ten million dollars a year, made life a horror for his subjects. No one was safe. Private conversation became a dangerous pastime. In passing through Constantinople, I was struck with the hushed seriousness of the whole community. Laughter and gaiety were absent. The residents would warn me at every turn not to talk in public. They had learned to live in an atmosphere where free speech was denied every one. The contrast to Persia was striking. I attended the celebrated salaamlukh to see the Sultan come in state to Friday prayers. It is a function which can only be attended by special permission, and tickets and places were reserved for us in the pavilion. How near we came to falling under the suspicion of the ever-present spies, I can never know. But just as the Sultan passed in his carriage, our three-year-old child piped up in a clear voice: "Papa, the king is a great killer." When I said "Hush," she repeated the words: "Papa, the king is a great killer." I quickly whispered to her: "The king loves his own little boys and girls." This satisfied and quieted her. She was evidently applying her knowledge of King Herod to the first king she saw. And out of the mouth of a babe the truth was spoken as truly as by Gladstone when he pronounced Abdul Hamid "the Great Assassin." At another time, when leaving Constantinople, our baggage was taken out and most minutely examined. When we had come down to breakfast in the hotel that morning we had noticed that all the waiters were missing. We now understood that they had been imprisoned on suspicion of a plot. The police thought maybe bombs had been concealed in our baggage to escape their inspection.

Through the reports of these spies, twenty-five thousand of the flower of Turkish manhood suffered death or exile, or fled, leaving their property to be confiscated. Many were exiled to distant parts of the empire. Many were dropped into the Bosphorus. Apropos of this a story goes that some foreign sailors had need to dive down near a vessel at Seraglio Point. They found themselves among a multitude of human corpses, whose heads were weighted down and their legs were moving to and fro by the force of the currents (McCallagh: "Abdul Hamid," p. 119). The press was strictly censored. Public discussion was prohibited. Liberal ideas were crushed. Schools for Moslems were repressed, except primary education of a poor quality. Foreign governesses were spied upon as well as their pupils and their fathers. Higher education was grudgingly allowed to officers because it was essential and medicine was carefully taught. It and sanitation were two things Abdul Hamid cherished. But electric lights and telephones were excluded. When Dr. Jessup wrote "The Mohammedan Missionary Problem," just after the Treaty of Berlin was signed, he thanked God for the bright prospects for Turkey, because Christian England had undertaken to see that reforms were carried out—having taken Cyprus as a vantage ground. Alas that it was otherwise ordered by Abdul Hamid. He became the enemy of England, and the Armenians became the victims of unspeakable and terrible massacres. It seemed as if the plan was to exterminate the Christians. The liberal Turks suffered much, but there was no general massacre of them. The number of them killed was as hundreds to tens of thousands of Christians.

THE YOUNG TURKS

The political reformers who had fled to Europe, and especially to London and Paris, and had agitated for reforms in the time of Abdul Aziz had been dubbed "The Young Turks." They published a paper, called *"Hurriat"* (Liberty). When Abdul Hamid abolished the Constitution of 1876, thousands of them again fled into exile. There their eager souls grew in longing for the freedom of their country. Among them was Hairedin Pasha, a Circassian. He had been governor of Tunis and Grand Vizier in the first year of Abdul Hamid. He believed that under Islam they could attain to the high standard of European civilization. He dismissed the corrupt officials and started out to do justice to Moslems and Christians alike. Unable to carry out his project he went again into exile and became one of the reorganizers of the Young Turk party. This was a secret organization, formed to work for liberty and reform. They published literature in Europe which they smuggled into and distributed in Turkey. In spite of repression many minds were permeated with modern ideas. They became impressed with their inferiority to Western nations and even to their subject Christian races in education and science. For years the ferment worked actively, especially among the younger men. Students abroad and in the government schools imbibed liberal ideas. The officers and surgeons in the military college were inspired with the spirit of reform. Many of the bolder propagandists suffered death, betrayed. Exiling to distant provinces spread the reform movement in those outposts. The espionage system was disgusting to the officers of the army, and the rank and file, too, became disaffected by continual neglect, poor pay, and hard service in Arabia and the fortresses.

In 1891 a committee of reformers was organized in Geneva. Later they perfected organization in Paris and other capitals and took the name of "The Committee of Union and Progress." Their policy was to liberalize and reform Turkey by (1) preserving its integrity, (2) avoiding European or any outside interference in its affairs, (3) giving equality to all races, (4) introducing parliamentary government and if necessary deposing the Sultan.

The movement was distinctly secular in its nature. It was a reflection of European political life. Its moving influences, its modes of thought came from Christian civilization. Islam was not paramount in its aims, but the nation, the people, independence, self-defence. The Young Turks explained away the traditions of Islam; discouraged fanaticism. They wished to bring religion into conformity with modern progress. They repudiated Pan-Islamism, which even the Egyptian Nationalists encouraged. One of their leaders said: "We Ottomans understand that the pursuit of Pan-Islamic designs of the visionaries would be contrary to our dearest interests" (Knight's "Turkey," p. 658). Therefore membership included Christians and Jews, who were to join Moslems in political action as friends and brothers. The Armenian and Jewish committees were persuaded to unite with them, and later unity of action was negotiated with the Macedonian committees of the Bulgarians, Greeks, and Serbs. Salonica was made headquarters of the Committee. This city had not been controlled by the spy-system as much as some others. Besides, according to Knight ("Turkey," p. 101), Freemasonry flourished there, though the name and nature of their meeting were always secret, for to be found to be a Mason was to incur the penalty of death. The Committee of Union and Progress was, he tells us, "to a large extent modelled on Freemasonry and a considerable portion of the early associates, Moslems, and some Jews, were of Masonic lodges of Salonica." In Macedonia the army corps and officers were won over. There were altogether fifteen thousand members enrolled in Macedonia. The soldiers of Asia Minor were brought into harmony with the movement. Propagandists were successful everywhere throughout the empire. The leaders were men of education, in professional and official life, averaging but thirty-two years of age.

THE REVOLUTION

The time was ripe. The plot was perfected, though European diplomacy knew it not. On July 23, 1908, the leaders, among whom were Niazi Bey, Enver Bey, and Mahmud Shevket Pasha, openly revolted and proclaimed a Constitution. From Salonica the demands of the revolutionists were presented by telegram straight to the Palace. The Sultan awoke to find himself without resource or subterfuge. In solemn conclave, where all the viziers knew and none dared to say the word, the astrologer Abul Huda was put forward and pronounced the talisman, "A Constitution." The next day Abdul Hamid issued a decree re-establishing the Constitution of 1876. The Young Turks became the rulers of Turkey. The Macedonian Corps became the royal guard. The Palace camarilla disappeared, the spies were dismissed, the prisoners of liberty were released, the exiles returned, separated families were united, a whole people breathed the first free breath in thirty years. The jubilee of liberty was sounded. Enthusiasm knew no bounds. The entire populace went wild with a delirium and frenzy of rejoicing. Transports of joy thrilled all hearts. Pæans of praise and gratitude burst spontaneously from all lips. Barriers of race and religion were broken down. Moslems and Christians and Jews sincerely fraternized, in an ecstasy of delight. Mullahs and priests embraced and kissed each other in the streets; they met in mass-meetings, speaking on a common platform and electrifying a united people with approval and exemplification of the motto, "Hurriyat, Musavat, Agviyat, Adalat" (Liberty, Equality, Fraternity, Justice). Demonstrations of various kinds were held. Conspicuous among them was the memorial service of the Armenians, killed in the massacres. The exiled Armenian Patriarch had returned. Ulema and Moslem people accompanied Greek, Bulgarian, and Armenian priests and bishops to the Armenian cemetery and prayed and held services for the victims of fanaticism and hate which seemed to have passed away. At the City Hall a mullah offered prayer for brotherhood, and Christians and Moslems joined together in the "Amin." At the time of the parliamentary election the ballot box was treated as a symbol of liberty. It was adorned with the flag, borne on camel-back in procession, surrounded by little girls dressed in white. Carriages followed, in which were seated Turkish mullahs, Greek and Armenian priests, and Jewish rabbis sitting side by side. At the voting table a mullah sat with a Greek priest on one side and an Armenian on the other. All over the empire, in Asia Minor, Syria, and Armenia, the people received the news of freedom with boundless joy and enthusiasm. The world read the reports with gratitude and something akin to awe.

Most wonderful of all, the veiled women of the harams issued forth from behind the pardas and the latticed windows, threw aside the veils, appeared in carriages with men, attended the theatre and the parks, wrote for the press, held public meetings and receptions, made addresses, demanded new rights, talked politics with men, stood in the street awaiting election returns—open-faced and without shame. It was decided by the government to admit women into the University, and to have special courses in hygiene and domestic economy. It seemed the day of woman's emancipation.

THE CONSTITUTION AND THE SHARIAT

The provisions of the Constitution were, in brief: the participation of the people in their government through representatives in parliament, thus limiting the autocratic power of the Sultan; the right of secure domicile and personal liberty; Islam to be the established religion, but all religions and races to have equality before the civil law; all subjects to be considered Ottomans and to serve in the army; popular education to be promoted. Adhered to and put into practice these principles would have made a really new political system in Moslem lands.

There were supreme difficulties in the way of accomplishing all this, even after the army had been won over and the despotic caliph cowed. On the religious side there were two great difficulties: (1) To show the Ulema and their party that the Constitution in general was in accordance with the Shariat; (2) To justify the provision that non-Moslems were to be on an equality with Moslems. The general question was settled in a way by the decrees of the Caliph and of the Sheikh-ul-Islam. The Sheikh proclaimed the legality of Constitutional government, holding that Islam was essentially democratic, that the first four "rightly guided" caliphs had been elected by the people, that the principles of liberty, equality, fraternity, and justice were compatible with the Koran and Islam. It was shown from the traditions that it is in accord with the Law to limit the power of the ruler by that of the people. For example, the Prophet has said: "Consult with them [the people] on every affair"; "Take counsel"; "Any obnoxious measure taken after consultation is preferable to a salutary measure taken arbitrarily"; "If any one should give you a good commandment in my name, even though I have not given it, do it"; "I am only a man. When I order you anything respecting religion, receive it; when I order you anything regarding the affairs of the world, I am only a man." It was cited also that the "rightly guided caliphs" and their commanders mentioned important events in the assemblies of the people on Fridays; that the Imam Ali even appeared before a tribunal, like any ordinary man, in a suit against a Christian. In an interview with some prominent Englishmen (C. R. Buxton: "Turkey in Revolution," pp. 172-74), the Sheikh-ul-Islam was asked: "Is a real Constitutional government permitted by the law of Islam?" He replied: "Permitted! It is more than permitted; the law of Islam is more liberal than the Constitution itself. . . . Our law, rightly interpreted, is in accordance with the principles of representative government. The wisest men, chosen by the people, are to direct the ruler, and if he rules without their consent he is going beyond his power. Now that this principle has been embodied in the law of the Constitution, that law itself is included in the law of Islam (!). Our Ulema are bound to help actively in carrying out the Constitution. . . . The law of Islam enjoins equality—not that the people can regard a Moslem as in every way the same as a

Christian; but political equality, equality before the law, they are bound to grant."

The crux of the matter lies in this provision—the equality of civil rights of Christians and Jews with Moslems. Is this possible under Islam? As an ideal this had been propounded in the Ottoman empire as early as the seventeenth century by the Koprulu family of viziers. The Christian governments had laboured to this end in the nineteenth century, especially for equal taxation, military service, and the right to testify. This equality of rights had been proclaimed in the Hatti Sherif: adopted in the Constitution of 1876, and now readopted. It said: "All subjects of the Ottoman empire are called Ottomans, whatever religion they profess." "All Ottomans are equal before the law. They have the same rights and the same duties in reference to the State." Of this provision Jurist says (*Moslem World,* 1913, p. 360): "The signing of the Constitution of 1876 was the death-warrant of Moslem law. . . . The two basic principles are essentially Christian—responsibility and equality." To bring the Moslem people into reconciliation with this provision the Committee sent Ulema through the land to instruct in the mosques and harmonize constitutional equality with Moslem ideas. After hearing the doctrine propounded, two old mullahs rose up in a mosque and protested; and one in Bagdad said: "Then this is the end of Islam." He was right as regards one of the working postulates of Islam, that the Moslems are the ruling class, and Christians and Jews subject races, suffered to live only so long as they continue in subjection. The Moslem regards himself as superior—not because of wealth, intellect, education, morals, or even conquest, but because of his religion. It is a revolutionary change of Moslem conceptions and of the customs of thirteen hundred years to put the Christian on an equality. To count the Christian's life and honour as equal to those of a true believer, to grant him equality before the courts in giving testimony and receiving punishment, in taxation, in the army as privates and as officers, in the elections, and in official life—this is a condition which the Moslem cannot contemplate with equanimity. The Young Turks might idealize, in the environs of Geneva or Paris, such a consummation, and the Sheikh-ul-Islam theorize about it in interviews with liberal statesmen, but to bring it into practical working was a superhuman task. Yet the Young Turks were sincere in their purpose and the Constitution was re-established on this ideal. They would have grafted on the Moslem state the best results of Christian civilization. They would have substituted patriotism for religious fanaticism. Yet this new fundamental law guards the law of Islam and leaves an opening for persecution and punishment of the apostate. For after declaring that Islam is the religion of the State, it is further declared in Article X that "individual liberty is inviolable. *Except* according to the forms and for the *causes* determined *by the Canon Law of Islam* (Shariat) and the civil code, no one can be arrested or suffer penalties."

The parliament assembled December 17, 1908. It was a striking assemblage, with deputies from Turks and Albanians, Kurds and Arabs, Greeks and Armenians, Syrians and Jews. It met in the historic St. Sophia. The Ulema of Islam, the Christian Patriarchs, the Ottoman princes, the ambassadors of Moslem and Christian States all gave dignity to the scene, while Sultan Abdul Hamid in person inaugurated the National Assembly. It was an occasion of supreme interest.

THE REACTION

Kaimal Pasha was made Grand Vizier. Around him was organized a party called the Ahrar, the Liberal Union. With them was Prince Sabah-ud-Din, a son of the Sultan, who had lived in exile. These favoured decentralization, giving to the Arabs and Albanians and such races large powers of local self-government. They were backed by the Sultan and the reactionaries for their own purpose. And with this party were British diplomacy and press, sowing the seeds they are now reaping. All were working against the Committee of Union and Progress.

The reactionaries organized an association called the Moslem League. Its organ was the *Volcan,* whose editor was a darvish. The League had more than five hundred agitators, of whom seventeen were journalists and a number were connected with the Palace, with Nadir Aga, one of the Sultan's eunuchs, as leader. The Sultan and his treasure-chest was back of it all. The cry of the League was, "The Sacred Law is in jeopardy! The Shariat! The Shariat is in danger! The Faith is fallen!" They were not lacking in pretexts for this party-cry. It was not difficult to find cause against the Young Turks. Mahmud Mukhtar Pasha had issued an order that military drill and discipline should not be interrupted by prayer times. Some of the officers had refused to join in the prayers and had mocked the soldiers for beliefs which they said were exploded. They had shown contempt for the ceremonial rites. The sentiment of one was quoted as: "Now, glory to God, every one is free to believe as he likes." When the League was discovered to be working among the soldiers the latter were forbidden to associate with the Hodjas and the Hodjas from entering the barracks. Officers even directed the soldiers to be ready to bayonet the Hodjas. They retorted by calling the Young Turks infidels, Freemasons, Jews, wine-bibbers, seducers of Moslem wives and destroyers of harams, who delighted to decorate their lodgings with pictures of naked infidel women. By such influences, aided by powerful bribes, the soldiers were weaned from their allegiance, even the Salonica regiment, which, as supporters of the Constitution, had been placed as guards of the Sultan's palace. On April 14, 1909, the soldiers rose in mutiny; in the Palace, the barracks, in the cavalry, the marines and the regulars, all officers who did not manage to escape were slain. The officers of the Committee and their journal, the *Tanin,* were wrecked. The night following Constantinople was terrorized and shuddered in wakeful, fearful anticipation, while the soldiers shot off more than a million cartridges. The next day in front of St. Sophia, the mutineers and the Ulema celebrated the restoration of the Shariat. Cries rent the air,—"Yashasun

Shariat-i-Paghambar!" ("Long live the Law of the Prophet!"). With sounding of trumpets and chanting of hymns, they rejoiced. On all sides and from every lip went up the shout, "Shariat!" "Shariat!" In the name of religion they had dared and won. The next Friday the Sultan held his salaamlukh, with a strange sight of soldiers on guard and officers conspicuous by their absence. The Sultan seemed again triumphant and absolute.

DEPOSITION OF ABDUL HAMID

But that was the Red Sultan's last salaamlukh. Like an avenging fury, the Constitutional army swept down from Macedonia upon the Capital, General Husain Husni Pasha sending a proclamation that "There exists not and cannot exist any law or power above our Constitution." Swift and sure was their victory. Parliament reassembled. It put to the Sheikh-ul-Islam this momentous question (April 22, 1909):

"What becomes of an Imam who has destroyed certain holy writings; who has seized property in contravention of the Shariat; who has committed cruelties in ordering the assassination and imprisonment of exiles without any justification under the Shariat; who has squandered the public money; who having sworn to govern according to the Shariat has violated his oath; who by gifts of money has provoked bloodshed and civil war and who is no longer recognized in the provinces?" The judgment of the Sheikh-ul-Islam, the highest tribunal in Turkey, was in few words: "He must abdicate or be deposed."

A Committee of Parliament—chosen by lot—waited on the Sultan, and by the mouth of a Salonica Jew this mighty despot, this Caliph-Sultan, heard the decree of deposition. His haram of several hundred concubines were scattered to the homes of their childhood, in the mountains of Albania, the huts of the Circassians, or the palaces of favourites. The Sultan, still well supplied with a retinue of three Sultanas, four inferior concubines, five female slaves, four eunuchs, and nine domestics, was exiled and confined in a Salonica palace. The last picture we have of the great assassin is, gathering his womenfolks about him and casting the lot, which proves unfortunate, for he exclaims "Bosh sheh!" ("Vanity, Vanity!") and breaks out into an oath—"Laanat Olsun!" ("Cursed be it!") (Francis McCallagh: "Fall of Abdul Hamid").

CONSTITUTIONAL RÉGIME; SUCCESSES AND FAILURES

Mahmud V Rashad was chosen Sultan and Çaliph and bound on the sword of Othman as a Constitutional monarch. The Young Turks took up the task of government with considerable hopefulness. The press was active, newspapers multiplied; new books were issued; modern text-books were adopted; schools were established; a reformed writing and spelling was introduced to facilitate the study of Turkish; recruits were ordered to be taught to read, as well as to use knives and forks; men of age began attending night school, and could be seen reading on the street corners. Several hundred youths were sent to Europe to study law, finance, politics, and industry; a maternity hospital was opened; lectures were delivered on religious liberty; much freedom of speech and travel was allowed. The white-slave traffic with Egypt was abolished, encouragement was given to the liberation of slaves, ladies-in-waiting were substituted as far as possible for eunuchs in the palace. Tramways were increased; telephones came into use; electric lights were no longer prohibited, but appeared in the mosques and on their domes. The dogs were cleaned out of the streets of Constantinople in spite of the prophecy that their leaving would be a sign that the city would be no longer Mohammedan.

In carrying out the provisions of the Constitution, the Young Turks found circumstances too much for them. Neither equality of the religions nor Ottomanization of the races was possible practically. Equality was violated in the arrangements for the new parliament, for the representation was so manipulated that out of 240 deputies, the Christians had only 37. The enlistment of Christian soldiers met with difficulties. The Turks were utterly unwilling to treat them as themselves. They limited the number in each regiment to twenty per cent. They did not accept them as officers; they did not desire that they should receive military training, but rather that they should be hewers of wood and drawers of water and makers of roads. The Christians began to flee the country to avoid the conscription. The Christian soldiers were in danger of demoralization and of losing their faith. The Patriarch of the Greeks and the Exarch of the Bulgarians tried to arrange that Christian soldiers should have their own worship and chaplains, should keep Sunday, and should not be permitted to become Moslems during their term of service. They insisted that they should be received into the military schools to be trained as officers. Civil offices, too, were not given to the Christians in proportion to their numbers, though they are very capable. In some places fifteen per cent of the police were allowed to be Christians.

Unwillingness of the Moslems to allow Christians to assume equality was one cause of the Adana massacres, though these were no doubt instigated by Abdul Hamid and the reactionaries. The peasantry were wrought upon by tales of how the Armenians were going to rise and rule over them. This massacre, 1909, in which twenty-five thousand Christians lost their lives, was more dastardly, cruel, and lustful than those that preceded it. However inadequate the punishment meted out may be considered, it was at least a sign of progress and a new thing in history that a Moslem government hanged for the murder of Christians more than a score of Moslems, some of whom were wealthy and some religious leaders. The Young Turks in their sane moments have tried to teach Moslems that they cannot kill Christians with impunity in times of peace. A Moslem was executed at Jerusalem for murdering an Armenian abbot. An Arab, looking on, said: " It is a black day for us, for a Moslem has been killed for killing a Christian." But these punishments were exceptional. The truth is that neither in the army, in the courts, in the government, nor in ordinary life, did the Christians receive liberty, equality, fraternity, or justice. Islam and the

Constitution did not work together. It is doubtful whether even a long period of peaceful progress would have accomplished it. Rather it was demonstrated that only power exerted from without can make the life and property of Christians safe under Moslem rule.

ATTEMPTS AT OTTOMANIZATION

Attempts were made in Arabia and Syria to bring the Arabs nearer to Turkish methods. These were met by hostility. The project was initiated of imposing on the Albanians the language, alphabet, customs, and military discipline of the Turks. A census was ordered and new taxes imposed. The Albanians resisted and rose in insurrection. Harassed by internal troubles and before it had time to put its house in order, Turkey became a prey to its neighbours. Austria annexed Bosnia and Herzegovina. Bulgaria declared her independence. Italy proclaimed war and annexed Tripoli and some islands. The Balkan States, Bulgaria, Servia, Montenegro, and Greece, formed an alliance, conquered their ancient foe and rent from her Macedonia, much of Thrace, Albania, Crete, and other islands. The seizure of Morocco by France added to the feeling of dismay and hatred. With thousands of Macedonian refugees to provide for, tension with Greece through boycotts and oppressions of her Greek subjects, with danger of Kurdish raids and Arab plots, with factional fights within and its revenues diminished and its expenditures for war preparations enormous, Turkey's plight was sorry indeed. Its one consolation was the deep sympathy which the Moslem world showed it in its misfortunes, sympathy shown in lamentations and tears, in curses on the Christians and in generous contributions. These attacks of the Christian governments had by this time driven from the minds of the Young Turks all thought of treating the Christians of the empire as equals; indeed, little remained that they should treat them all as enemies. They found it necessary to show a loyalty to Islam which they did not possess, and to foster and strengthen the fanaticism of the Moslems in order to utilize it.

Though bent on carrying out the policy of Ottomanization of everything, yet necessity made the Young Turks dependent on the brain and experience of Christians. So after the Balkan War foreign advisers were called in. German officers took charge of the army and Gen. Liman von Sanders became commander of the corps at Constantinople. To the British was signed the navy; to the French, finance and the gendarmerie. Others were to assist in reforms in Armenia and Kurdistan. With all this it appears that Pan-Islamic agitation was taken up from Constantinople. Agents and tracts were sent out. *The Near East* says (April, 1914): "The publication of Pan-Islamic, anti-Christian, anti-European literature has increased markedly of late." The European name for the capital, Constantinia, was erased from the coinage and Dar-ul-Khalifate ul Aliyah (the abode of the High Caliph) substituted, corresponding to the official title of the city, Dar-i-Saadat, the Seat of Prosperity. The change has one advantage, in that the coins can be used in the new capital without recoining. Stamps were ordered to be printed in Turkish alone, the French being deleted. Signboards, which were often in three languages, must be only in Turkish. Turkish names must be given to the schools and other institutions of the non-Moslems. The street-sweepers of Pera had badges with number and title in both French and Turkish. They went on strike, complaining that the Frangi letters on their necks interfered with their prayers. Their petition was granted. Efforts were begun to curtail and even abolish the privileges of the Christian races and to annul the status granted to them by Mohammed the Conqueror, and even to change the privileges conferred by the Caliph Omar. These privileges were granted to regulate the condition of those subjects who were denied the rights of full citizenship enjoyed only by Moslems under their law. Each race or religion has had an organization (millat) with a large measure of self-government. The Patriarch was considered the head of the race as well as of the religion and administered many matters ordinarily in charge of the civil magistrate. The abrogation of these privileges must depend upon the establishment of real equality in law and practice which has not yet been attained.

ABOLITION OF THE CAPITULATIONS

Another step towards Ottomanization was the abolition of the Capitulations, which was put into effect September 9, 1914. These capitulations are treaties which the Sublime Porte has made with reference to foreign subjects living within its borders. They are named from the capitula or sections into which the treaties are divided. In Byzantine times the emperors had made such arrangements with regard to resident Europeans. These regulations were confirmed by Mohammed II. They were founded on an ancient principle of law that the State would not extend rights and privileges under its laws to foreigners and that their own State must take the trouble of governing them. Moslem rule made special regulations more necessary, for it would not grant the privileges under the Sacred Law to any except Moslems and could not expect subjects of independent Christian States to take the inferior position of the rayats or subjugated Christians. Hence a special arrangement, mutually agreeable, was entered into which allowed each nationality to be judged by its own consul and laws. Each group formed a separate colony, enjoying what have been called extra-territorial rights. These were extended under the favourite nation clause to all who made treaties. At first the powerful Sultans entered into this arrangement somewhat as a matter of grace and accommodation. They were relieved of the trouble of governing the Genoese, Venetians, and other colonies, and the power of the Sultans was not limited by this in any way in which they cared to exercise it. But when Turkish power declined, these privileges became extended and acted as a restraint on Turkish authority. These capitulations granted freedom of religious worship, freedom from the jurisdiction of the Turkish courts, with right of trial by one's own consul, protection from molestation from natives or from the police, exemption from taxes or arrest, inviolability of domicile. They arranged the rate of custom-duties, which could not be changed without the consent of the foreign governments. They permitted foreign post-offices in connection with the consulates.

These privileges were at times greatly abused. By selling or granting the right of citizenship or by receiving many into nominal service at the embassies, the number enjoying these privileges was wrongfully increased. One French ambassador received $80,000 for passport privileges. The Austrians and Russians enrolled several hundred thousand subjects in Wallachia and Moldavia. Governments which charged enormous duties at their own ports, limited Turkey to an eight- or eleven-per cent duty. There was no doubt of the gross injustice of the conditions. Besides it was galling to the pride and self-respect of the Turks and a sign of their inferiority. Efforts were made to annul them in 1856 and 1862, after the adoption of the Code Napoléon. Especially since the adoption of a Constitution declaring equal rights to all races and religions, the Turks felt that the time had come to abolish such restrictions. On the face of it their contention is right. But some considerations make it evident that the fulness of time had not come for their abolition. For the equality of Christians with Moslems before the courts is not yet put into practice; the judges are all Moslems, and the testimony of a Christian does not yet count for much as against that of a Moslem; the courts are notoriously corrupt, and have not yet been reformed. The *Tanin* declares that the judges continue to oppose the reform of the judiciary and that when a European adviser was employed to purge and regulate the courts he was stoutly resisted.

Reform, it says, "is a fight against the whole force of the magistrates, their methods, their ignorance, their inability, their mental state." This difficulty is not insuperable, for if Greece and Japan can judge all foreigners, and if Great Britain can have Moslem justices in India who are worthy of confidence, such may be at length developed among the Turks. Indeed, there is testimony to assure us that in the Shari courts upright judges are not wanting.

The abolition of the Capitulations was celebrated in Turkey as an Independence Day,—as "the dawn of a new era." Flags were flying for three days, amid great rejoicings and congratulations. It was regarded as a great and glorious event—as a fact accomplished —in spite of the unanimous protest of the Legations.

Following this, new laws have been issued. Duties have been raised from fifteen to one hundred per cent; an income tax (Temettu) has been fixed on foreigners and their occupations, exception being made for certain classes as teachers and clergy. Most disquieting is the new law regarding schools, which directly affects those of the missions. All schools must be formally authorized, must state the name of their responsible director, of the text-books and curriculum, must teach Turkish equally with the chief language of the school, and the history and geography of Turkey in the Turkish language. Think of it! The history of Turkey must be taught, and according to the Turkish representation of the facts. But further the law declares "that religious knowledge and history and the teaching of the creed of the denomination to which the school belongs *shall not be given to pupils who do not profess that religion."* Nor must such pupils be made to attend prayers. This strikes at the foundation of educational mission work, the largest branch of the American work in Turkey. This has already been specifically applied, as at Beirut College.

At another point the Ottomanization programme shows itself. After the massacre of the Christians by the Druses in 1860, the Lebanon district was placed under a special administration. Its privileges have been declared null. An army of seventeen thousand was sent in and all administration was taken over by the Turks. The Christian governor's authority was reduced to a shadow. The patriarch of the Maronites was stripped of his privileges.

The aim of this movement and of these new laws is to reduce the whole empire to a uniform basis under Ottoman law, to abolish all special laws and privileges. The non-success of the attempt in Albania does not argue well for its wisdom.

TURKEY AND THE PRESENT WAR

On the opening of the present European war Turkey began general mobilization, calling to arms Christians and Jews as well as Moslems. Many non-Moslems were excused on the payment of fifty pounds. After three months, on November 7, 1914, Turkey entered the conflict on the side of Germany, and proclaimed the jihad.

Why did the Turks enter the war? According to their own word, they believed that the day of deliverance for Islam had come, "the day of vengeance against the oppressors," the day of triumph over those who had despoiled their heritage. "We are fighting," says the editor of the Turkish *Yourdou*, "for the freedom of the Turkish race and of Islam." The *Tarjuman* says: "The Turkish expeditionary army on the West and on the East carries the message of salvation and life to the Moslems living there." Halidah Khanum, the famous writer, graduate of the American College, says: "This war is an absolute necessity; how eagerly our brethren in Russia await the army of the caliphate!" (*Orient*, January 25, 1915). Sir Edwin Pears, a high authority, confirms this opinion, saying that popular sentiment was with the war party because they hoped to get back some of the territory they had lost.

ENGLAND OR GERMANY: WHICH?

Why did the Turks enter the war on the German side? From a conviction of self-interest. It appears to them that Russia, Great Britain, and France are the countries that are holding Moslems in subjection, while Germany has been content with financial advantages. It need not be counted strange that they believed Germany to be their friend. The German emperor had assumed that position, had supported the Red Sultan at the time of the Armenian massacres, had twice visited him in 1889 and 1898, had stood by the grave of Saladin at Damascus and announced that, "The three hundred millions of Mohammedans that are scattered through the world may rest assured that the German emperor will eternally be their friend."[1]

When the star of Abdul Hamid was setting, the Germans won the friendship of the Young Turks, which the British lost by inexplicable diplomacy. After the Balkan War, the German ambassador publicly declared: "The time has come when the Fatherland may attach to the Asiatic provinces the warning, 'Touch me not!'" So when the present war was declared, it is no wonder that the crowds made a great demonstration in front of the German ambassy. The Ambassador spoke to them of the struggle as one for the real welfare of Islam before which there was victory and a glorious future. In this connection we may recall the telegram which a great mass-meeting of Persians and their sympathizers sent from Stamboul to the Kaiser, beseeching his help against England and Russia on behalf of Persia. Germany had played its game of diplomacy so as to impress the Moslems, of Turkey and Persia at least, with her friendship. Of small importance, and intended only to inspire the populace, were the reports that the Kaiser had become a Mohammedan and had adopted the name Haji Mohammed Wilhelm, and was wearing a fez, as the photograph showed, and that his haram was coming to visit the Sultan in the captured dreadnaughts of the British; that the Germans had become true believers and in proof of their anti-Christian feelings had sent views of the ruined churches of

* When I saw the glaring metal tablet at Baalbek, placed to commemorate the Kaiser's visit, I thought it exceedingly incongruous in those sublime ruins.

Belgium; that they had appointed a Mohammedan governor of Belgium, and the Belgians themselves were desirous of becoming Moslems. Even a consular agent of Germany in Persia is said to have professed to be a Mohammedan in order to win the Persians to the jihad.

Lest you be too much astonished at these things, behold the other great Protestant Power of Europe vying with Germany in being the friend and assister of Islam. Sardar Wingate of the Sudan said in his proclamation on behalf of the British Government (*Near East,* January 1, 1915): "From the religious aspect also we [Great Britain] have brought the holy places within a few days' journey of Khartum. We have subsidized and assisted the men of religion. We have built and given assistance to the building of new mosques all over the country. The Kadis and others have received free and thorough education in the Koran and in the tenets of the Mohammedan religion. . . . Great Britain will continue to improve in every possible manner the facilities for the practice of the Mohammedan religion." The High Commissioner in Egypt, representing King George, in the formal address to the new Sultan Husain Kamal, declares that "The strengthening and progress of Mohammedan institutions in Egypt is naturally a matter in which his Majesty's government takes the deepest interest." Lieut.-Col. A. C. Yate, member of Parliament, at a session of the Central Asian Society, presided over by Sir Mortimer Durand, said: "If ever a great Mussulman confederacy was to be formed, it must be done with the fullest sympathy and support of the

British Empire. The day might come when Great Britain might stand forth *as the champion of Islam*, of Turkey, Persia, and Afghanistan in alliance with the Mussulmans of India."

THE PROCLAMATION OF THE HOLY WAR

The Jihad, or Holy War, was proclaimed with due ceremony, before an immense crowd at the Mosque of Mohammed the Conqueror at Constantinople. By legal custom, questions were asked and formally answered by the Fatva-amini, this constituting a lawful declaration. In this the call is made to all Moslems, "old and young, living in all parts of the world," including those living under the governments of Russia, England, and France, to join battle against the enemy, with their persons and their property; otherwise their conduct is "a great revolt against the Omnipotent and liable to celestial punishment, and if they fight against the Sultan they are to be punished with hell-fire." The proclamation was repeated all over the country and with special ceremony at Jerusalem. The concourse gathered at the Dome of the Rock, the rock-top of Mt. Moriah, the altar of Abraham. The Kazi of Medina was brought to add impressiveness to the occasion. Just as he rose to read, a thunder-storm interrupted him. In a lull he began again, when a fierce wind tossed the flag from its staff at his feet. The Kazi was alarmed at these evil omens and tremblingly read the proclamation, after which he fell into a fit, and died within three days (*Near East*, 1914, p. 384). Far and wide throughout all

Islam the proclamation of the Jihad was sent. Through the press, through tracts, and travelling agents the Holy War was urged upon the faithful. Bulletins were scattered by aeroplanes over the armies of the Allies in Belgium and France to call the Moslem soldiers of Algeria, Senegal, and India to allegiance to Islam. Let me give some extracts from a proclamation of the Jihad: "To the millions of Islam! 'God will punish them in your hand; ye will overcome them!' (Koran). Oh, ye faithful, what do ye wait for? How often have the savage Russians, the traitorous English, the Frenchmen born of impure parentage, planted their unclean flags upon your holy mountains. Oh, ye helpless people of India, of the Oxus, of Tunis and of the orphan isles, and you wretched tribes of Turkey. Ye have become slaves of the people of the Cross. If you desire honour and glory, houris and damsels, behold all are in the grasp of your sword. Attack your enemies from every side. Whenever you meet them, kill them. Quicken the failing proclamation of the Unity. Listen to the will of God, the desire of your prophet, the command of the Caliph that you give no rest to the enemy. If you have no arms, *tear his throat with your teeth.* Jihad! Jihad! Oh, Moslems! The Great God is ordering you to fight everywhere. God will give you the victory. He gives you the houris and the damsels of heaven."

Turks and Germans expected great things from the Jihad. Ali Fahmi Mohammed (in *The Near East*) declared: "Egypt would revolt against England in a world-wide conflict or any serious rising in India."

Hafiz Bey Ramazan, an Egyptian Nationalist, had been assured that the Kaiser expected to plan his attack in connection with an uprising in India and Egypt. Grothe (quoted by Hurgronge: "The Holy War," p. 36) anticipated that on Turkey's proclaiming the Holy War, the Moslems would attack their masters "here with secrecy and ruse, there with fanatical courage," and especially to the undoing of England. Mr. Carl Peters, the African traveller, voiced this expectation (quoted from Professor Vambery in "Islam: A Challenge," p. 239): "There is one factor which might fall on our side of the balance and in case of a world-war might be made useful to us: That factor is Islam. As Pan-Islamism it could be played against Great Britain as well as against the French Republic; and if German policy is bold enough, it can fashion the dynamite to blow into the air the rule of the Western Powers from Cape Nun, Morocco, to Calcutta."

The ambitious scheme had in some minds this consummation, that there should be in the world two great empires; the Caliph should be ruler of all Islam and the Kaiser of all Christendom.

It is not strange that many persons with a knowledge of the intense disloyalty and hatred that prevails among Moslem subjects of Christian Powers and of the propaganda that had been carried on through so many years, should have anticipated great results from the call to the Jihad. They miscalculated indeed, but did not misjudge Moslem feelings. The Moslem people did not make a general uprising. We need not, however, give too much value to the proclamations of loyalty issued in Egypt, India, Zanzibar, Algeria, and Central Asia. These might be diplomatic utterances accompanied even by secret disloyal plottings. But two reasons account for the failure of the call to the Jihad. The first and greatest was the conviction that the Jihad did not promise success. The Moslem leaders of Asia and Africa could not believe that the united force of Great Britain, France, and Russia could go down in defeat. These are the great and conquering empires whose power they have felt. They looked upon Turkey as broken, overcome by Italy and by her own late subjects, the Balkan States. Besides if the Germanic Alliance should be victorious, they felt that they would only be changing one Christian master for another, and as one Moslem expressed it, quoting Shakespeare:

> "Thus must we from the smoke into the smother."

In addition to this the wily head of Pan-Islamism was gone and the Islamic world has a suspicion of, if not a detestation for, the Young Turks as a set of worldly, Europeanized men with little care for the faith as such, and of the Committee of Union and Progress as a sceptical group of Crypto-Jewish Dunmas and wine-bibbing modernists, who are playing with the jihad as a political instrument. Besides they felt the incongruity of fighting for the faith of Islam in union with an army partly composed of and commanded by Christians.

However, had the Austro-Germans conquered the Allies and the campaigns of Turkey in Egypt, the Caucasus, and Persia been successful, the Moslem world would have been agitated to its depths and its widest extent. There is no doubt that Egypt, Tripoli, Algeria, Morocco, the Sudan from east to west, including the powerful Sanusiyahs, would welcome an opportunity to cast off the hated infidel yoke. Persia would rejoice to attack the Russian bear, could it feel assured that its teeth were extracted and its paws disabled. As to India we hear well-worded expressions of loyalty from the official class, but we do not hear from the great sixty millions of steadfast Sunnis who, no doubt, would join the Hindus to throw the British into the Indian Ocean, if confident of ultimate victory. The twenty million Moslems of Russia are of the same mind. In all these lands there are few Moslems loyal to their Christian rulers. To be so is contrary to the law, instinct, and spirit of Islam. They would prefer to be as Afghanistan, with a civilization of the Middle Ages and under the old-time absolutism of a Mohammedan ruler, than to have the culture and education of Aligarh College, under the British Raj. Albeit their progressive men hope for twentieth-century civilization with the Mohammedan faith and political independence. To obtain the latter they would welcome the first favourable opportunity, not because the Turks proclaim a jihad, but because it is the deep and fervent desire of their hearts. Convince them of a successful issue, and rebellion will follow. In this lies the danger in a repulse of the Allies at the Dardanelles. For their retreat might be the signal for a tremendous upheaval in other Moslem lands. It will create a serious problem for the Christian colonies and camps in Africa and Asia if the Jihad becomes universal, while the forces of Christian nations are engaged in Europe.

The Turk, wherever his hand reaches, is waging his Holy War with terrible reality. See it in action with all its old-time fanaticism. Tens of thousands of Christians in Urumia and Salmas, Persia, have fled for their lives, abandoning all. Their villages, homes, and churches have been destroyed, and their women ravished. The tribal Nestorians of the Kurdish mountains have been driven into the Alpine fastnesses to perish of hunger, or to surrender to death or Islam. Their patriarch, Mar Shimoon, is a fugitive in a foreign land. Look over the mountains and plains of Asiatic Turkey and see the ruthless Holy War waged against the defenceless Armenians. Their strong men butchered in cold blood or drafted into the army to be slaughtered in the van. The old men and children set adrift in the wildernesses to perish. All the goodly women subjected to unspeakable dishonour or carried off to the harams of the Turks and Kurds and forced to Islamize. Thousands of villages and towns and districts depopulated. Hundreds of thousands of Christians, Armenians, Nestorians, Jacobites, Greek Orthodox, Roman Catholics, and Protestants mercilessly destroyed, with the diabolical purpose to wipe out Christianity from Turkey. This is the ripened fruit of the reform movement of the Young Turks.

We write over that movement and the attempt to establish Constitutional government, as over that of Persia: "Failure! Mene, mene, tekel! Weighed in the balance! Found wanting! To be divided!" A righteous issue of the war will be the dismemberment of Turkey, with the remnant deprived of the power ever to proclaim a jihad or to persecute its non-Moslem peoples.

A review of present-day movements among Moslems shows that Islam is neither dead nor moribund. It is full of life, action, agitation, of cross-purposes, the resultant of contrary religious and intellectual forces. Some are striving for the reform of the social, intellectual, political, and religious life of Islam; some are mighty to conserve and spread the old Faith; not a few would strengthen the old fanatical zeal and hatred of its people and call into exercise its persecuting spirit. All these movements in Islam are energetic, aggressive, determined, and anti-Christian.

Upon the Church of Christ, Islam is an urgent call to duty, to faith and obedience. Facts and conditions voice anew the command of Jesus Christ: " Go, preach the Gospel to the Moslems." The call is for a contrite heart, recognizing the long neglect of the Church; for a sincere love which will overcome our crusader spirit and quench thought of vengeance in prayer for their repentance and forgiveness; for heroic faith because of the supreme difficulties of the task; for unfailing courage, knowing that the conversion of Islam is the most arduous work that the Church has undertaken. The need of and hope for Moslems is a movement Christ-ward.

INDEX

D

N

T

U

V

W

PROBLEMS OF WAR AND PEACE, Etc.

ANNA FITZ GERALD VAN LOAN

The Power to Right Our Wrongs

Evidence from Facts that Christian Principles are Best Aiding Humanity. 12mo, cloth, net $1.00.

"This book demonstrates, from carefully taken premises, that the principles which now control and maintain peace in civic and national affairs could, and should, be applied to avert international conflict, thereby furnishing a practical method of ushering in an era of world-wide peace."

GAIUS GLENN ATKINS, D.D.

The Maze of the Nations and the Way Out

The Prize Essay in the One Thousand Dollar competition promoted by the Carnegie Church Peace Union. 12mo, cloth, net 75c.

Dr. Atkins' main contention is that the only way to insure a lasting peace among the nations of the earth, is by eliminating the causes of war. A thoughtful, ably-written essay, containing suggestions for the pacification of the world, of real and practical value.

THOMAS CAPEK (Editor)

Bohemia Under Hapsburg Misrule

A Study of the Ideals and Aspirations of the Bohemian and Slovak Peoples as Related to and Affected by the European War. 12mo, cloth, net $1.00.

"The whole forms a fairly complete survey of the character, achievements, and aspirations of Bohemians, past and present."—*N. Y. Times.*

HENRY D. ESTABROOK

The Vengeance of the Flag

And Other Occasional Addresses. 8vo, net $2.00.

"This man Estabrook—he is a surpriser. Takes a man's breath away to read his speeches. A man can't let go when he has once laid hold. It's like grasping the poles of a battery."—*Omaha Mercury.*

COMPARATIVE RELIGIONS

SAMUEL G. WILSON, A.M., D.D.

Bahaism and Its Claims

A Study of the Religions Promulgated by Baha Ullah and Abdul Baha. 8vo, cloth, net $1.50.

Bahaism is a revolt from the fold of Islam which in recent years has been bidding vigorously for the support of Occidental minds. Many of its principles are culled from the Christian religion which it insidiously seeks to supplant. What this Oriental cult is, what it stands for, and what it aims at, is told in a volume which forms a notable addition to the History of Comparative Religions.